John Sch. Risley

The Law of War

John Sch. Risley

The Law of War

ISBN/EAN: 9783337233402

Printed in Europe, USA, Canada, Australia, Japan

Cover: Foto ©ninafisch / pixelio.de

More available books at **www.hansebooks.com**

THE LAW OF WAR

BY

JOHN SHUCKBURGH RISLEY, M.A., B.C.L.

Lordinges, (quod he) ther is ful many a man that crieth "Werre, Werre," that wote ful litel what werre amounteth.—*Chaucer.*

LONDON:
A. D. INNES & CO.,
BEDFORD STREET.
1897.

Richard Clay & Sons, Limited,
London & Bungay.

PREFACE

IN time of peace the average individual is not wont to concern himself deeply with the principles or problems of International Law. He is quite content to leave questions of extradition and commercial treaties and other subjects of "the rules of peace" to the lawyers, statesmen, and diplomats to whom such matters appertain. At the same time, he is sometimes apt to talk in a light-hearted way about *War*, without perhaps much knowledge of its laws or consequences.

My aim in writing this work has been simply to furnish him with an exposition of the rules which actually govern the relations of states in time of war in a simple and compendious form.

I trust that its contents may be found to be sufficiently full and accurate, always remembering that, as Sir R. Phillimore justly observes, International Law is a subject which is "not susceptible of precise mathematical accuracy," consisting as it does of rules which vary infinitely in point of certainty and acceptance. The rules which have met with an absolutely universal acceptance are comparatively few in number: and with regard to those rules which have been and continue to be the subject of difference amongst states, the utmost that can be done is to set forth opposing doctrines with impartiality and clearness, in all cases keeping the statement of the rule carefully distinct from any criticism or speculation, where such has been attempted.

Some few of the most important cases have been inserted in the text, an addition which it is hoped will increase the interest of the subject as well as the clearness of the rule illustrated.

I have availed myself freely of the learned and elaborate works of eminent International Jurists, but, except in the case of quotations at length, I have refrained from constant acknowledgment of my obligation, which is "as great as it is obvious." I must, however, make a special acknowledgment of my indebtedness, in writing the last chapter, to Mr. Waraker's *Naval Warfare of the Future*, and Mr. Lawrence's essay upon the same subject, although I have found myself at issue with some of the arguments of the former and with the conclusions of the latter.

The freedom of International Law from the technicality which hedges most if not all branches of municipal law is a feature which should especially commend a study of its principles to the general reader; and such a study, moreover, can alone enable him to appreciate the magnitude of important international questions in which his country may be interested, and which he himself may, in however small a way, help to decide.

I venture to express a hope that this work, whilst disclaiming any pretension to the character of a legal text-book, will be found useful as a "first guide" to any such seekers after knowledge, and possibly also to law-students by way of an introduction to more elaborate treatises.

JOHN SHUCKBURGH RISLEY.

8, *Stone's Buildings,*
Lincoln's Inn.

CONTENTS

Part I.—INTRODUCTORY

CHAP.		PAGE
I.	The Nature of International Law	1
II.	The History of International Law	11
III.	The Sources of International Law	25
IV.	The Law of Persons and the Rules of Peace	37
V.	Modes of settling International Disputes	49

Part II.—THE LAW OF BELLIGERENCY

I.	The Nature of War	67
II.	The Commencement of War	77
III.	Enemy Character	93
IV.	The Conduct of War	106
V.	The Conduct of War (*continued*)	119
VI.	Military Occupation and Prize	134
VII.	Intercourse between Belligerents. The Termination of War	152

Part III.—THE LAW OF NEUTRALITY

CHAP.		PAGE
I.	THE RIGHTS AND DUTIES OF NEUTRAL STATES	171
II.	DUTIES OF ABSTENTION	179
III.	DUTIES OF PREVENTION	188
IV.	THE ALABAMA CLAIMS	208
V.	DUTIES OF SUFFERANCE. CONTRABAND	225
VI.	BLOCKADE	239
VII.	MARITIME CAPTURE AS AFFECTING NEUTRAL SUBJECTS	249
VIII.	THE RIGHT OF VISIT AND SEARCH	265
IX.	ENGLAND AND THE DECLARATION OF PARIS	280
	INDEX	303

PART I
INTRODUCTORY

THE LAW OF WAR

PART I

CHAPTER I

THE NATURE OF INTERNATIONAL LAW

THERE have been various classifications by publicists and text-writers of the rules comprising that body of law which was formerly known as the Law of Nations, but which is now more generally termed International Law.

By far the most natural and simple division of these rules, however, appears to be into— {Classification—}

1. Normal International Law, or rules regulating the relations of states in time of peace, and {1. Rules of Peace.}
2. Abnormal International Law, or rules regulating the relations of states in time of war. {2. Rules of War.}

These two branches may, in more simple and homely language, be styled the Rules of Peace and the Rules of War.

It is only with the latter branch that this work purports to deal, and its rules may be disposed under two main headings, viz.— {Rules of War divided into—}

1. The Law of Belligerency, or rules regulating the relations of belligerents *inter se*. {1. Belligerency.}
2. The Law of Neutrality, or rules regulating the relations of belligerents with neutrals. {2. Neutrality.}

But before proceeding to consider these rules *scriatim*, it will be as well to begin at the beginning of the subject, to ascertain what is the nature of International Law as a whole, to briefly review its origin and history, to show how it has been built up by enumerating the sources from which it springs, to notice, in passing, the subjects that are dealt with by the other branch of the law, the Rules of Peace, to describe the means of settling international disputes short of war, and so finally to come in due order to a detailed account of the rights and duties of nations comprised in the Rules of War.

§ 1. *The Definition of International Law.*

It would be possible to fill several pages with the definitions of International Law that have from time to time been laid down by various writers on this subject. The reader's patience will not, however, be taxed to such an extent. He would probably throw the book down in despair, and give up any attempt to acquaint himself with a subject which seems capable of presenting itself in a different phase to well-nigh every mind that has grappled with it. Nor, having regard to the saying of the old Roman jurist, "Omnis definitio in jure periculosa," will any new definition be here attempted. It would serve no useful end to quote any of the early definitions framed by publicists at a time when International Law was in its infancy. These definitions were constructed with reference to the connection between International Law and the Law of Nature—in other words, they defined the source of International Law rather than explained its nature and characteristics. Of the multitude of modern definitions it will be sufficient for the purposes of this work to quote but one, that of Kent—a definition which explains lucidly in simple language the nature and objects of International Law, and the sources from which it is derived.

Kent's Definition.

International Law, says Kent, is "that collection of

rules, customary, conventional, and judicial, which independent states appeal to for the purpose of determining their rights, prescribing their duties, and regulating their intercourse, in peace and war, imposed by opinion and based upon the consent of nations."

§ 2. *Its Name and Nature.*

It is a singularly significant and characteristic fact, that the very title of International Law, no less than its contents, should have been a matter of uncertainty and debate. Gentilis and Grotius and the early publicists, who wrote in Latin, termed it the Jus Gentium, which was not a peculiarly happy name, inasmuch as it caused considerable misapprehension, and tended to obscure the true influence which was exercised by Roman Law upon the development of International Law. *Jus Gentium.*

Richard Zouch, Professor of Roman Law at Oxford University, about the middle of the seventeenth century, invented a new title, "Jus inter gentes," which was a great improvement, indicating as it did that the rules comprised by it formed a new and distinct code regulating the relations of states, and not to be confused with the body of Roman Law called Jus Gentium. However, when Latin ceased to be the polite language of science, and was everywhere superseded by the vernacular, Jus Gentium or Jus inter gentes became translated in English into the "Law of Nations." This title misses the preciseness of that of Zouch. It is far too vague and general; for it would include general principles of justice common to all or most civilized nations, and would therefore contain rules applicable to the relations of individuals as well as to those of states. This, it may be observed, is an objection to which the original title of Jus Gentium was also open. *Jus inter gentes.* *Law of Nations.*

Towards the end of the eighteenth century the expression "International Law," an exact equivalent of Zouch's Jus inter gentes, was invented by Jeremy Bentham. He *International Law.*

confesses, in his *Principles of Morals and Legislation*, that the term is a new one, but says "it is calculated to express in a more significant way the branch of law which commonly goes under the name of the Law of Nations, an appellation so uncharacteristic, that, were it not for the force of custom, it would seem rather to refer to internal jurisprudence."

The title is euphonious, compact, and self-explanatory, and has been generally adopted by English and American writers, Droit International being the accepted French equivalent. It may therefore be said that "International Law" is now universally recognized as the title of the body of rules regulating the intercourse of states.

<small>The nature of International Law.</small> But this title has not been unchallenged. John Austin and his disciples have denied that such a body of rules has any claim to be entitled "Law" at all; an objection which not merely calls in question the propriety of its formal name, but sets in issue the very nature and binding power of its contents.

The key to the positions taken up by the opposing sides in this controversy is really a simple one. If the word "Law" were susceptible of but one meaning, one contention would be clearly right and the other wrong. But with the word "Law" are associated many shades of meaning, from the widest and most comprehensive down to the most precise and particular.

Law is, in fact, an algebraical symbol, to quote Sir Henry Maine, to which various values may be assigned; and the controversy between the Austinians and the supporters of "International Law" is therefore purely a jurisprudential one, into which it would be out of place in a work of the present scope to enter, however briefly, were it not for the fact that the criticism and objections of Austin, and the answers by which they have been met, afford the reader the clearest possible demonstration of the nature and limitations of International Law.

§ 3. *In what sense, if any, is it "Law"?*

The answer to this question depends, as already indicated, upon the breadth of meaning to be ascribed to the word "Law." It is a contest between popular usage, which is naturally loose, and a scientific definition, which is perhaps of no great practical value. Without entering into the merits or demerits of the Austinian system it will be sufficient to state, that Austin found Law proper to consist of rules imposed by a determinate superior, either divine or political—*i. e.* the Law of God and Positive Law. On analyzing the latter he found it to be composed of the following ingredients. A command addressed by the sovereign or supreme power in the state to the citizens or subjects of that state, enjoining upon them certain acts or forbearances, and enforced in courts of justice by a sure and certain sanction, or penalty in case of disobedience.

Austin.

Austin then turns to International Law, and finds that it does not contain any one of the necessary elements which constitute Positive Law. It does not consist of commands; it is not issued by any one sovereign or central power; it is not addressed to individuals; and it has no sure and certain sanctions, because there is no international court to administer them. Therefore, he says, International "Law" (so called) is not strictly Law at all, but merely amounts to Morality.

It may be readily conceded that International Law is not Positive Law as defined by Austin, but without attempting a detailed criticism of that definition, it must be pointed out that it rests upon an arbitrary assumption that all law implies a command to the exclusion of every other idea; and that it is not applicable to law in all states of society, or under all political systems. It is not open to Austin, having arbitrarily assigned a narrow meaning to the word "Law," to characterize as incorrect any wider employment of the term. Within his own

International Law is not "Positive Law" as defined by Austin.

limits he is undoubtedly correct, but the question is whether "Law" can with propriety be confined within such narrow limits.

<small>But many of its rules are as binding as those of Positive Law.</small>

Coming from theory to actual practice, if the nature and stringency of the rules comprising International Law be examined, we shall be entitled to inquire in respect of many of them—"How do these rules differ from laws proper?" Take, for example, the rules that a state has the right to exercise internal control, to settle its form of government, that it has rights of ownership over its soil, or any of the other rights which are implied by its mere existence as one of a group of equal independent states. These rules are universally recognized, and owing to the doctrine of the "Balance of Power," are as stringently enforced as any positive law in the strict sense of the term. And yet the title of law is to be denied to them, because they fail to satisfy the requirements of a scientific definition!

In actual practice, moreover, it will be found that International Law is fully recognized by the municipal law of every country as being a body of true law. Its principles have long been applied in municipal courts, *i. e.* Courts of Admiralty and Prize Courts, the mere existence of the latter being evidence of the reality of International Law.

In Hughes *v.* Cornelius, a case decided about the year 1681, it was unanimously held by the Court of King's Bench, that the decision of a Prize Court constituted by a belligerent on a question of lawful prize was conclusive, although erroneous.

In Triquet *v.* Bath, a case decided in 1764, Lord Mansfield said, "I remember in a case before Lord Talbot, of Buvot *v.* Barbut [decided 1736], ... Lord Talbot declared a clear opinion 'that the Law of Nations in its full extent was part of the law of England.' ... I remember too Lord Hardwicke's declaring his opinion to the same effect; and denying that Lord Chief Justice Holt ever had any doubt as to the Law of Nations being part of the law of England upon the occasion of the arrest of the Russian Ambassador."

And in Lockwood *v.* Coysgarne, decided in 1765, Lord Mansfield declared that the Law of Nations was in full force in these kingdoms.

Many of its principles have been expressly incorporated by statute into municipal law for the purpose of enabling the executive to carry them out more effectually. The statute of 7 Anne, c. 12, dealing with the privileges of ambassadors, the Foreign Enlistment Act 1870, the Territorial Waters Jurisdiction Act 1878, and the Neutrality Acts of the United States, may be quoted as examples.

Hall puts the case very clearly. He says, "It is impossible, in dealing with International Law, to ignore the two broad facts, that it is habitually treated as law, and that a certain part of what is at present acknowledged to be law is indistinguishable in character from it."

There can be no doubt that International Law exhibits an ever-increasing tendency to lessen the gulf which Austin asserted to exist between itself and "Positive Law."

Its authors have become more determinate; national conferences have been held, at which representatives of all or most of the great states have been present, for the purpose of framing rules, which, emanating from such a central authority, would have the force of true commands, while the unanimity which produced the rule would insure a certain sanction in case of disobedience. It is not pretended that these conferences, except perhaps the Geneva Convention of 1864, have effected so much; but the mere fact that they have been held is of some significance. Much good work in the way of consolidating and harmonizing the principles of International Law has also been done by the Institute of International Law, founded in 1873, and composed of eminent advocates and jurists belonging to all nations.

International Law practically, if not theoretically, a body of true law.

The general view taken at the present day is that International Law is so real and important a factor in the life of every state, and its principles approximate so closely to the characteristics of municipal law, that it forms practically, if not theoretically, a body of law which it would be idle and pedantic to describe by any other title.

Hall sums up the position occupied by its rules as follows:—" That they lie on the extreme frontier of the law is not to be denied; but on the whole it would seem to be more correct, as it certainly is more convenient, to treat them as being a branch of law, than to include them within the sphere of morals."

According to Halleck:—" These rules cannot perhaps with strict propriety be called laws, in the sense of commands proceeding from an authority competent in all cases to enforce obedience or punish violations. But, like the laws of honour, they are rules of conduct imposed by public opinion, and are enforced by appropriate sanctions. They are therefore, by their analogy to positive commands, properly termed laws; and they are enforced not only by moral sanctions, but by fear of provoking general hostility, and incurring its evils, in case of violating maxims which are generally received and respected among nations."

In conclusion, it may be added, with reference to the name and nature of International Law, that Kent, in rejecting the title of "Law of Nations," accepts that of "International Law" as a "definite and expressive term, which, though not altogether accurate, is convenient and now in common currency."[1]

---

[1] It is important to arrive at some conclusion as to the nature of International Law, before treating of the rules and principles which it contains. I have endeavoured to show that it has well-founded claims to be called "law," and as such it will be treated throughout this work. Consequently all such words as "law," "right," "duty," "legal," "illegal," and the like will be freely used without an apologetic explanation upon every occasion that the word is not used in the strict "Austinian" sense.

§ 4. Public and Private International Law.

The use of the expression "Private International Law," a name which has been generally assigned to a certain body of rules and principles, has assisted to obscure the true nature of International Law proper.

Private International Law consists of the rules and principles which determine within what limits Courts of Justice will apply foreign law and recognize foreign jurisdiction, and to what extent they will give effect to foreign judgments. *Private International Law is really municipal law.*

It deals, for example, with questions of status, the validity of marriage, the legitimacy of children, and conditions of divorce, with rights arising upon contract, and with questions affecting movable property. It recognizes foreign claims to criminal jurisdiction, and enables a litigant within certain limits to reap the benefit of a foreign judgment in his favour.

It is, therefore, in some sense, international, but with International Law proper it has nothing whatever to do, seeing that it is concerned, not with the relations of states, but of private individuals, and is, in fact, pure municipal law.

There appears to be one connecting link between International Law proper and Private International Law, namely, the rules which deal with the relations of a belligerent state on the one side, and a neutral private individual on the other, i. e. the laws of contraband and blockade. But the link is only an apparent one. The real relation is not between the neutral individual and the belligerent state, but between the latter and the neutral state to which the individual belongs. *An apparent link between Public and Private International Law.*

A neutral state, with a view to avoiding endless disputes with the belligerents on either side, is invested by International Law with certain duties of sufferance towards the belligerents. These include the duty of allowing a belligerent to prevent neutral subjects from carrying on certain forms of trade, which are innocent in time of peace, but prejudicial to the belligerent in time of war. In preventing such trade the belligerent state is brought into contact with the neutral individual, but the latter is under no duty to the belligerent, and his responsibility is simply the outcome of expediency and convenience.

This is, no doubt, an anomaly; but it illustrates the fact that International Law regulates the relations of states alone; and unless an injury done by a state to an individual is also an injury to the individual's state, it is, so far as International Law is concerned, no injury at all.

To sum up, therefore, International Law may be described as being in practice, if not in strict theory, *a body of true law*, regulating the relations of states in time of peace and war.

CHAPTER II

THE HISTORY OF INTERNATIONAL LAW

IN the earliest stages of society, of which there are any traditions or records existing, there was no conception of international right or duty in peace or war.

It was only natural that the Jews, chosen to be a "special people," should have had no sense of duty in relation to the surrounding nations. Not only were they prohibited from all peaceable intercourse, but the commandment was "Thou shalt smite them and utterly destroy them" (Deut. vii. 1—8), "Thou shalt blot out the remembrance of Amalek from under heaven" (Deut. xxv. 17—19). Where there was to be perpetual warfare there could be no rules of peace. Even the sanctity of ambassadors was violated, *e. g.* Hanun's treatment of David's envoys, and there was no glimmering of international sentiment to regulate intercourse in time of peace, or restrain violence in time of war. The Jewish era.

In the state of society described by Homer, piracy was an ordinary respectable calling, war was most literally what Bynkershoek calls a "concertatio per vim vel per dolum," and (not to take it too seriously) the views held in Olympus on the subject of neutrality were extremely vague and unsatisfactory! Ancient Greece.

Leaving the traditions, and coming to the history of ancient Greece, it may be said that Greece furnished for the first time in the world's history the conditions necessary to the development of any international sentiment and usage. Greece was composed of a group of independent states, knit together by common moral, religious, and political ideas incident to their common ancestry and historical antecedents. Had the Greeks possessed the Roman genius for law, the genesis of International Law might have been antedated by about 2000 years; but, although they evolved nothing approaching to an international system, Greek history discloses a perception of many of the rudimentary principles of International Law, which were recognized and acted upon, even if in a somewhat desultory manner. The recognition of many of these principles was due to the influence of a common religion. On this ground they respected ambassadors and heralds (as did also the ancient Egyptians) and observed treaties and truces for the burial of the dead; the sacred truce of Olympia was a kind of early Treuga Dei, and the Amphyktionic League was a religious, not a political association.

The Delphic Amphyktionic oath prohibited the utter destruction of an Amphyktionic town and the cutting off of the water-supply of a besieged city; other rules of war, moreover, were recognized in theory, such as the prohibition of poisoned arrows, the giving of quarter to the vanquished, and the ransoming of prisoners; but when once war was begun, there was in fact little or no check to the violence and ferocity of the hostilities. The pages of Thucydides record countless instances of the relentless cruelty, treachery, and devastation practised in Greek warfare.

The Amphyktionic League.

The Amphyktionic League made no attempt to check violence or settle contentions between Greek states, to soften the ferocity of war, or maintain the principles of honour and justice. It was powerless to execute its sentences, and therefore was, as Thirlwall says, "almost powerless for good, except in cases where the honour and dignity of the Delphic sanctuary were concerned, and in these it might safely reckon on general co-operation from all the Greeks." Its political insignificance may be gathered from the fact that it is not even mentioned by Thucydides, Xenophon, or Aristotle.

But there was one Greek institution of an international character which deserves more than a passing mention. This was the Xenia or Proxenia, the hospitium publicum or public hospitality existing between two states, an institution which developed out of the sanctity of private hospitality. Where it existed, persons called proxeni were appointed in each state as the recognized agents of the state for which they acted. Sometimes a state sent out one of its own citizens as proxenus to reside in the other state; sometimes it selected one of the citizens of the latter; and in some cases the office became hereditary in a particular family, as in the case of the family of Callias at Athens, who were the hereditary proxeni of Sparta. The duties of the proxenus were to receive persons who came from the state which he represented, especially its ambassadors; to procure them admission to the Assembly, and seats in the theatre; to mediate between the two states in case of dispute; and to take care of the property of a citizen of the state for which he acted who happened to die in the country. In many respects, therefore, the institution of Xenia affords a curiously exact prototype of the consular system of modern International Law.

Xenia.

Even had the Greeks been able to establish anything like a code of International Law, it would have suffered a lengthy eclipse during the supremacy of Rome; and might even have remained hidden and lost until the revival of learning, in which case it would not have illumined the darkness of the Middle Ages or accelerated the growth of modern International Law.

In the early days of Rome the Jus Fetiale, administered by the Collegium Fetialium, was really the germ of what

Rome.

might have been a system of pure International Law, but the rise of the Roman republic to the mastery of the world rendered any system of Jus inter gentes impossible. The Jus Fetiale consisted of customary rules regulating the solemn rites used in demanding satisfaction for an injury, and, in case of refusal, declaring war; and also rules for the making of peace, the framing of treaties, and the protection of ambassadors. It was administered by a College of Priests whose functions were few and formal, and with the increasing power of Rome it dwindled into a mere "obsolete collection of formalities, no longer supported by the religious feelings of the people."

Besides the Jus Fetiale, the Romans had a far more important and extensive body of law called the Jus Gentium; but this was something very different from the Jus Gentium of Grotius and the other early publicists, and had in fact nothing whatever to do with the Law of Nations. The Jus Gentium of Roman Law, originally consisting of local customs of the Italian tribes, adopted as an alien code in Rome, developed into a body of equity coexisting side by side with the ancient Jus Civile, and ultimately identified, owing to the teaching of the Stoics, with the Jus Naturale.

There can be no doubt that the early publicists who wrote in Latin, all identified to a greater or less extent the Law of Nations with the Roman Jus Gentium, and to this misconception is due the battle of learning which was waged round the vexed question as to whether International Law was or was not, either in whole or in part, equivalent to the Law of Nature.

With the exception of that branch of Roman law regarding titles to land, which was imported by the publicists into International Law (a natural consequence of the doctrine of territorial sovereignty), the latter owes few of its actual rules to Roman Law. But Roman Law, in the hands of Grotius and his learned successors, was the guiding and animating spirit under whose influence and direction modern International Law was built up. It provided, not concrete rules, but a certain standard of reasonableness to which the rules should conform.

The classical writers make occasional allusion to a vague and shadowy Jus Belli, or customary rules for the carrying on of war. These rules in actual practice had but little authority, and were easily and wilfully disregarded, the conduct of Roman warfare being marked by unbridled and wanton savagery, alike under the Republic and the Empire. *Jus Belli.*

The great Empire of Rome was divided into the Eastern and Western Empires, A.D. 364, Valentinian being Emperor of the West, seated at Rome, and Valens of the East, at Constantinople. This was the beginning of its total disruption. Incursions had been going on from time to time since the days of Augustus, the great Teutonic tribes, the East Goths and West Goths, the Franks, Burgundians, and Vandals, having all made various settlements within the bounds of the empire. And in A.D. 476 Rome was taken and the Emperor deposed by Odoacer, a chief of the Heruli; and Western Europe was overrun by the wild and warlike hordes of Germany. From this time until the beginning of the ninth century the Empire of the West continued nominally under the sway of the Eastern Emperor at Constantinople. The Roman Empire was nominally re-united, but the actual power was in the hands of the barbarous tribes who had made settlements there. To this fact was due the origin and increase of the power and importance of the Pope. About A.D. 606, Boniface III. procured Phocas, the Emperor of the East, to confine the title of Pope to the Prelates of Rome, and to establish the supremacy of the Pope over the whole Christian Church. The Emperor having no real authority in Rome, the power of the Pope thenceforth increased unrivalled and unrestrained. It reached its zenith about *Division of the Roman Empire.* *Power of the Pope in the Western Empire.*

the eleventh century, by which time the Popes had "carried their pretensions so far as to hold themselves out as lords of the universe, arbiters of the fate of empires, and supreme rulers of the kings and princes of the earth." The dealings of Innocent III. with King John at the beginning of the thirteenth century, and the proclamation of Boniface VIII. that "God had set him over kings and kingdoms" at the end of that century, illustrate the enormous powers arrogated by the Pope in the Middle Ages.

Towards the end of the eighth century the Pope and the Roman people, seeing no prospect of help from the Emperor at Constantinople, sought the assistance of the Franks, in order to free Italy from the Lombards, who were in possession of Ravenna and threatened Rome.

New Western Empire.

The result of this invitation ultimately was, that in the year 800 A.D. the great Frank Charlemagne was crowned by Pope Leo III. as Charles Augustus, Emperor of the Romans, and a new Germanico-Roman Empire of the West was formed, destined to consolidate Western Europe and play a chief part in the history of the world.

Rivalry of Emperor and Pope.

As far as International Law is concerned, the Eastern Empire at Constantinople may now be dismissed from consideration, the object of this short historical outline being simply to show how International Law in its early dawning in Western Europe came to be affected by two predominating and rival influences—those of the Emperor and the Pope.

During the earlier portion of the Middle Ages, every important question of politics had some bearing on religion, which could bring it up for examination and settlement before the Pope, who thus, as it were, discharged the functions of an International Judge and Arbitrator, as a matter of almost unquestioned right until the end of the thirteenth century. On the other hand, the Emperor claimed to be ruler of the civilized world: there was no group of equal independent nations to whom rules of

International Law could apply; there were imperia in imperio, whose disputes and wars were feudal or private rather than international. In the words of Westlake, "vague notions of supremacy in the Pope, or even in the Emperor, beyond the acknowledged limits of the Holy Roman Empire, tended, so far as they had any influence, to keep quarrels of rulers and cities on a level with those of private individuals."

The rivalry between the Empire and the Papacy no doubt delayed the consummation of an international system; but there were many influences at work in the Middle Ages, all tending towards the creation of an international sentiment, and the accumulation of a mass of international usage, which, on the final triumph of the doctrine of territorial sovereignty, developed into a system of International Law applicable to the relations of equal and independent states. Of these influences none was greater than that of the Church. The spread of Christianity mitigated to some extent the savage violence of mediæval warfare, and the Crusades preached by the Church fostered and glorified the institution of chivalry, which dictated "humane treatment of the vanquished, courtesy to enemies, and fidelity, honour, and magnanimity in every species of warfare." The Crusades further had the effect of giving an enormous impetus to maritime commerce between the East and West of Europe. This extension of commerce led to the formation of treaties, and consequent suppression of piracy and plundering of wrecked ships, to the remarkable maritime codes of commercial towns, to the institution of the consulate, and to the development of the laws and customs of embassies. *Christianity. Crusades. Chivalry.*

By far the most celebrated of the early maritime codes is the Consolato del Mare, which contained the maritime rules and usages observed by states and cities bordering on the Mediterranean. Its date is not even approximately known, but it is beyond all question very ancient. The *Early maritime codes.*

first edition which can now be traced was published at Barcelona in 1494. The Rooles of Oleron formed a code prepared from the Consolato del Mare, under the direction of Queen Eleanor, Duchess of Guienne, and named from her favourite island of Oleron. It was revised by her son, Richard I., Duke of Guienne and King of England, for the use of the English maritime courts—a fact which proves the antiquity of the Consolato del Mare. Another very ancient code was the Lex Rhodia, applying primarily to the island of Rhodes, and later generally to the Ægean Sea. Among other more local codes were the Lois de Westcapelle, the Coutumes d'Amsterdam, the Laws of Antwerp, and the Leges Wisbuenses, originally ordinances of the town of Wisbuy in Gottland, and adopted afterwards by the Swedes and Danes.

To these mediæval codes a considerable portion of modern International Law directly or indirectly owes its origin.

There was one other great influence at work helping to pave the way for the establishment in its due time of a system of International Law. This was the study of Roman Law. After the fall of the Western Empire, Roman Law continued to spread through the medium of German compilations, such as the *Breviarium* of Alaric and the *Lex Romana Burgundorum*, into the Gothic, Lombard, and Carlovingian kingdoms, and in fact into the whole of Western Europe. This spread was systematic and continuous, and the finding of the Florentine copy of the Pandects at the siege of Amalfi in A.D. 1135 still further extended the study of Roman Law, and sowed the seed which bore rich fruit in the labours of Suarez, Gentilis, and Grotius.

The earliest traces of International Law in the Middle Ages relate rather to the state of war than of peace. If nations came in contact at all in a barbarous age, it was

Study of Roman Law.

on the battle-field. The influence of Christianity and chivalry in limiting the violence of war has already been noticed, and canons were passed by some of the Lateran councils with the same object. Not that any such limitations were of much practical avail, as witnessed by the enormities committed by Tilly's brutal soldiery at Magdeburg, and as witnessed pre-eminently by Grotius himself, who says that he had many weighty reasons for writing, and chiefly the "bellandi licentia vel barbaris gentibus pudenda," for which the Thirty Years' War, which commenced in 1618, was especially conspicuous. Human passions have been found "stronger than legal formulæ," not only in ancient and mediæval times, but also, as history shows, in more recent and enlightened days. The point is, that in the Middle Ages a body of international usage regarding the conduct of war began to accumulate, later to develop into the modern Rules of War; and the extension of commerce, the study of Roman Law, and the growth of the doctrine of territorial sovereignty gradually paved the way for the formation of the Rules of Peace.

The Reformation in the sixteenth century broke down the authority of the Pope, and finally destroyed his quasi-international judicial powers; and the Peace of Westphalia, 1648, consummated the disintegration of the great Roman Empire, and brought to an end the paramount control exercised by the Emperor in Europe. The removal of these two predominant external authorities left Western Europe in the hands of a group of independent states, who were absolute masters of the territory occupied by their people, and subject to no external control whatever. It was then that the need was first felt for some code to regulate the relations of equal independent states without appealing to any external superior; and the need was met by a succession of international jurists, dominated by the principles of Roman Law, from whose writings the true beginning of modern International Law may be said to date.

Peace of Westphalia.

International Jurists.

Territorial Sovereignty.

The doctrine of territorial sovereignty depended upon the feudal idea, the essence of sovereignty consisting not in the personal rule over so many subjects, but in the possession of and jurisdiction over so much territory. The growth of this doctrine advanced *pari passu* with the decay of feudalism as an institution, the submission of feudal lords and petty princes to the supreme power of the king, and the consequent centralization of authority in every state. This idea of national unity was perhaps first stimulated by the Crusades, and it afterwards found expression in Grotius' doctrine of the territorial sovereignty of states.

Grotius.

Grotius published his great work, *De Jure Belli Ac Pacis*, at Paris in 1625. He wrote to illuminate the popular darkness on the subject of that Law of Nations which had been slowly growing into existence, dimly perceived and little understood, through the Middle Ages; and its basis he conceived to be the absolute equality and territorial sovereignty of states.

The Reformation had already done much in accomplishing the discomfiture of the Empire and the Papacy, and in 1648 the Peace of Westphalia set the seal upon the complete triumph of territorial sovereignty. A system of true International Law then became possible. The theories of Grotius became practically realizable, and were adopted by the nations of Europe almost with one consent. "It is scarcely too much to say," writes Phillimore, "that no uninspired work has more largely contributed to the welfare of the commonwealth of states. It is a monument which can only perish with the civilized intercourse of nations, of which it has laid down the master principles with a master's hand. Grotius first awakened the conscience of governments to the Christian sense of international duty."

The Law of Nature and Positive Law of Nations.

The teaching of Grotius, very briefly, was that there was a system of natural justice, the expression of natural reason, or, in other words, a Law of Nature binding upon states and regulating their relations; and, in addition to this, there was a positive Law of Nations, consisting of their actual customs and usages, also binding upon them so far as it was not inconsistent with the principles of the Law of Nature. Grotius connected the Law of Nations, or Jus Gentium, with the Law of Nature, in order to enhance the dignity and procure the acceptance of his system, and this object was fully realized in the event.

"The notion that the Jus Gentium was an international code of antiquity, based upon the Law of Nature, brought about a wholesale adoption of its rules, especially those which regulated proprietary rights; and thus modern International Law was filled with principles and details taken directly from the legal system of ancient Rome. We see therefore that Grotius reared the magnificent fabric of his system on the foundation of a double mistake. It was a speculative error to suppose that the so-called Law of Nature was a positive code actually existing among men; and it was an error of fact to suppose that the Jus Gentium was regarded by the Roman lawyers as a body of rules for the settlement of disputes between nations. Yet, had it not been for these errors, it is difficult to see how he could have found materials for the construction of his system, and it is certain that if it had been constructed it would never have been received and acted upon."[1]

Grotius owed a considerable debt to three of his predecessors, Balthazar Ayala, Francisco Suarez, and Albericus Gentilis, Professor of Jurisprudence in the University of Oxford. Ayala in his *De Jure et officiis Bellicis* (1582) first systematically reduced the practice of nations in the conduct of war to legitimate rules; and in his first and third book Grotius closely followed the arrangement of the subject mapped out by Albericus Gentilis in his *De Jure*

Grotius' predecessors.

[1] Essays upon some disputed questions in modern International Law. By the Rev. T. J. Lawrence.

Belli (1598). Suarez in his treatise, *De Legibus et Deo Legislatore* (1612), first showed that the Law of Nations comprised both principles of justice and the actual usages of states, although his book is curiously enough neither mentioned nor referred to by Grotius. It is not to be inferred, however, that the latter adopted the theories and principles of earlier writers without acknowledgment, for in the Prolegomena to his great work he mentions both Ayala and Gentilis as having been of service to him, and of the latter he says, "cujus diligentia sicut alios adjuvari posse scio et me adjutum profiteor." Certainly, whatever he borrowed he improved, and, in the words of Hallam, "the book may be considered as nearly original, in its general platform, as any work of man in an advanced stage of civilization and learning can be. It is more so, perhaps, than those of Montesquieu and Adam Smith."

The great publicists who succeeded Grotius debated his theory of International Law. Puffendorf, who was the first Professor of the new science at Heidelberg University, in his *De Jure Naturæ et Gentium* (1672) entirely denied the authority of general usage, and identified the Law of Nations with the Law of Nature. Bynkershoek, on the other hand, who flourished and wrote at the beginning of the eighteenth century, separated International Law from the Jus Naturale, and maintained that international usage, which Grotius called the positive Law of Nations, alone constituted the true Law of Nations binding upon states.

Puffendorf.

Bynkershoek.

The controversy is no longer of importance. It dealt with the source or origin rather than the nature or characteristics of International Law. No doubt many of its rules did owe their existence to the theories of natural or divine law, but their authority no longer depends upon the truth of such theories. Rules are now observed because they are in themselves just or reasonable or expedient.

Therefore the modern view is that International Law consists of rules actually observed, *i.e.* of international usages, and has progressed beyond the sphere of influence of the Law of Nature.

As regards the history of the actual rules of which International Law is composed, it is the usual custom of writers to divide the subject, starting from the Peace of Westphalia, into periods punctuated by such great landmarks as the Peace of Utrecht, 1713, the Treaty of Paris, 1763, the French Revolution, the Treaty of Vienna, 1815, and so on, summarizing the contemporary practice of nations and opinions of writers during each period. Such a detailed review would be out of proportion in a work of the present scope, but, in dealing with the Rules of War, in Parts II. and III., some brief account will be given of divergent practice and opinion, where any particular rule has been, or still is, a subject of controversy and debate.

Speaking generally, it may be said that the Rules of War are more voluminous and more certain than the Rules of Peace. They are certainly more ancient. The early writers, Suarez excepted, evidently considered war the most important branch of the law, and one to be considered before any other. This is clear from the very titles of the works of Ayala, Gentilis, and Grotius. Rules of War more certain than Rules of Peace.

The Rules of Peace were to a large extent constructed by Grotius and the early publicists, being the logical outcome of the doctrine of territorial sovereignty : whereas it has been already seen, rules of war in some rudimentary form have existed from very early times. Their volume and certainty are due partly to the existence of Prize Courts, which have given birth to a mass of authoritative case-law, and partly to the fact that, neutrals and belligerents being alike interested parties in a great war, there has been greater co-operation amongst states in settling doubtful points than is possible in the case of an isolated dispute between two nations in time of peace.

The Law of Neutrality was the latest branch of Neutrality.

International Law to develop. There is but one chapter on the subject in Grotius, in whose day neutrality was a thing almost unknown and impossible. In the great religious wars by which Europe was torn from the Reformation down to the Peace of Westphalia, no nation could stand aloof as neutral. All were ranged on one side or the other, and ally and foe were the only two possible characters.

The modern Law of Neutrality may be said to date almost entirely from the great wars at the end of the eighteenth and beginning of the nineteenth centuries, arising out of the revolt of the English North American colonies and the French Revolution. And the account given in Part III. of the rules comprised in this branch of the law, will show that England, France, and—more than either—the United States have played the leading parts in its formation and development.

CHAPTER III

THE SOURCES OF INTERNATIONAL LAW

In his Prolegomena Grotius describes International Law as "Jus illum quod inter populos plures aut populorum rectores intercedit, sive ab ipsa natura profectum, aut divinis constitutum legibus, sive moribus et pacto tacito introductum."

Natural Law, Divine Law, and Usage are the three sources of International Law. Of these the second includes the first, for Divine Law is either revealed or unrevealed; and unrevealed Divine Law being, in the words of Phillimore, "intuitive law written by the finger of God on the heart of man," is nothing else than the Law of Nature. Wheaton says to the same effect, "the Law of Nature may more properly be called the Law of God or Divine Law, being the rule of conduct prescribed by Him to His rational creatures, and revealed by the light of reason or the Sacred Scriptures."

To Grotius and Puffendorf the Law of Nature was the great fountain-head of International Law. Bynkershock and other publicists have, on the other hand, declared the actual usage of nations to be the sole source of the law; while other writers again appear to deduce the law from treaties, from judicial decisions, from expert opinion, and from a variety of other independent sources. These divergences of opinion are in reality very easily reconciled. They depend upon the divergences of meaning comprised

Three senses of the word "source."

in the word "source," which may, from a jurisprudential point of view, be correctly used in two senses—formal and material. It may also be used in a third loose and general, or "popular," sense.

Formal.

Formally, the sole source of all law is the authority which gives it binding force. In this sense the source of municipal law in every state is the Legal Sovereign, however it may be constituted. There is no pre-eminent international sovereign; therefore the formal source of International Law is the consent of nations, tacit or express, which alone gives, or can give, binding force to the rules of which it consists. This is indicated most clearly by the definition of Kent quoted on page 2.

Material.

Materially, the sources of law are numerous. The source of a rule of law in this sense is the immediate fact or group of facts which originally called it into existence, or the influences which have contributed to its development. In this sense the Law of Nature has been doubly a source of International Law. So far as it consisted of a vague, shadowy, ideal code, a *recta ratio* to which all law ought to conform, its influence was carried by the early publicists into every branch of International Law. So far as it was a real code, identical with the Roman Jus Gentium, it contributed not only material rules of Roman Law, but also a "rich treasury of principle and definition," without which the labours of Grotius and his successors had probably been but vain. The opinions of experts, the extension of commerce, the humanizing influence of Christianity, and even mere sentiment, such as that of chivalry, have all been, directly or indirectly, material sources of International Law. But by far the widest of such sources is the actual usage of nations, as evidenced by histories of wars, negotiations, and treaties, by the decisions of Prize Courts, and other international tribunals, and by similar records.

Popular.

Coming to the third sense of the word source, it is used in a loose and popular manner to express the quarter to which recourse must be had in order to become acquainted with the provisions of particular rules of law. In this sense a treaty or judicial decision is something more than mere evidence of usage. It is, as far as it goes, an independent source from which a rule or facts bearing upon some rule of International Law may be ascertained. Divine Law has influenced and coloured the rules of International Law, but it is not in the present sense a source of them. The rules of war are not to be found in the Bible. Yet the teaching of the Bible has inspired them with a spirit of mercy and humanity. Similarly with the Law of Nature, or unrevealed Divine Law. This cannot now be regarded (whatever may have been the theories of the early publicists) as a concrete code from which definite rules can be ascertained. It is, in fact, the abstract principle of justice, the "constans et perpetua voluntas jus suum cuique tribuens." It is the conscience of nations supplying them, just as an individual's conscience supplies the individual, with a test by which rules are to be judged, rather than constituting a source from which they are to be derived.

In its popular use the word source is, therefore, not quite so extensive as in its material sense. But it is something more than merely equivalent to a "repository," for it suggests an idea of authority. The opinions of Grotius and the decisions of Sir William Scott, for example, are commonly said to be "authoritative sources," although authority can only be actually conferred by the consent of nations who accept opinions or decisions as binding rules.

In the largest and loosest sense the sources of International Law may be described as follows:—

1. *History.* History.

History records "what has been generally approved and what has been generally condemned in the variable and contradictory practice of nations," both in peace and war. It of course relates much of the matter contained in treaties, judicial decisions, and other records enumerated below as separate sources of the law, but it also sets forth the general usages of nations that have arisen independently of treaty or judicial decision, and are not to be found in any such records. History is, therefore, the most comprehensive source of International Law.

Municipal Law.

2. *Municipal Law.*

The marine ordinances and commercial laws of a particular state show how the principles of International Law are understood and practised by that state. By themselves they are only "particular admissions of general principles"; but when the ordinances and commercial laws of the great maritime countries agree, they form "a court from which there is no practical appeal." Such was the character of the Consolato del Mare, the great maritime code which met with almost universal acceptance in the Mediterranean in the Middle Ages.

Various principles of International Law have at times been incorporated by states in their municipal law. For example, the Neutrality Act of the United States, and the British Foreign Enlistment Act, although they go beyond the acknowledged requirements of International Law, contain the law upon certain subjects as understood and practised by two great powers, and are *pro tanto* sources of International Law. No rule can attain absolute authority until it is universally accepted by all the powers, but it increases in weight in proportion to the extent of its adoption. Every pronouncement, therefore, by every state upon a rule of International Law is of importance, and is *pro tanto* a source from which the nature of that rule may be ascertained. The qualification contained in the words *pro tanto* must not be overlooked. States, or "normal international persons," are nominally and theoretically equal; but in fact they occupy different grades of importance, undefined but well understood, and the voice of a first-rate power necessarily commands greater attention than that of one of lesser rank. If the opinion of Portugal and Liberia upon a question of maritime law should counterbalance the united opinion of England and France, the whole system of International Law would be impossible and absurd.

Therefore the authority of a rule depends not only upon the number, but also upon the importance of the states which give their adhesion to it. It is necessary to bear this in mind in order to estimate the *value* of municipal law as well as of manifestoes, diplomatic notes, instructions to armies in the field, treaties, and the like, as sources of International Law.

It is not for a private individual to attempt to estimate the relative value of national acts. It is simply his province to point out that all municipal laws containing principles of International Law, and all national acts of a similar limited character, do not carry the same weight, but they may all be accurately described as being *pro tanto* sources of the law.

3. *Official Proclamations and Manifestoes.*

Proclamations and manifestoes are not infrequently issued by states on the outbreak of war. A belligerent state can, in its discretion, issue both a proclamation to its subjects and a manifesto to the other belligerent state and to neutral states, explaining its attitude with regard to principles and facts which may be in question. A neutral state may see fit to issue a proclamation to its subjects, warning them to abstain from taking part in the hostilities, and explaining its views of neutral duty. Such proclamations and manifestoes can only be binding upon the states by whom they are issued and upon their subjects. To give only one instance, in 1877, at the outbreak of the Russo-Turkish War, Great Britain issued a proclamation of neutrality, quoting the provisions of the Foreign Enlistment Act, and warning British subjects of the penalties they would incur for offences under that Act. They were also warned that they would commit breaches of blockade, and carry contraband at their peril. A letter was also addressed simultaneously by the Foreign Office to the other principal secretaries of state, laying down rules to regulate the use of British harbours, ports, coasts, and territorial waters by the ships of the belligerents.

Army Instructions.

4. *Instructions for the Government of Armies in the Field.*

Instructions are now issued by many governments to their military forces. They are codes containing the laws of war as understood and accepted by the states who issue them. As sources of International Law they therefore stand upon the same footing as the municipal laws, proclamations, and manifestoes of individual states.

Diplomatic Documents.

5. *Diplomatic Notes and State Papers.*

These documents exhibit the views and opinions of particular states upon particular questions more clearly and correctly than any other records. Such statements upon points of International Law are prepared for a government by its official jurists. The profound learning and sound reasoning contained in some of these State Papers, coupled with the high reputation of their authors, have invested them with more than ordinary importance. Some of them have even become absolutely authoritative.

In the *Life of Sir Leoline Jenkins*, state adviser to Charles II. and James II., it is recorded that "his answers or reports of all matters referred to him, whether from the Lords Commissioners of Prizes, Privy Council, or other great officers of the kingdom, were so solid and judicious as to give universal satisfaction, and often gained the applause of those who dissented from him, because they showed not only the soundness of his judgment in the particular matters of his profession, but a great compass of knowledge in the general affairs of Europe, and in the ancient as well as modern practice of other nations. His opinion, whether in the Civil, Canon, or Laws of Nations, generally passed as an uncontrovertible authority, being always thoroughly considered and judiciously founded."

Perhaps the most celebrated of all State Papers is the English Memorandum on the Silesian Loan. Sir George Lee was the principal author of this State Paper, to which is affixed the name of Murray, afterwards the great Lord Mansfield.

This "Answer to the memorial of the King of Prussia" has been universally received and acknowledged throughout Europe as a correct and masterly exposition of the law of reprisals.

6. *Treaties.* Treaties.

Treaties are only binding upon the states who are parties to them, like the contracts of private individuals, and the doctrine that they affect any other state is essentially unsound. The only treaties which could conceivably do so are those which "enshrine a principle," and they are extremely rare.

It follows that treaties to which every civilized state has become a party, such as the Convention of Geneva, are absolutely authoritative sources of International Law.

By far the greater number of treaties, however, are mere bargains, commercial contracts of sale or exchange, which are not concerned with principles of International Law. All other treaties have theoretically been distributed into two classes, those declaratory of the existing law as understood by the parties, and those declaratory of the law as the parties wish to have it amended. The former are (or ought to be) treaties which enshrine an *existing* principle or rule of International Law; the latter are evidence not of the rule but of the exception, and they are of value in showing how an exceptional usage may by a series of treaties be so widely adopted as to finally become universal.

As soon as a usage becomes universal no more treaties are required to give it binding force, and, therefore, when one finds a principle enshrined in a treaty binding only on two or three states, it is difficult to resist the conclusion that it is not yet an accepted principle of International

Law. If it were, a treaty which could lend it no additional strength or sanctity would be wholly unnecessary.

Practically, then, there is no distinction between the two classes of treaties mentioned. The first class, which affect to declare the existing law as understood by the parties, do not in reality state the law as it is, but as the parties wish it to be. The latter class openly propose to amend the existing law. They are frankly "amending acts," whereas the former are amending acts disguised as "declaratory acts."

The Declaration of Paris, 1856, is usually quoted as the stock example of a "treaty which enshrines a principle." But of the four rules which it contains only one—the rule that neutral goods in an enemy's ship are free, except contraband—confirms previously existing usage; of the other three, two directly reverse it.[1] Similarly the "three rules" of the Treaty of Washington and the Declarations of the two Armed Neutralities, though affecting to declare the law as understood by the parties, were substantial amendments of it.

Briefly therefore, a treaty which enshrines a principle may in almost every instance be translated as a treaty which enshrines an exception; and an exception can only be binding upon the parties who have agreed to be bound by it. Treaties mark the transition of the exception into the rule, and are, *pro tanto*, sources of International Law.

Judicial Decisions.

7. *Decisions of International Tribunals.*

International tribunals, however and in whatever country they may be constituted, in theory administer one and the same law. Hence international case-law is almost as rich and valuable a source or repository of International Law (especially of the rules of war) as English case-law is of the principles of English common law.

---

[1] The previous practice of nations relating to blockade was so varying and inconsistent, that it is impossible to say in general terms that it was either confirmed or reversed by the Declaration of Paris.

International tribunals are of two kinds—mixed tribunals appointed by the joint consent of two or more states, and ordinary Prize Courts erected in belligerent countries in time of war. The former usually consist of Boards of Arbitration constituted to effect a peaceable settlement of disputes between two or more countries. The fact that varied interests are represented in the constitution of such Boards would at first sight appear to offer a strong guarantee for their fairness and efficacy. It is, however, in reality a source of weakness. The members of International Boards have not, in general, been men of such eminent learning and ability as Judges of Courts of Admiralty and Prize, and in the great majority of cases arbitration leads merely to a compromise of international differences and not to any enunciation of principle. It is not sought to belittle the practical utility of arbitration for settling certain classes of international disputes (see p. 51), but the decisions of arbitrators are not, in general, fruitful sources of legal principle. Boards of Arbitration.

Prize Courts are *ex parte* tribunals erected in a belligerent country to determine all questions connected with maritime prize in time of war. In theory, as already stated, the law administered in Prize Courts is International Law and everywhere the same; but practice has not always corresponded with theory, and, as is perhaps only natural in moments of intense national excitement and irritation, decisions have at times been given in Prize Courts at variance with acknowledged principles of International Law. Prize Courts.

The whole value of such decisions depends upon the inflexible impartiality of the judge who pronounces them. In this respect judicial decisions are like the opinions of text-writers, and the State Papers of official jurists, the authority of which is measured to so large an extent by the reputation of their authors.

No better example can be given than the decisions of

D

Sir William Scott, afterwards Lord Stowell, whose commanding genius and master-hand played so great a part in the building up of the law of neutral and belligerent rights in maritime war. It has been said that the courts of great maritime countries must almost necessarily feel an unconscious bias in favour of the captor, and that England has been the leading champion of belligerent rights at sea.[1] Yet during one of the most critical periods in her history, when England was struggling for her very existence, there arose a Judge in the English Prize Court whose spotless integrity was unquestioned by England's bitterest enemies, whose word nations have been content to accept as law, and whom posterity has acclaimed second only to Grotius as the most commanding figure in the history of International Law. There have been other eminent international judges, such as Chief Justice Marshall and Justice Story, to name only two, but there is no name that carries with it such overwhelming authority as that of Sir William Scott, whom the great American judge, Mr. Justice Story, calls "the ornament of all ages and of all countries, the intrepid supporter equally of neutral and belligerent rights, the pure and spotless magistrate of nations."

Opinions of Writers.

8. *Opinions of Writers.*

The works of publicists and text-writers are important sources of International Law. Materially, the law has derived a greater proportion of its principles from the works of Grotius and the other great writers than from any other source. And, in the popular sense of the word source, text-books form by far the most convenient and accessible source of information as to its rules. In this sense, all such books, so far as they merely state acknowledged rules, are sources of International Law, but the personal opinions and suggestions of their authors differ very considerably in value.

[1] Until the Declaration of Paris, at least, this was undoubtedly the case.

Certain of the great publicists have acquired so wide and acknowledged an authority that their unanimous opinion upon any point is conclusive. It is sufficient to mention Grotius, Puffendorf, Bynkershoek, and Vattel as perhaps the four greatest names. These and other great writers have been constantly referred to as authorities in the Courts of all nations. They are, as Phillimore says, " the umpires in international disputes "; and " no civilized nation that does not arrogantly set all ordinary law and justice at defiance will venture to disregard the uniform sense of the established writers of International Law " (*Kent*).

Where, however, the doctors disagree, it becomes necessary to estimate the value of their opposing contentions. Although no writer can presume to estimate the relative value of national acts, such as treaties or municipal laws, certain criteria may be suggested by which, in a broad and general manner, it may be possible to measure the value of individual opinions.

In the first place, the value of an opinion entirely depends upon its author's reputation for sound judgment and freedom from special bias. The requirement of strict impartiality is fatal to the claims of a very large number of jurists to authority. The functions of a text-writer are twofold—to *record* existing rules and usages, and to *interpret* and criticize those rules. The due discharge of these two functions leads to the suggestion of new rules for future adoption. Any confusion of the two distinct functions is an almost certain indication of bias; and some writers have even gone so far as to suppress the existing rule entirely, substituting in its place the rule as, in their opinion, it ought to be.

It is unpleasant to have to record that a large proportion of modern continental writers are animated by an inveterate hostility towards England. "It is impossible," says Creasy, "to become familiar with the writings of continental jurists without observing the ill-will with which they regard the naval ascendency of England." M. Hautefeuille is a conspicuous example. Phillimore (a most temperate critic) characterizes Hautefeuille's *Des droits et des devoirs des Nations neutres* as "disfigured throughout by the blindest prejudice," and comments upon its author's "violent and unreasoning hatred of England." Sir W. Harcourt has also subjected this "bulky libel on Great Britain" to his scathing and trenchant criticism in the *Letters of Historicus*. Similar complaint may in various instances be made of Heffter, Calvo, and other writers; and upon matters connected with neutral and belligerent rights at sea, modern continental opinion has by its partisanship forfeited almost all claim to authority.

If, however, a jurist's reputation for impartiality is above suspicion, his opinion must needs be of a certain value, in estimating which many things have to be taken into consideration. Was his country at peace or war when his opinion was expressed? Upon what reasoning is it based? Has it been acted on since? How does it accord with previous and subsequent usage? All these and other questions have to be answered in order to arrive at the true value of the opinion.

It follows that it is impossible to distinguish any particular writers as authoritative. There is no single writer, not even Grotius himself, who is of absolute authority upon every question. The only general statement possible is that certain writers enjoy a higher authority than others; that this measure of authority is based upon their evident impartiality, and that their opinion, unless founded upon unsound reason or at variance with well-settled usage, meets with a corresponding proportion of respect.

CHAPTER IV

THE LAW OF PERSONS AND THE RULES OF PEACE

INTERNATIONAL Substantive Law may be divided into the Law of Persons and the Law of Things, the latter consisting of the normal and abnormal rights of nations—in other words, of the Rules of Peace and the Rules of War.[1] Some short account must first be given of the International Persons with whom both branches of the Law of Things are concerned, by way of prelude to a brief review of the Rules of Peace and the more detailed description of the Rules of War in Parts II. and III.

A. *The Law of Persons.*

The persons with whom International Law deals are either normal or abnormal. A normal international person is constituted by a permanent community of human beings, enjoying political organization and independence, possessed of some considerable tract of territory, numeri-

_{International Persons.}

_{Normal.}

---

[1] The subjoined table may assist to make the division of the subject clear to the reader.

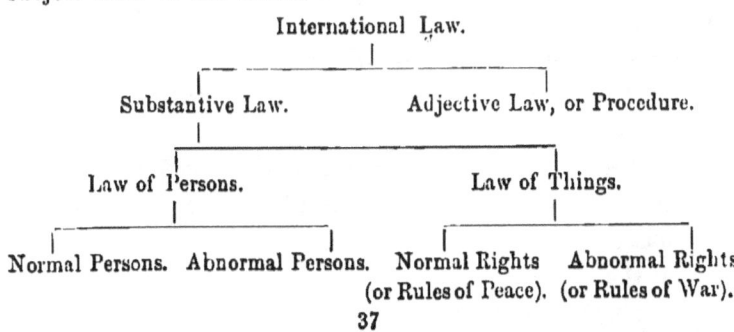

cally of some considerable size, and obeying the dictates of modern civilization. As regards the numerical and geographical size of a state it is impossible to fix any requisite minimum, but it must be large enough to be, in Bentham's words, "capable of indefinite duration."

<small>Questions of National status.</small>

A state possessing all the above characteristics is entitled to recognition as a normal international person; but whether it actually possesses them is a question of fact which every other state is entitled to judge for itself. Such questions arise when an existing state, originally lacking one or more of the characteristics of a normal international person, lays claim to recognition, as in the case of the Ottoman Empire, which was only admitted by the European Powers as a normal international person by the Treaty of Paris, 1856.

Questions of national status also arise, when a new state comes into being by the division of some existing state into two distinct states, or by the union of two previously distinct states, or by the successful revolt of a province or colony from the parent state. In the last-mentioned case, third powers cannot with safety or propriety recognize the revolted province until the parent state has done so. This principle was acted upon by the European Powers in general in the recognition of the United States of America, and of the revolted Spanish colonies in South America; and in 1862 Great Britain, upon the same principle, refused the application made for recognition by the Confederate States in the American Civil War.

Normal international persons are the proper subjects of International Law in its entirety; and, if a state lacks any of the above characteristics, it is an abnormal international person to whom the principles of International Law have only a partial or limited application.

<small>Abnormal.</small>

Abnormal international persons may be classified as follows :—

1. *The members of a Confederate Union.*
The international personality of its members is not entirely merged in that of the confederacy. They may retain a separate Jus legationis, a right of making treaties, or even the power of making peace and war, subject to the interests of the confederacy. They are therefore abnormal international persons, the confederacy as a whole constituting a normal international person, as in the case of the Germanic Confederation from 1815 to 1866.

A Federal Union, *e. g.* the United States or Switzerland, and an Incorporate Union, *e. g.* Great Britain, are also normal international persons, but their members are not international persons at all. The State of New York and the Kingdom of Scotland have no international personality of any kind.

2. *Semi-sovereign States.*

These states have not free control over their external relations, but otherwise enjoy full internal independence. They are either "protected states,"[1] or "states under suzerainty," the former being states which, although originally independent, have been placed under protection in such a way as to restrict without extinguishing their international personality; the latter being states which, although originally dependent provinces, have acquired some measure of independence, and, consequently, an abnormal international personality. A few examples will suffice.

The Ionian Republic was under British protection from 1815 to 1864, and the republics of Andorra and San Marino may be cited as modern instances of protected states. Roumania and Servia were states under suzer-

[1] The "protected states" of our Indian Empire are not protected states proper, because in their case protection amounts, so far as International Law is concerned, to extinction of international personality altogether.

ainty until the Treaty of Berlin, when they became independent, and Egypt is still nominally a state under Turkish suzerainty.

3. *Neutralized States.*

States of this kind, while otherwise enjoying full internal and external independence, are bound by treaty to abstain from hostilities, except for the purpose of repelling aggression and vindicating their neutrality. Other states are bound to respect and to assist in maintaining the neutrality of such states. Switzerland was neutralized in 1815, and Belgium in 1830, in this manner.

4. *Barbarous States.*

States outside European civilization, *e. g.* Turkey or China, which exhibit the other characteristics of a state, are abnormal international persons until they become sufficiently civilized to be entitled to recognition as normal international persons. Such states must enter into the concert of nations by some formal act signifying their acceptance of International Law in its entirety. Turkey was formally admitted by the Treaty of Paris, 1856.

5. *Trading Corporations.*

Such corporations as the East India Company formerly, and the British South Africa and Niger Companies at the present time, sometimes hold so important a position as to acquire locally a quasi-international status. One such corporation, the International Association of the Congo, has even developed into a new state, the Congo Free State, under the presidency of the King of the Belgians, and the guarantee of the great powers.

6. *Rebel Provinces or Colonies.*

A colony or province in revolt may under certain circumstances be recognized as a belligerent power or abnormal international person.[1] Strictly, rebels are liable

---

[1] This perhaps requires some explanation. On the outbreak of war between two *states*, the belligerents become invested with certain

to be treated as traitors and criminals. It is a "concession of pure grace" for a parent state or third power to recognize rebels as belligerents. Rebels cannot *claim* such recognition, but, when once they have established their independence in fact, they are entitled to claim recognition as a new state, or normal international person; and every existing state is bound to consider their claim. The difference between these two kinds of recognition is well illustrated by the attitude of Great Britain towards the Confederate States in the American Civil War.

On the grounds of humanity, if the rebellion amounts to an actual war, rebels are generally recognized as belligerents by the parent state; and similar recognition may be accorded by foreign powers in self-defence, if war is actually being carried on, and the interests of the foreign power are affected. When hostilities extend to the sea, there is a presumption that the interests of all maritime nations will be affected, and Great Britain was therefore perfectly justified in recognizing the Confederate States as belligerents in 1861. The effect of recognition is, shortly, to place rebels in the position of an ordinary belligerent state, both as regards belligerent and neutral rights and duties.

B. *The Rules of Peace.*

Adopting the lines of Austin's scheme for classifying Private Law, the Law of normal international rights consists of primary or antecedent rights and secondary or remedial rights. Primary rights are either "*in rem*," as

International Rights.
1. Normal: The Rules of Peace.
2. Abnormal: The Rules of War.

---

abnormal *rights*, but they do not thereby lose their normal status, or become abnormal international *persons*. A rebel colony, on the other hand, which has never had any international personality at all, acquires one by recognition as a belligerent power. It acquires, in fact, *the abnormal rights of a normal international person in a state of war*. It may therefore be said to be an abnormal international person, and this personality may be conveniently described as being that of a "belligerent power."

against all the world, *e.g.* a right to property, or "*in personam*," as against a particular state, such rights arising from treaties or other contracts. Secondary rights arise when some primary right has been violated by another state.[1] The procedure by which all international rights are enforced is not of course the legal procedure of a court of law, but is either war or the methods of compelling redress, short of war, described in the following chapter.

The Primary Rights of nations in time of peace may be arranged under three broad headings.

<small>Inherent Rights.</small>

1. *Inherent Rights.*

Every state has certain rights arising out of and inseparable from its mere existence as an independent state. It has a right to settle the form of its government and the model of its social institutions, a right to erect fortifications and maintain military and naval forces upon any scale, and generally to exercise full control within its dominions. It has a right to exclude or admit foreign persons, ships, and property to its shores, and generally to regulate its external intercourse with other states.[2] It

---

[1] It has been objected to Austin's scheme that, being a classification of rights, it contains no place for crimes, which are breaches of absolute duties to which no rights correspond. The classification of International Law is free from this objection, because no absolute international duties exist, and there can therefore be no international crimes. However grievously one state injures another, it commits no "crime," and is not liable to "punishment." The injured state retaliates not by way of punishment, but in self-defence, in order to obtain indemnity for the past and security for the future. As in a private duel, the injured party is exposed to risk equally with the aggressor, and does not occupy the secure position of a Public Prosecutor. No doubt the concert of states will in the end see that a wanton aggressor is practically "punished," but this does not alter the fact that states are not subjects of any international criminal law.

[2] There is no absolute "right of legation," but diplomatic agents of various grades are now so invariably accredited and received by all states, that this is sometimes described incorrectly as a right. A state cannot compel another to receive its minister any more than

has necessarily a right to exist in safety, a right to freedom from interference at the hands of other states so long as it does not interfere with them, and, in the last resort, a right of self-preservation if its safety be placed in great and immediate peril. Lastly, it has a right of equality with all other independent states. Every state has, in short, the right to "live its life its own way," to use Hall's phrase, and to "continue and develop its existence" uninterfered with. This right is of course subject to the right of all other states to self-preservation, which may justify intervention by one or more of them if the state in question live its life in such a way as to endanger their safety.

Intervention is *primâ facie* a hostile act, an infringement of the right to exercise internal control. It is justifiable in two cases. The first is on the ground of self-preservation, when the acts or omissions of state A endanger the good order, the institutions, or external safety of state B. If, however, the danger is caused by the existence of a certain form of government, or the prevalence of certain ideas in state A, intervention cannot be justified. Excessive armament abroad should be met by measures of precaution at home, and it is only when the danger is great and imminent that intervention is, in the last resort, justifiable on this ground. Secondly, a state may lawfully intervene in a civil war, if invited to do so by both contending factions. Intervention on humanitarian grounds, *e.g.* to prevent a massacre or a religious persecution, may sometimes be justified by the circumstances, but the cloak of humanity may be abused to conceal ambition and aggression, and such intervention is therefore condemned by many writers.

Intervention.

---

compel it to enter into a contract or treaty. It has the power, rather than the right, to send diplomatic agents and make contracts, the consent of some other state being a necessary factor.

2. Rights of Property and Ownership.

Property Rights.

The right of every state to acquire and alienate property is only limited by the doctrine of the "Balance of Power." The concert of states will not permit any of its members to aggrandize itself to such an extent as to threaten the independence and security of the rest. This doctrine has been upheld and vindicated ever since the humiliation of the Empire was consummated by the Peace of Westphalia in 1648. It is as old as International Law itself,[1] and was never more jealously maintained than it is at the present day. The property over which a state can exercise a right of ownership is either territorial or non-territorial.[2]

Territorial property is either land or water, and includes lakes, rivers, canals, and maritime territory. Non-territorial property comprises public vessels and private vessels covered by the national flag.

Territorial Property.

With regard to territory, a state is said to have a "right of eminent domain," because the immediate property in land is in private individuals, only an ultimate property therein residing in the state. But, as between states, with whom alone International Law is concerned, a state's territory is its property; and for the same reason private vessels are, collectively, the property of the state under whose flag they sail.

Lakes and Rivers.

Every state is owner of the rivers and lakes lying entirely within its boundaries, but it is seldom that the whole river or lake, if constituting a state boundary, can be claimed.

---

[1] According to Bacon, there is one rule "which ever holdeth: which is that Princes do keep due sentinel that none of their neighbours do overgrow so by increase of territory, by embracing of trade, by approaches, or the like, as they become more able to annoy them than they were."

[2] It is quite competent for a state to hold property on the footing of a private owner either within its own limits or in another country, e. g. the Suez Canal shares held by the British Government. This, however, has clearly nothing to do with the right of ownership as between states.

Where such a claim is established, e.g. Turkey's rights on the Danube, it carries with it a right to a sufficient margin on the other side for defensive and revenue purposes. As a general rule, however, the boundary follows the centre of a lake, or of an unnavigable river, or, if the river be navigable, the centre of its deepest channel, known as the thalweg. Where a river intersects several states, each state is owner of the portion lying within its boundaries. It has been usual for all riparian states to permit each other by treaty to navigate the whole river from source to mouth on payment of tolls. No such right, however, exists apart from treaty, as has been sometimes contended, a fact which is amply demonstrated by the history of the controversies relating to the Rhine, the Danube, the Mississippi, and the St. Lawrence. The navigation rights on these rivers were all settled by treaty.

Canals are on the footing of artificial rivers, and as regards navigation rights are subject to the same principles. In the case of inter-oceanic canals these are of great importance.[1] Maritime territory includes inland seas and the straits leading to them, bays, gulfs, mouths of rivers, ports, harbours, and the sea for the space of three miles from low-water mark round the coast. An inland sea whose shores belong entirely to one state is a private sea, e.g. the Sea of Azov. Otherwise it is a public sea.

Canals.

Maritime Territory.

A strait leading into a public sea, and more than six miles wide, has in any case a strip of high sea in its centre. If it is less than six miles wide, and its shores belong to different nations, each has a right over it for three miles, but the boundary lies in the centre. If, however, both

---

[1] The Suez Canal was in its inception politically a Turkish river, and commercially the property of a French company. After 1875, when the British Government purchased the Khedive's shares, it became practically a British highway. Its anomalous status has now been terminated by neutralization, and it is open to the ships of all nations on payment of tolls.

shores belong to the same state, it is a private strait, *c. g.*
the Bosphorus, Dardanelles, and straits leading into the
Baltic. The owner of such a private strait must permit
innocent passage to merchant ships.

There is no well-settled limit to the size of a gulf or
bay that may be claimed as territory. Great Britain
formerly claimed " King's chambers," or the waters within
lines drawn from headland to headland. France has claimed
the Bay of Cancale, seventeen miles wide at the mouth,
and Great Britain the Bay of Fundy, and the United
States Delaware Bay, both of vast extent. The Dutch
claim to the Zuyder Zee has always been held a good
one. The true principle is probably that stated by Grotius,
that the size of a gulf or bay claimed is immaterial, provided that its area is small compared to that of the land
upon which it is attendant.

With regard to marginal or territorial waters, the "three-mile limit" was laid down by Bynkershoek towards the end
of the seventeenth century. In the Middle Ages it was
held that the sea could be appropriated contrary to the
doctrine of the Roman law that the sea is a res communis.
The preposterous claims of Spain and Portugal in the New
World led to a reaction. In 1609 Grotius published his
Mare Liberum, which was followed in 1635 by Selden's
Mare clausum and other treatises. The controversy was
practically terminated by Bynkershoek, who laid down the
principle that "dominium maris finitur ubi finitur armorum vis." Effective control from the shore was the test. At
that time the range of artillery was three miles, and the
three-mile limit was gradually adopted by all states, and
claims to the high sea abandoned. This limit, notwithstanding the increased range of modern artillery and
consequent proposals to extend it, has been maintained
ever since.[1]

[1] So far as regards Great Britain, by the Territorial Waters Jurisdiction Act, 1878, "any part of the open sea within one marine league

3. *Rights of Sovereignty.*

The most important right arising from the sovereignty of a state is its right of jurisdiction, or control over persons and things. Every state has a territorial jurisdiction over its territory and ships on the high seas, and over all persons whether subjects or not, and all things in or upon such territory and ships. This right is limited only by the doctrine of exterritoriality. Every state has also in principle a personal jurisdiction over all its subjects beyond its territorial limits, but can only enforce it in the limited cases to which the doctrine of exterritoriality applies. Lastly, all states have a concurrent jurisdiction on the high sea against pirates.[1]

Exterritoriality is a fictitious attribute of certain persons and things, who are considered from motives of courtesy and convenience to be outside the territory in which they really are for the purposes of jurisdiction. They are therefore not subject to the local jurisdiction, but to the personal jurisdiction of their own country. This attribute attaches to sovereigns, ambassadors, and armies whilst in a friendly foreign country, and to public ships in foreign waters. A private vessel in foreign waters is, however, subject to the local jurisdiction, and exterritoriality only attaches to her if she is driven into a foreign port by stress of weather or illegal force, or if a crime other than piracy has been committed on board on the high seas, in which latter case her country has jurisdiction.

---

of the coast, measured from low-water mark, shall be deemed to be open sea within the territorial waters of Her Majesty's dominions" for the purposes of that Act. And, generally, the "territorial waters of Her Majesty's dominions" are defined to be such as are "deemed by International Law to be within the territorial sovereignty of Her Majesty."

[1] Up to the early part of this century this applied also to slave-traders, slave-trade being considered a kind of piracy; but the suppression of the trade is now carried out under various treaties entered into for that purpose.

Asylum.

A state has also the right in virtue of its territorial sovereignty to shelter or adopt foreigners. This right of asylum is restricted by extradition treaties, under which foreigners guilty of certain serious crimes defined by the particular treaty are given up to the courts of their own country. Extradition treaties never extend to include political offences. The conditions upon which a state exercises its right to naturalize foreigners are immediately determined by its own municipal law, but they are also affected by treaties entered into with other states. The legal effects of naturalization are necessarily confined to the territorial jurisdiction of the naturalizing state, but if the adoption is also a good one by the law of the naturalized person's original country, it holds good all the world over. Treaties enable states to confer such valid and permanent adoption.

Naturalization.

The right of the state to compel resident foreigners to perform military or police service for the maintenance of internal order in time of war is likewise derived from its territorial sovereignty. The possession of territory is a source of responsibility as well as of right, and a state is *primâ facie* responsible for all acts or omissions occurring within its territory by which another state or its subjects suffer injury. This responsibility is the subject of more particular discussion in dealing with neutral duties in Part III.

CHAPTER V

MODES OF SETTLING INTERNATIONAL DISPUTES

IT is the supreme interest of all nations that peace should not be disturbed; and in cases of international dispute, it is the solemn and sacred duty of every state to exhaust every possible mode of settlement before appealing to the terrible arbitrament of war. International disputes may be settled, short of actual warfare, by measures taken via amicabili or via facti, that is to say, in a pacific or a forcible manner. *[Via Amicabili.]*

A pacific mode of settling an international dispute may be agreed upon by means of negotiation between the states who are actual parties to the dispute, by mediation, arbitration, or by an international conference.

1. *Negotiation.* *[Negotiation.]*

The object of negotiation is to bring about an "amicable accommodation" or "compromise." The distinction between these is not very clear. The terms, however, which are used by Vattel and Halleck, clearly point to some peaceable arrangement arrived at by concessions on one or both sides. An amicable accommodation would seem to be the wider term of the two, although Halleck says it is only a particular kind of compromise; for whereas every compromise is an amicable accommodation (in the ordinary sense of that expression), not every amicable accommodation is a compromise. For instance, if one state were to withdraw its claim entirely, and acknowledge the justice of the position taken up by the other claimant, the result would be an amicable accommodation, though it would hardly be a compromise. But it is unnecessary to enlarge upon a mere matter of terminology or classification. It is sufficient to state the broad fact, that negotiation between the parties may bring about some peaceable settlement (by whatever name it may be called) of the subject-matter of the dispute.

Negotiation may either lead to an immediate and final settlement of the dispute, or to a supplemental agreement to accept mediation or refer the matter to arbitration. At the least it constitutes in every case the first step towards a peaceable settlement.[1]

Mediation.

2. *Mediation.*

As the result of negotiation, states may accept an offer by some third power, or extend an invitation to some third power, friendly to both sides, to mediate in their quarrel; but, unless the offer be accepted by, or the invitation proceed from, both parties to the dispute, any interference from a third power amounts not to mediation, but, so far as the non-accepting or non-inviting state is concerned, to intervention and possibly even to an act of war. Intervention, as pointed out in the last chapter, is *primâ facie* an infringement of the right of settling its own affairs possessed by every state in virtue of its sovereignty, equality, and independence, a right that can be only overridden by the paramount right of all states to security. The only broad ground of intervention generally recognized as justifiable is a menace to the security of one or more states by the home or foreign policy of another state, the danger being serious and imminent.

---

[1] There have been numberless instances of settlements of this kind. The British American Fisheries, the Maine Boundary, and Oregon questions may be quoted as examples, all being disputes between Great Britain and the United States, which were settled by treaties in 1818, 1842, and 1846 respectively.

Mediation, therefore, is to be distinguished both from intervention and from arbitration. It is not the office of the mediator to *decide* the quarrel as an arbitrator does, but merely to offer counsel and advice, to endeavour to smooth difficulties and reconcile conflicting opinions, and by bringing the disputants to a peaceable understanding to avert the horrors of warfare. It is a delicate and difficult office, and can only be discharged by a mediator who is free from the faintest suspicion of interest in the subject-matter of the dispute. In the twenty-third Protocol to the Treaty of Paris, 1856, the Plenipotentiaries expressed a wish in the name of their governments, that recourse might be had, before appealing to arms in cases of serious international disputes, to the "good offices of a friendly Power." They could scarcely do more than express a wish. It is impossible to compel mediation or any other form of peaceable settlement of international differences, where large interests are at stake, or national feeling runs high. Attempts at mediation by friendly powers were rejected both before the outbreak of the American Civil War, and the Austro-Prussian and Franco-Prussian Wars.

Every serious international dispute is attended with peculiar circumstances which may make mediation possible or impossible, and there are no rules which can be laid down on this subject. In the words of Phillimore, "much must depend upon the subject of dispute, upon the character of the disputants, and upon the position and authority of the state which tenders its good offices."

3. *Arbitration.* Arbitration.

This is the decision of the dispute by some third power or body agreed upon by negotiation between the disputants. The question of arbitration has been a very prominent one of late years, owing to the attention that has been excited by well-intentioned schemes for the formation of a permanent International Court of Arbitration for the settlement of all international disputes. Before proceeding to consider the constitution of such a court, there are certain rules, generally recognized, which may be stated, relating to the composition and proceedings of ordinary courts of arbitration.

The submission to arbitration must be in writing, and is usually affected by a preliminary treaty, which formulates the subject-matter and the conditions of the submission, and, not unfrequently, the rules and principles to be applied. This was the case in the Treaty of Washington, 1871, which provided for the Geneva arbitration. Otherwise the arbitrators may lay down and apply special rules, and settle their own procedure.

The contending parties appear by counsel, and, speaking generally, the proceedings are modelled on those of an ordinary Court of Justice. The submission may be made to a sovereign or head of a state as sole arbitrator, to one or more private individuals, or the choice of the whole or part of the tribunal may be entrusted to foreign states. In the first case the sovereign usually places the affair in the hands of experts, and gives their decision in his name: as, for example, in the arbitration by the Emperor of Germany in 1872 in the San Juan Boundary question, which arose out of an obscurity in the Treaty of Washington, 1846, settling the Oregon dispute.

Where an uneven number of arbitrators is appointed the opinion of the majority will govern the award, but if an even number, and they are evenly divided, the arbitration fails—unless they are empowered by the conditions of submission to call in an umpire, in which case his decision will be final.

The death of an arbitrator before the award *ipso facto* dissolves the arbitration, but when once the award has been formally delivered, it is binding upon the parties to the submission, and cannot be altered or re-considered without a new agreement.

The decision of the arbitrators may be disregarded where they have clearly exceeded the limits of their authority, or where the award is tainted by fraud, collusion, or glaring partiality, or amounts to an open denial of justice.

Hall points out that this leaves ample room, under the influence of personal or national prejudice, sentiment, or erroneous theories of law, for the commission of grave injustice; and that, as states are unwilling to stir up foreign opinion against themselves by rejecting awards, unless vital issues are involved, arbitration is therefore only adapted for the settlement of minor international controversies.

It should be noted that no state is bound to accept a proffered arbitration, nor to give any reasons for its refusal, unless indeed it has bound itself by treaty to decide a certain class of disputes with one or more countries by means of arbitration. There have been examples of such an arrangement of late years, for example in the Convention of Paris, 1873, for a Universal Postal Union, and the commercial treaty between Great Britain and Italy, 1883. These certainly appear to be steps in the direction of realizing the dream of philanthropists and peace societies—compulsory international arbitration.

The total abolition of warfare has been dreamt of by the benevolent from the Treuga Dei, or Peace of God, of the mediæval priests down to our own day. Grotius himself regarded it as both "utile" and "necessarium" that "conventus quosdam haberi Christianarum potestatum, ubi per eos, quorum res non interest, aliorum controversiæ definiantur." But the modern conception of an International Court of Arbitration may be said to rest upon the proposals of Bentham and Kant, and, more lately, of Mill; and the constitution of such a court has been advocated upon something like the following lines:—
Every state to select a certain number of representatives,

who must necessarily be men of the highest reputation, the widest learning, and the strictest integrity. Publicists or Jurists to be chosen rather than Diplomats, who might, however unconsciously, be affected by official bias; and all members to be paid a sufficiently princely salary to place them above the possibility of corruption. In case of a dispute between any two states, a committee of the Court to be formed, selected partly by the Court and partly by the two disputants, to arbitrate. The award of the committee to be binding upon the disputing states. In short, the spirit of belligerency to be stamped out by an overwhelming league of neutral powers.

Such a court would undoubtedly be free from many of the objections urged against ordinary boards of arbitration. It would be permanent, and not merely a temporary tribunal erected for the peaceable settlement of some particular dispute. Its decisions would therefore be a series of legal precedents, and possess a continuity lacking in isolated awards, which are often more in the nature of compromises than legal decisions. Further, if it was unanimous, or if the majority in favour of one view was so overwhelming as to make the Court practically unanimous, it would have the power, unpossessed by an ordinary board of arbitration, of enforcing its decisions as surely as the Central Authority of an individual state has that power within its own jurisdiction. But if the Court was evenly divided, and a particular view was supported by only a bare majority? Herein lies the essence of its weakness and impracticability. In theory, all the nations represented would be equal, but in fact, their representatives, even if men of the highest ability, and actuated by the purest motives, could never be accorded equal authority and importance. The voice of Greece could hardly carry the same weight in maritime matters, for example, as the voice of England or France. It is useless to disguise the fact, that the strong powers have too much to lose and too little to gain by International Arbitration ever to lend themselves to the formation of such a court for the decision of questions of more than minor importance.

It has been well pointed out by Sir Henry Maine, that England in particular would fare badly, and be regarded as an "unpopular litigant" in an International Court. "The truth is," he says, "our country is thought to be very wealthy, and to be able to bear the burden of a money award against it better than any other community. It is believed to be comparatively careless of its foreign policy, and not to show much sensitiveness under a judicial rebuff. Lastly, there is a general impression that it has so contrived its international relations as to escape from its fair share of the anxieties and sufferings which fall upon other states through war, apprehension of war, and preparation for war."

In other words, England is regarded by some, at all events, of the other states with a certain amount of jealousy, which could not fail to prejudice her interests in an International Court. It cannot be expected that England, or any other nation, will submit its most vital interests to the decision of any such court, however perfectly constituted. There are some questions which can only be decided by grim fighting, questions which nations will not trust dispassionately to the chances of litigation. The issues fought out at Blenheim and Waterloo could never have been decided by a Court of Arbitration.

It has been suggested that a permanent International Court, with restricted powers and limited jurisdiction, might be established for the decision of certain classes of international controversies; but, in addition to the general objections already stated, there would be the enormous practical difficulty of obtaining any international agreement as to what the limits of its jurisdiction should be. The result would probably be that its jurisdiction would be extremely narrow, and its utility would hardly justify its existence.

Much has no doubt been done, by treaties, the writings of distinguished jurists, and the labours of the Institute of International Law, to consolidate the law and thereby remove occasions of strife, and reduce the chances of war; but to bind nations down by the chains of compulsory arbitration, and abolish war entirely, is a dream beyond all hope of realization by the united efforts of all the jurists and peace societies in the world. In the words of Burke, "As to war, if it be the means of wrong and violence, it is the sole means of justice among nations; nothing can banish it from the world."

<small>Conference.</small> 4. *International Conference.*

Conferences or Congresses have been held from time to time, where there are questions at issue in which several states are interested, and they agree to send delegates to discuss these questions in a fair and conciliatory spirit, with a view to arriving at an amicable settlement.

The London Conference of 1831, for the settlement of Belgian affairs, and the Conference at Geneva in 1864, resulting in the "Convention for the amelioration of the condition of soldiers wounded in armies in the field," afford good examples of an International Conference.

They have been held either before the outbreak of hostilities, with a view to their prevention, or after the termination of a war, for the purpose of settling questions which may have arisen incidentally during the war, and may be likely to lead to future disputes. These Conferences or Congresses are not confined to the late belligerents, but other states are invited to send representatives. The Congress of Paris, 1856, the Brussels Conference, 1874, and the Berlin Congress, 1877, are memorable examples.

<small>Via Facti.</small> After all milder measures have proved ineffectual, there are various modes of terminating international disputes, *by forcible means*, short of actual war. These are retor-

MODES OF SETTLING INTERNATIONAL DISPUTES

tion, reprisals, embargo, pacific blockade, or seizure of the thing in dispute.

1. *Retortion.*

This is equivalent to retaliation, which may be either amicable or vindictive. *Retorsion de droit*, or amicable retaliation, is a remedy for any departure from ordinary international courtesy; for example, an aggressive law passed by one state as to the access of foreigners to its shores may be met by similar measures in other states. It is not really a forcible mode of settlement at all, and is usually employed where a state has acted in an unfriendly though not strictly illegal manner. *Retorsio facti*, or vindictive retaliation, on the other hand, implies the infliction of the same amount of evil on an aggressive state that it has inflicted on the state aggrieved. It is literally an eye for an eye, and is hardly worth dwelling on as a mode of settling international disputes, as the adoption of such a course would merely precipitate the outbreak of war. The general modern view is that vindictive retaliation is a purely belligerent act, and cannot constitute one of those semi-peaceable "acts of police" by which an aggression can be met without actually going to war.

2. *Reprisals.*

Reprisals are a means of redress consisting in some active or passive interference with the rights of a foreign state, which has inflicted some injury upon the state so interfering, either in its collective capacity or upon one of its individual citizens or subjects. Reprisals are passive (or negative) when a state refuses to fulfil a perfect obligation, which it has contracted, *e. g.* the payment of a debt as in the case of the Silesian Loan, or to permit another nation to enjoy a right which it claims. They are active (or positive) when they consist in the forcible seizure of the property or subjects of the offending state as a means of compelling satisfaction.

Where the injury has been inflicted on the state as a whole, the reprisals are termed general; special reprisals being confined to cases where the injured party is an individual.

It was formerly the practice to sell the property seized by way of reprisal immediately, pay the injured subject compensation out of the proceeds, and restore the balance to the state of the aggressor. It is recorded that Cromwell on one occasion took reprisals against France in this manner on behalf of an English Quaker. But it is now usual to hold the property of the offending state until a satisfactory reparation is made for the alleged injury; if this is done the property is restored, but if war ensues it is lawful prize. The right of granting reprisals is vested in the Sovereign or Supreme Power of the state, but they must only be granted in a case where justice has been openly denied, or so unreasonably delayed as to amount to a denial, and with full knowledge of the causes which justify them.

An individual injured by a foreign state must first appeal to its Courts, and not until justice has been there denied him has his own Government any claim to interfere on his behalf. If the injury be to the state, compensation must be properly demanded, and not until the claim is refused can the injured state rightfully resort to reprisals.

General reprisals consist in a general permission to all the subjects of the state to make attacks upon the property and persons of all subjects of the offending state. They are an extreme step, and constitute in practice, though not in theory, a state of war, as they amount to a declaration of hostilities unless satisfaction is promptly made by the aggressor.

Special reprisals are those which a state allows one of its subjects, who has suffered an injury from another state, to take for himself, by granting him letters of marque or reprisal, authorizing him to indemnify himself upon the property of subjects of the state from which he has received injury.

The French Ordonnance Sur la Marine of 1681 contained provisions for the issue of *Lettres de Représailles*, and more anciently in England the statute of 4 Henry V. cap. 7, enacted that in case of any of his subjects being oppressed by foreigners in time of peace, the "King will grant marque in due form to all that feel themselves in this case grieved." Such licences have, however, entirely fallen into disuse, and the expression "letter of marque" is now used to signify the commission issued to a privateer in time of war.

The most memorable case relating to reprisals is that of the Silesian Loan in the middle of the eighteenth century. In 1744 Great Britain was at war with France and Spain, Prussia being neutral. Towards the end of 1746 Prussian subjects commenced to load French cargoes on their ships, while using neutral vessels of other nations to carry their own trade. Thereupon several Prussian ships were captured by the English, and subsequently condemned. By way of reprisal, the King of Prussia confiscated a loan of £80,000 payable by the Prussian Government to certain British subjects, and secured on the revenues of Silesia.

In the controversy which ensued between Great Britain and Prussia, the views of the former were embodied in a long and celebrated document prepared by Sir George Lee and Mr. Murray (afterwards Lord Mansfield). The principles laid down therein as to the rights and liabilities of neutral trade were those which prevailed until the Declaration of Paris; and with regard to reprisals, it was laid down that they are only allowable in two cases—where a violent wrong is done and upheld by the sovereign authority, or where there is a denial of justice in the Courts, or by the Government of a state, in a case admitting of no doubt; finally, that in no case can it be lawful to confiscate a debt due to private individuals by way of reprisal for wrongs done, or alleged to have been done, by their Government.

The matter was ultimately settled by the Treaty of Westminster, 1756, by which Great Britain paid Prussia £20,000 in discharge of all claims, in consideration of Prussia agreeing to pay off the loan according to the original contract.

The British view as to reprisals, and the injustice of confiscating private debts to meet public claims, met, and still meets, with universal approval.

Embargo.

3. *Embargo.*

Embargo and Pacific Blockade are sometimes, perhaps generally, considered to be specific forms of reprisals. But they may be employed in a somewhat wider manner. The principle of reprisals is strictly compensation: to do the wrong-doer as much injury as he has done you, to repay yourself the amount of your loss, and no more. Embargo and Pacific Blockade, however, have been used to bring international controversies to a head without any idea of exact compensation for injury. The object has been to bring an aggressor either to his knees or else to a declaration of war.

Hence, as Phillimore says, embargo "stands, as it were, midway between Reprisals and War."

An embargo is a seizure of property belonging to the Government or individual members of the state which has committed the alleged injury, and the seizure may extend to the persons to whom the property belongs. It is provisional in its inception, a sequestration to compel satisfaction by the wrong-doer; and, if war follows, the property becomes lawful prize. Otherwise it is restored to its original owner. These principles are illustrated by the following cases :—

The "*Boedes Lust*" (5 C. Rob. 233).

Disputes having arisen in 1803 between Great Britain and Holland, an embargo was laid on Dutch property.

This vessel, belonging to certain persons in Demerara, then a Dutch settlement, was seized. War was afterwards declared, and before it terminated, Demerara came under British control. Consequently it was urged that the ship was not, at the time of the adjudication, enemy property. Sir William Scott, in pronouncing a decree of condemnation, expounded the nature of an embargo very clearly, stating in effect that the seizure under an embargo is at first equivocal, and, if a reconciliation follows, the seizure is converted into a mere civil embargo, and the property restored; but if hostilities ensue, the property then becomes liable to confiscation.

Great Britain and the Kingdom of the Two Sicilies, 1839.

This dispute arose out of a grant by the latter to a French company, infringing the English sulphur monopoly conferred by treaty in 1816. Great Britain laid an embargo on all Neapolitan and Sicilian vessels at Malta, and ordered her fleet to seize all such vessels at sea. Eventually, by the mediation of France, the grant to the French company was rescinded, and the ships restored.

The case of Don Pacifico, 1850.

Don Pacifico was a Jew born at Gibraltar, and therefore a British subject. In 1847, his house at Athens, where he resided, was wrecked by the mob in an anti-Jewish riot. He claimed £26,000 damages from the Greek Government, in which claim he was supported by the British Government. The Greek Government replied that he ought to have appealed in the first place to the local Courts of Justice, and refused to make any compensation. Great Britain thereupon laid an embargo on all Greek merchant vessels, and captured and detained all those found upon the sea. After a dignified protest from the Greek Government, the claim was eventually referred to certain commissioners, who awarded Don Pacifico £150. The action of Great Britain was defended at the time on the ground that the Greek courts were so corrupt that it was a mere farce to appeal to them, but it is not denied by Phillimore and other English writers, that her proceedings were high-handed, and a violation of the principles which she herself had laid down as to reprisals in the Silesian Loan.

It is to be noted that the prevalence of treaties between various states, stipulating for time for removal of persons, ships, and property in the event of war breaking out between the parties, bids fair to make the institution of hostile embargo ineffective. For if such a treaty existed between states A and B, and A on some dispute declared an embargo on B's vessels, B by immediately declaring war would of course terminate the embargo, and the vessels would have to be released under the treaty; but in the absence of any such treaty, embargo will continue to be a means of bringing about the peaceable settlement of international disputes.

Pacific Blockade.

4. *Pacific Blockade.*

This consists in the blockading by one or more powers of the coast, or some portion of the coast, of another power without at the same time rupturing the peaceable relations which exist between them. This practice hardly seems to fall within the principle of Reprisals; it is generally condemned in America, but has been regarded with favour in Europe, where it is recognized as a convenient and salutary method of coercing a weak but aggressive power, and preventing the latter from presuming upon its weakness. It is a method, moreover, that the general concert of powers can effectually guard from abuse.

The earliest instance of a Pacific Blockade occurred in 1827, when France, Great Britain, and Russia blockaded all the coasts of Greece occupied by Turkish forces, with a view to coercing Turkey. This blockade was followed by actual war, the Turkish navy being annihilated at Navarino, October 20, 1827. There have been many instances of Pacific Blockade since, *e. g.* of the Tagus by France, 1831;

of the ports of Holland by France and Great Britain, 1833; and of Mexico by France, 1838.

In the latter instance vessels of third powers were seized and brought in for condemnation, and in the earlier cases they had been sequestrated and restored without compensation.

In 1850 Great Britain, on blockading the Greek ports, established a milder precedent, only seizing Greek vessels; and the principle that Pacific Blockade only extends to the ships of the blockaded country thus laid down is now generally admitted by all the great powers in Europe, with the exception perhaps of France. It was acted upon in 1886, when parts of the Greek coast were blockaded by the fleets of Great Britain, Austria, Germany, Italy, and Russia, in order to compel Greece to abstain from attacking Turkey. That blockade extended to Greek ships only, ingress and egress being freely permitted to all ships of other nations.

France, as appears from the conduct of the French blockade of Mexico, 1838, and of Formosa, 1884 (which was the subject of a protest from the British Government), would make no distinction between the incidents of Pacific and Hostile Blockade. But it is clear that to seize all vessels, when a blockade purports to be pacific, is to arrogate in time of peace the right of interfering with trade only permissible in time of war, to disclaim the character but exercise the privileges of a belligerent.

In 1887 the Institute of International Law made a declaration approving of Pacific Blockade when applied only to the ships of the blockaded country, notified officially, and maintained by a sufficient force.

The last instance of a Pacific Blockade was the French blockade of Siam, in July 1893, but, the ultimatum of France being speedily accepted by Siam, the blockade was of such a short duration that its character was necessarily indeterminate, and it is impossible to say whether France would have adhered to her peculiar views or have conducted the blockade on the generally recognized principle adopted in 1886.

Seizure.

5. *Seizure.*

Seizure of the thing in dispute, or of the persons committing the offence, is also a step short of war, which compels the state who also claims the thing in dispute, or to whom the persons belong, to join in arriving at a peaceable settlement, or else to declare war.

It is hardly a method of settlement, but, like Reprisals, Embargo, and Pacific Blockade, in certain cases it may hasten the termination of an international quarrel, by inducing the disputants to resort to one of the friendly methods of settlement previously described.

Failing that, and when all the modes of settlement mentioned in this chapter have failed, there remains only War to decide the quarrels of nations.

PART II
THE LAW OF BELLIGERENCY

CHAPTER I

THE NATURE OF WAR

WAR is in fact an armed contest between states or communities: in law it is a substitute for international litigation.

The following definitions illustrate its twofold aspect:— *Definitions.*

"Bellum est publicorum armorum justa contentio," and "Bellum est contentio publica armata justa."—*Albericus Gentilis.*

"Bellum status per vim certantium."—*Grotius.*

(This includes private and every other description of warfare.)

"Bellum est eorum, qui suæ potestatis sunt, juris sui persequendi causa, concertatio per vim vel per dolum."—*Bynkershoek.*

(War may be carried on "quomodocunque libuerit," he says. It will be seen that modern usage is less savage.)

"War is the exercise of the international right of action, to which, from the nature of the thing and the absence of any common superior tribunal, nations are compelled to have recourse, in order to assert and vindicate their rights."—*Phillimore.*

This emphasizes the legal aspect of war, and is an amplification of Bacon's description—"the highest trial of Right."

Just Causes of War. *Just Causes of War.*

Grotius, in the second chapter of his first book, entitled

"An bellare unquam justum sit," makes an elaborate examination of the arguments contained in the Old and New Testaments, and the writings of the early Fathers of the Church, and comes to the conclusion that a righteous self-defence is not forbidden by God. This conclusion is followed up by three later chapters in the same book, "De causis justis," "De causis dubiis," and "Monita de non temere etiam ex justis causis suscipiendo bello," chapters which contain moral counsel rather than attempt to lay down legal rules, and which, it has been well said, are "valuable sermons written in the universal language of Christendom for the guidance of Christian states."

Grotius has been followed by numerous other writers in this inquiry, which is, strictly speaking, out of place in a treatise on International Law.

The jurist is solely concerned with the rights and duties of nations in peace and war. The latter is to him simply an event modifying and altering the normal relations of states without any reference to its justice or injustice; this question being, in fact, not one of International Law at all, but of ethics. "The voluntary[1] or positive law of nations makes no distinction between a just and an unjust war. A war in form, or duly commenced, is to be considered as to its effects as just on both sides. Whatever is permitted by the laws of war to one of the belligerent parties is equally permitted to the other."—*Wheaton.*

The mere fact that there is no supreme judge to decide what is just and what is unjust renders it useless to attempt to frame rules of war with reference to abstract justice, for it is possible for two nations to seriously

---

[1] Voluntary as opposed to necessary. The terms "voluntary" and "necessary" law of nations are used by Vattel; the latter being the Law of Nature, which he considers equivalent to the Law of God, *necessarily* binding upon all states, and the former the rules due to actual usage and custom, *voluntarily* observed. It is these rules only which comprise what is now understood by International Law.

disagree, and yet for each of them to sincerely believe in the justice of its claim; and it often happens in a war that neither party is wholly in the right or the wrong, as the points at issue may be numerous and complicated.

Just causes of war have, nevertheless, been distributed by writers of authority under two broad heads, the *redress* and the *prevention* of injuries; but what is usually known as the doctrine of the Balance of Power is a practical consideration at the present day of greater importance than theorizing on just and unjust causes of war.

All nations keep so close a mutual watch over the opinions and actions of each other, that it may safely be asserted that no nation would now be permitted by the general concert of powers to embark upon a war of plunder or mere ambition, or any other war contrary to the principles of abstract justice which are universally recognized. There is a modern tendency for the body of states to interfere even where no great principle is at stake; but not until an International Court with unlimited powers has been erected will it be possible for just and unjust causes of war to be defined with clearness and authority. And when such a court is a *fait accompli* there will be "no more war," and consequently no just causes of war to determine.

In short, it is impossible to determine what are just or unjust causes of war; and it is unnecessary to determine, because in actual warfare the actions of both belligerents, if they are to be governed by any rules at all, must be governed by the same rules irrespectively of the justice or injustice of their opposing claims. If International Law had the power to define wrongs as plainly, and punish them as certainly, as municipal law does, it would be possible to invest the state wronged with special rights, and the aggressive state with special disabilities in war: but these, in the present state of International Law, could not be enforced, and would be simply disregarded.

Therefore both parties to a war are considered to have equal rights unaffected by what may be called the "merits of the case."

Different kinds of Wars.

<small>Classification of Wars.</small>

Wars have been variously classified by writers who have approached the subject from different points of view. The character of the military operations in a war is the chief consideration with military writers, and they therefore generally class wars as offensive or defensive, without any reference to the nature or origin of the dispute. A war which is offensive from a military point of view, may be entered upon with a purely defensive object, *e. g.* a war to prevent aggression and maintain the balance of power. The historian chiefly regards the nature and objects of wars, and therefore treats them as wars of independence, wars of conquest, wars of propagandism or religious wars, national wars, civil wars, and so on; or he classes them geographically with reference to the barbarous or civilized character of the combatants.

But these classifications are of no value from a jurist's point of view. So far as he is concerned, the character of a war depends entirely upon the international legal status of the combatants, and wars have been consequently classified by the publicists as "perfect" and "imperfect," or as "public," "private," and "mixed." These two classifications are practically identical.

<small>Perfect and Imperfect.</small>

A perfect war is one in which one whole nation is at war with another nation, and all the members of each nation are authorized to commit hostilities against all the members of the other, in every case and under every circumstance permitted by the general laws of war.

An imperfect war is limited as to places, persons, and things.

<small>Public, Private, and Mixed.</small>

A public war is a contest between independent sovereign states carried on on either side under the direction and with the sanction of the supreme authority, which has the sole right of making war in every state, or of delegating the exercise of this right to inferior authorities in remote possessions, or to commercial corporations exercising, under the authority of the state, sovereign rights in respect to foreign nations; *e.g.* the old East India Company or the British South Africa Company.

A mixed war is a term which has been applied to a civil war between different members of the same state; Grotius regarding it as "public" on the part of the established government, and "private" on the part of those resisting its authority. *Primâ facie*, such a contest is an insurrection or rebellion, and the insurgents are liable to be punished as traitors according to their own municipal law. But where an insurrection attains to any considerable proportions, and the rebels carry on warlike operations according to the rules of war, it is usual for the established Government, on the ground of humanity, to accord them recognition as belligerents. In other words, they acquire an abnormal international personality (cf. p. 40), and become entitled to all belligerent rights as defined by International Law. Such recognition may be also accorded to insurgents by foreign powers whose interests are affected or likely to be affected by the hostilities. In 1861 the Federal Government of the United States impliedly recognized the Confederate States as belligerents by issuing a proclamation on April 19, placing their coasts under blockade. This was the clearest evidence of an existing war, and Great Britain, whose American trade was thereby gravely affected, was consequently justified in recognizing the Confederate States as belligerents by issuing a proclamation of neutrality on the following 14th May.

A private war is one carried on by individuals, or bodies of individuals, without the authority or sanction of the state to which they belong. The individuals may of course belong to the same state, or to different states. In either case they must be dealt with, not by international law, but by municipal law; in the first case that of their own country, and in the second, speaking generally, that of the country where they commit hostilities.[1] The family and clan feuds and vendettas of a by-gone age were kinds of private war, but in International Law private war, having no concern with states, has no place. On the whole it does not seem a very useful or profitable task to classify wars, the essential point being, that every contest in which the combatants on either side possess the legal status of International Persons, whether normal or abnormal, is a war for the purposes of International Law. Moreover, as barbarous communities and tribes occupying fixed territories are now regarded as abnormal international persons, although they recognize International Law, and observe the rules of war, slightly, or not at all, it is clear that practically all international passages of arms are to be regarded as war, and save where both combatants are savage tribes, every kind of warfare, whether on a large or small scale, must be carried on in accordance with the rules of war.[2]

---

[1] The Government of the country may elect to hand over private disturbers of its peace to the courts of their own country. This was the course pursued by the Transvaal Government with reference to the British South Africa Company's force under Dr. Jameson, in January 1896.

Warfare against Savages.

[2] When a civilized nation is at war with some barbarous tribe it may become impossible to carry out the milder usages of modern warfare. The laws of war are largely based upon the rule of reciprocity, but there are limits to the right of retaliation, and a civilized belligerent is never justified under any provocation in meeting the atrocities of savage races with barbarous measures condemned by International Law.

If savages use poisoned weapons or murder prisoners of war in cold blood, civilized troops must not imitate them. Strong measures of reprisal, such as burning their towns and villages, or refusal of quarter, are justifiable, but in the interests of the troops themselves, as well as of humanity and civilization, the extreme rights of civilized warfare must not be outstepped.

If civilized troops bring themselves down to the level of savages

Limits to violence in war.   <small>Violence in War.</small>

War, as Bacon says, is "no massacre or confusion, but the highest trial of right"; and its conduct is regulated by a code of rules which impose limits more or less distinctly defined to the violence which may be used in military operations. The fifteenth and sixteenth centuries have been described as an age of haughty cruelty and savage vengeance, of plot and treason, treachery and lack of faith. There was no reverence for law, human or divine, and the licence of warfare was horrible beyond description. The religious wars culminating in the Thirty Years' War were especially cruel and bloody. It has been already seen (Part I. chap. ii.) how the brutal savagery of early and mediæval warfare found some alleviation in the mitigating influence of Christianity, chivalry, the Crusades, Roman law, and the writings of Grotius; and the result has been the building up of a body of International Law which has reduced the horrors of warfare, and contributed in no small measure to the moral and material welfare of the world.

The precise restrictions placed upon particular military operations will be noticed in their due place, but, speaking generally, the Rules of War are pervaded by one grand animating principle—to obtain justice as speedily as possible at the least possible cost of suffering and loss to the enemy, or to neutrals, as the result of belligerent operations. On this principle, for example, the wanton devastation of territory, the slaughter of unarmed prisoners, <small>The General Underlying Principle.</small>

---

in their method of conducting war, how are the latter to be persuaded that the civilized laws of war differ at all from their own? How are they to be influenced towards humanity and civilization except by example?

And as to the troops themselves, if they adopt a cruel and barbarous method of warfare, it deteriorates them morally, destroys their discipline, makes them less effective when pitted against a civilized foe, and tends to import barbarous practices into civilized warfare or the poisoning of an enemy's wells are recognized forms of illegal violence.

Other Theories.

There have been upholders of a harsher theory. Bynkershoek laid down that every form of violence and deceit, except absolute perfidy, is a lawful weapon against the enemy; and it has been said that the more cruel and bloody a thing war is made to be, the less chance there is of its occurring. From this point of view, the deadly engines of war and enormous armaments now maintained by the Great Powers are forces tending towards peace. But these armaments are maintained not to diminish the chance of war by increasing its possible horrors, but merely to preserve the balance of power. That the policy of nations has not been to increase but to diminish the horrors of warfare is sufficiently proved by the Convention of Geneva, 1864, and the Declaration of St. Petersburg, 1868.

Rousseau's Theory.

The limitation of violence in war was ostensibly supported (although it needed no such support) by a plausible theory, originally propounded by Rousseau, to the effect that war is a relation of states alone, and that an individual is a stranger to the war, both in person and property, except when he is actually fighting or contributing to the prosecution of hostilities.

This doctrine was wholly unknown to Grotius, Puffendorf, Bynkershoek, and the other early publicists, and it is only of importance because it was adopted by M. Portalis in opening the French Prize Court in 1801. He laid it down as follows:—"La guerre n'est point une relation d'homme à homme, mais une relation d'état à état, dans laquelle les particuliers ne sont ennemis qu'accidentellement, non point comme hommes, ni même comme citoyens, mais comme soldats; non point comme membres de la patrie, mais comme ses défenseurs."

The doctrine is in every way an objectionable fiction. As a matter of theory, a state apart from the individuals who compose it is an abstraction to which force cannot be applied; and, as a matter of fact, the doctrine is unsupported by history or the best opinion. Sir William Scott said, "A military war and a commercial peace is a thing not yet seen in the world," and most writers of authority have dismissed the doctrine as absurd and impossible. Moreover, it has had no influence upon practice, for the usages of modern warfare, from the beginning of the century down to the Chino-Japanese War of 1894, have been absolutely at variance with it.

Its crowning weakness is that it has been used by certain continental writers as "an insidious weapon of spite wrapped up in a specious cloak of humanity," for the purpose of attacking the right of capturing private property at sea, and the right of resistance by the civil population against an invasion. It has been used, that is to say, to attack the interests of England and the smaller continental states respectively. The limitation of violence in war cannot be based upon such a discredited doctrine as this.

Hall, in speaking of the increasing mildness of the usages of war, says, "It would be more rational to attribute it to a reaction from the excesses of the Napoleonic wars, to the influence of a long peace, and above all, to the general softening of modern manners, than to a principle which has been seen to be at variance with practice, which perhaps is not seriously adopted even in theory in any country, except by writers, and which is certainly repudiated in England and the United States."

For the latter Kent may perhaps be allowed to speak. He says, "When the sovereign of a state declares war against another sovereign, it implies that the whole nation declares war, and that all the subjects of the one are enemies to all the subjects of the other."

It is probably needless to hazard a conjecture as to the future of this doctrine, but it may certainly be suggested that its adoption as a principle of International Law, so far from limiting the violence of war, would enormously increase it. War would simply consist in conflicts between armies and fleets, and bloodshed would be the only weapon. An enemy can now be brought to terms by the crippling of his commerce as well as, and sooner and more completely than, by the killing of his subjects. But if the doctrine in question were adopted wholesale slaughter would be the only means of victory. (Cf. Part III. chap. ix.)

Arrangement of the Subject.

<small>Arrangement of Subject.</small>

It will be convenient to treat war chronologically from its outbreak to its termination. It will therefore be shown how the date of its commencement is to be determined and with what formalities, if any, it ought to be declared; what is the immediate effect of its outbreak, and what are the rules of conduct in the field by which belligerents are bound in carrying out military operations; finally, how it may be determined, and what are the effects of its termination.

CHAPTER II

THE COMMENCEMENT OF WAR

1. *By whom it is commenced.*   By whom commenced

The people in their collective capacity exercised the right of making peace and war in Greece and Rome, as did also the popular assemblies amongst the ancient Germans; and in early days this right resided in our own Witanagemot.

The right is, however, now vested in the supreme power of every state, whatever may be its constitution, and in England it is the sole prerogative of the Crown, acting under the advice of its responsible ministers.

2. *Is a formal declaration necessary?*   Formal declaration.

It is important that the outbreak of war should be capable of reference to a definite date, because the effect of such an outbreak is to invest the states at war with the character of belligerents, and all other powers with the character of neutrals, and to clothe every state with the rights and duties incident to the character it thus acquires.

It is especially important in the interests of neutrals that the date of the commencement of a war should be clearly fixed, as the seizure of contraband in a neutral ship, or the exercise of the right of search, or of any other purely belligerent right, depend for their legitimacy upon the existence of a state of war, and any such proceeding before the outbreak of war would be a grave outrage, and would, unless full compensation were forthcoming, amount to a *casus belli*.

How then is the precise date of the commencement of war to be ascertained?

There are two possible dates—the actual commencement of hostilities, or the issue of some formal declaration or manifesto by one or both of the contending states.

In early times the declaration of war was a very solemn and picturesque thing. At Rome under the Jus Fetiale it was an elaborate rite, and such it has continued to be even to our own day amongst the North American Indians and other barbarous tribes. Down into the Middle Ages solemn declaration and defiance by heralds was the recognized method of commencing war. It is stated that the latest instance of the employment of a herald was in 1657, when Sweden declared war against Denmark by a herald sent to Copenhagen.

It is not surprising that Gentilis and Grotius and all the great publicists before Bynkershoek, dominated by the spirit of Roman Law, by ideas of chivalry, and by long-established practice, should have insisted upon the necessity of a formal declaration of war. This continued to be the opinion of the vast majority of writers down to the end of the eighteenth century, but in the present century the opposite view has found favour with a considerable number of jurists. In this matter, however, expert opinion can be said to have had little weight, as the actual practice relating to the manner of commencing war has for the whole of the last three centuries been varying and inconsistent.

<small>Varying practice.</small>

In the age of transition from mediæval barbarism to modern civilization, an age when Cervantes could successfully burlesque chivalry, and the conditions of warfare were rapidly and materially changing, the notion that a state should give its enemy timely notice to enable it to prepare for attack began to appear "quixotic," and declaration of war by heralds began to die away, and finally disappeared.

<small>Historical Examples.</small>

In the sixteenth century there was no declaration of war before the invasion of the Spanish Armada, and in the seventeenth and first half of the eighteenth centuries wars were seldom preceded by any declaration, though in some cases declarations were issued after hostilities had commenced, a practice which occasioned disputes as to whether the war really dated from the commencement of hostilities or from the declaration.

In the Thirty Years' War Gustavus Adolphus invaded the dominions of the Emperor of Germany in 1630 without making any previous declaration, and the wars between England and Holland in 1652 and 1665 were commenced without any declaration, though one was issued in the latter case after hostilities had been some months in progress.

The War of the Spanish Succession was commenced and carried on for some months in 1701, yet no declaration was made on either side until the middle of 1702: and in the Seven Years' War hostilities commenced at the beginning of 1756, though no declaration of war was made by the French until May 15 in that year.

After the Seven Years' War manifestoes for the information of neutrals, published within the territory of the state declaring war, began to supersede the declarations formerly sent to the enemy. And yet most of the wars during the next hundred years, especially those at the end of the eighteenth and the beginning of the nineteenth centuries, commenced without either declaration or manifesto.

During the last half-century there has been a reaction in favour of the old formality of declaration or manifesto, a mere formality as regards the other belligerent, and, in its essence, a statement of claim, or defence and counter-claim, for the satisfaction of neutrals.

The Crimean War, 1854, the Austro-Italian War, 1866, the Franco-Prussian War, 1870, and the Russo-Turkish War, 1877, were all formally commenced, the two latter by express declaration to the enemy sent by France and Russia respectively. There was no declaration of war between France and China in 1884, but this is explained by the French contention that a state of war was not actually in existence between the two nations—a contention strangely at variance with their actions (cf. p. 63). In 1894 formal declarations of war were issued by China and Japan simultaneously on August 1, although naval and land engagements had taken place on the preceding 25th and 29th July.

<small>Declaration unnecessary.</small>

The exact importance and value of a declaration may be regarded as having been settled at the beginning of this century, and the decision of Sir William Scott, that a declaration of war is, legally speaking, unnecessary, has been accepted as being beyond dispute.

<small>Cases.</small>

The " Eliza Ann." (1 Dods, 244.)

During war between Great Britain and the United States in 1812, the *Eliza Ann*, an American ship, was captured by the British in Swedish waters. Sweden had previously issued a declaration of war against Great Britain, but, as the latter did not reply to it, the declaration was only unilateral. Sweden then made claim to the ship as a neutral state in whose waters it had been captured. Sir William Scott said, " It is said that the two countries were not, in reality, in a state of war, because the declaration was unilateral only. I am, however, perfectly clear that it was not the less a war on that account, for war may exist *without a declaration* on either side." The capture was accordingly held valid.

The " Teutonia." (L. R. 3 A. & E. 394; 4 P. C. 171.)

In 1870 a Prussian ship was due to deliver a cargo at Dunkirk. On July 16 off that port a pilot told her captain that war had broken out between France and Prussia, and he put back to the Downs. By the instructions of her owner two days later the captain, instead of going to Dunkirk, put into Dover. As a matter of fact war was not declared until July 19. The consignees of the cargo sued for non-delivery at Dunkirk. Sir R. Phillimore held that war might exist *de facto* so as to affect the subjects of belligerent states, either without a declaration on either side, or *before a declaration*, or with a unilateral declaration only; and the master was excused from liability for refusing to enter Dunkirk, war being so imminent as to make that port unsafe for a Prussian vessel.

The Judicial Committee of the Privy Council, on appeal, dissented from Sir R. Phillimore as to the *de facto* existence of war on July 16, but agreed that after the pilot's information the master was entitled to pause and make inquiries, and that he had not exceeded the limits of a reasonable time in so doing. Therefore the appeal failed. The general principle, as stated by Sir R. Phillimore, that war may exist without actual declaration, was fully admitted by the Judicial Committee. In Sir Matthew Hale's words, " nations slip suddenly into a war without any solemnity; and this ordinarily happeneth among us."

A great many wars have developed out of a series of reprisals, and it is difficult to say where reprisals have ended and warfare has commenced. In such cases, if no declaration at all is issued, the war can clearly only date back to the first act of hostility; if a declaration is issued, it may determine the commencement of the war, but will not do so as a matter of necessity where it has been preceded by acts of hostility affecting neutral interests, *e. g.* the institution of a hostile blockade.

This is merely repeating the principle already stated, that a formal declaration of war is not legally necessary; and the declarations and manifestoes of modern times have been issued for the satisfaction and information of neutrals, rather than as a formal commencement of hostilities against the enemy. When a nation is forced to resort to war as the only means of exacting redress for injuries inflicted upon it by another nation, it conciliates international opinion, and justifies itself to the world in general by explaining its motives and objects in making war, and to this end issues a declaration or manifesto.

The following conclusions seem to be warranted:—

Commencement of War.

As between Belligerents

1. War, as affecting belligerents *inter se*, commences from the date of an absolute declaration if its issue precede any act of hostility. In all other cases the war dates from the commencement of hostilities. Thus, if a conditional declaration, such as an ultimatum addressed to an offending state, is followed by war, the war will date from the commencement of hostilities and not from the conditional declaration.

As affecting Neutrals.

2. War, as affecting any neutral power, commences from the date at which the neutral power has, or may reasonably be supposed to have, knowledge of its existence. If a declaration or manifesto is issued, the neutral's knowledge of course dates from the official announcement: in all other cases the conduct of neutrals is entitled to the most favourable construction, and hostilities must have become so open and notorious that ignorance of them on the part of the neutral is impossible before the liabilities attaching to their neutral character will be enforced by the belligerents.

In modern times, however, questions as to the commencement of war are not likely to arise, because the rapidity of communication, the activity of the press, and the publicity accorded to all matters of domestic and international policy combine to make the outbreak of a war immediately known all over the world. Every state is in fact cognizant of the precise date of its commencement, whether it be the date of an official notification or the date of the commencement of actual hostilities.

Its general effects.

3. *The effect of the commencement of war.*

The outbreak of war between two states is an event which almost entirely alters the whole of their international relations. Many of the treaties existing between them are suspended or annulled, all friendly intercourse is broken off, and trading with the enemy, except by express permission, becomes illegal. A belligerent also acquires rights over the property of the other belligerent, and over the persons and property of its subjects found in his territory. Such, as between the belligerents, are the consequences of an outbreak of war, the nature and extent of which must now be considered.

But the outbreak of war is a matter of universal concern. When a state commences war, the persons and property of its own subjects, of the subjects of its allies, of the subjects of neutral powers, and of the subjects of the enemy and its allies, are all affected in various ways.

It is in this aspect of war that usage demonstrates most clearly the absurdity of the theory that "war is a relation of states and not of individuals," and that the latter are only affected in the character of actual combatants. In the rules regulating the conduct of armies in the field, war is dealt with purely from the point of view of the combatants, the fighting representatives of the contending states; and in that limited aspect of war the theory does not meet with so many glaring contradictions. Yet, to take one example, even here its upholders find such recognized military measures as contributions and requisitions rather awkward obstacles to surmount.

It will be convenient to state the effect of the commencement of war upon enemy persons and enemy property, without at present pausing to inquire in each case what persons and property are to be considered hostile. A momentary assumption of their hostility will save repetition, and in the next chapter will be found a description of the various circumstances which impress an enemy character upon persons, property, and territory.

4. *The effect upon treaties.*   Effect upon Treaties.
Treaties binding upon one or both of the belligerents are alone affected by the outbreak of war. Taking into

consideration the vast number and complex provisions of the treaties by which states are bound, or have at different times been bound, it is not surprising to find wide divergences, both in opinion and practice, as to the effect exercised upon them by the commencement of war. It is impossible to arbitrarily distribute treaties into distinct classes, so as to be able to lay down with certainty the particular effect which war will have upon every particular treaty. The factors which, broadly, determine that effect are the subject-matter of the treaty, the parties to it, and the permanent or temporary character of the objects it was designed to achieve.

<small>Three possible effects.</small>

War may affect treaties in three possible ways. It may suspend their operation during the war, in which case they will revive, *ipso facto*, at its termination; or it may annul them, in which case they can only be revived by express agreement at the end of the war; or it may leave them untouched. A treaty is not an indivisible whole, and, where it deals with a variety of matters, it is within the bounds of possibility that some of its provisions will be merely suspended, others annulled, and others remain unaffected by the outbreak of war.

Two propositions only may be advanced with any certainty:—

<small>Treaties contemplating War.</small>

1. Treaties which expressly contemplate the existence of war, and provide for matters only arising in time of war, are obviously neither suspended nor annulled by the commencement of war. They are practically suspended or dormant during peace, and it is war which calls them into active operation. The Geneva Convention, 1864, as to the treatment of the wounded, is an example of such a treaty. The Declaration of Paris, 1856, is not, as will appear hereafter, strictly a treaty, but it was an international agreement as to rules regulating the conduct of certain hostilities in

future wars; and, as such, so long as it exists, will continue binding upon its signatories in the event of war breaking out between any of them.

2. Treaties whose object has been to create some permanent state of affairs by an act done once for all, are unaffected by the commencement of war, whether the parties to them consist of the belligerents alone, or of one or both of the belligerents, and third powers in addition. This proposition is supported by common-sense and actual fact. Treaties effecting permanent settlements at the end of great wars, such as the Treaty of Vienna, 1815, or of Paris, 1856, cannot be affected by the mere commencement of any subsequent war, although that war may end in a treaty modifying or abrogating the previous treaties.

Treaties of Settlement.

Similarly a treaty ceding territory—an act done once for all—whatever be the parties to it, remains unaffected by the outbreak of war.

As regards all other treaties, which do not fall within either of the above classes, no authoritative rules can be laid down. Without attempting any exact classification, they appear with reference to their subject-matter and signatories to be capable of distribution under two broad headings :—

Other Treaties.

1. Treaties whose object has been to constitute a continuous course of conduct, binding upon one or both of the belligerents, and one or more third powers.

Treaties binding Belligerent and other States.

Treaties of this kind should logically, if not annulled—and there seems no reason why they should be annulled—either continue or be suspended according as the course of conduct provided for is, or is not, consistent with the existence of war and the requirements of the laws of neutrality.

86 THE LAW OF WAR

Treaties binding Belligerents alone.

2. Treaties binding the belligerents alone, other than those described above, making permanent settlements by an act done once for all.

All intercourse between belligerent states being prohibited, it is clear that all such treaties as deal with their social and commercial relations must be at least suspended, and possibly annulled.

Various distinctions have been suggested by various writers, and varying treatment has been adopted by belligerent states with reference to treaties. The entire absence of certain rules has given rise to the modern practice of settling by treaty at the end of the war the exact status of treaties and conventions binding the belligerents at its commencement. But it is worthy of note that these *ex post facto* settlements have been so varying and inconsistent in principle that they do not afford a basis for the formulation of any general rule or rules as to the effect of the outbreak of war upon treaties.

Effect upon Belligerent's own subjects.

5. *The effect upon the persons and property of a belligerent's own subjects.*

When a state declares war, all its subjects become enemies of all the subjects of the opposing belligerent, and all intercourse, commercial or otherwise, between them is necessarily suspended, with the following consequences.

Contracts.

The fulfilment or enforcement of contracts with or debts due to an enemy subject, existing at the outbreak of war, is, as a general rule, suspended until its termination,[1] no action being maintainable by a subject of one belligerent in the courts of the other during the continuance of hostilities.[2]

Some contracts are of such a nature that they are not merely suspended but extinguished, the contract of partnership being an example, inasmuch as the partners

---

[1] Wolff *v.* Oxholm. 6, Maul. and Sel. 92.
[2] Alcinous *v.* Nigreu. 4, E. and B. 217.

THE COMMENCEMENT OF WAR

cannot take up their joint business on the conclusion of the war at the precise point where they abandoned it when war commenced.[1] All contracts entered into with an enemy subject after the outbreak of war and during its continuance are void, except contracts made under the stress of necessity.[2] An example of the latter is afforded by ransom-bills, which are, shortly, contracts by the master of a prize to pay the captor a sum of money in lieu of the prize being destroyed or taken into port, and in consideration of exemption from capture for the rest of her voyage. (Cf. chapter vi. of this Part.)

Another consequence of the outbreak of war is, that all trading with the enemy, except under a royal licence, becomes illegal; and if a subject embarks his property in such an enterprise, it becomes liable to confiscation.

Trading.

The rule is so strictly applied that it has been held that a royal licence authorizing a homeward trade from the enemy's possessions does not cover the outward trade thereto, although intimately connected with and almost necessary to the existence of the homeward trade,[3] and a cargo purchased before but shipped after the outbreak of war is, if captured, liable to confiscation.[4] If, however, a loyal subject endeavours, in good faith, to remove his property from the enemy's country as soon as possible after the outbreak of war, it will be exempt from liability to capture.[5]

A cartel ship, whose business is to effect exchange of prisoners under a safe-conduct from the enemy, loses her protection and becomes liable to capture by either belligerent if she engages in trade.[6] And a contract, such as a policy of insurance, made in furtherance of illegal trading

[1] Griswold *v.* Waddington. 15, Johnson's Reports, 57.
[2] Antoine *v.* Morshead. 6, Taunt, 237.
[3] The *Hoop*. 1, C. Rob. 196.
[4] The *Rapid*. 8, Cranch. 155.
[5] The *Grey Jacket*. 5, Wallace, 342.
[6] The *Venus*. 4, C. Rob. 355.

with the enemy, is, like other contracts made during the war, void.¹

Personal conduct.

As to the personal conduct of subjects, in England under the Treason Act of 25, Edward III., British subjects adhering to the Queen's enemies, and giving them any aid or comfort, either within the realm or without it, are guilty of high treason, and punishable with death; and there is probably no country in which such conduct on the part of a subject is not considered a treasonable offence.

Special statutes are sometimes passed by a belligerent state on the outbreak of war relating to the conduct of its subjects during the war. An instance occurred at the beginning of the Crimean War, when an English statute was passed making any dealing with securities issued by the Russian Government during the war a misdemeanour.

6. *The effect upon the persons and property of the subjects of an ally.*

Effect upon subjects of an ally.

Allies, says Bynkershoek, "unam constituunt civitatem"; and this being so, the effect of the commencement of war upon the subjects of a belligerent state, and upon the subjects of its ally or allies, is identical, and what has been already said of the former holds good as to the latter.

The unity of allied states is such that a belligerent cruiser may lawfully take a prize into a port belonging to an ally, and it may there be condemned by the ally's Prize Court; and a merchant ship of one ally trading with the enemy may rightly be captured by a cruiser belonging to the other of two allied states.²

7. *The effect upon the persons and property of the subjects of neutral states.*

Effect upon subjects of neutral states.

The outbreak of war brings into operation all the laws

---

[1] Potts v. Bell. 8, Term Reports, 548.

[2] The *Neptunus*, 6, C. Rob. 403. Cp. the *Nayade*, 4, C. Rob. 251, *infra*, p. 97.

of neutrality, and these are binding upon all neutral states and their subjects, the latter, as individuals, being especially affected as to their persons by the laws concerning foreign enlistment, and as to their property by the laws of contraband and blockade.

These topics are all discussed in their appropriate places in Part III., which deals with the relations of neutrals and belligerents.

8. *The effect upon the persons and property of the subjects of the enemy.*

At the outbreak of war a vast majority of the enemy's subjects will, together with the bulk of their property, be within the limits of the territory of their own state. The commencement of war, therefore, does not immediately affect them, in person or property, unless and until their country is invaded by their enemy. The incidents of a military occupation are described in chapter vi. of this Part. <small>Effect upon subjects of the enemy.</small>

The persons and property of enemy subjects in neutral states are for the same reason not immediately affected by the commencement of war. They are out of hostile reach. But on the high seas, where no state has exclusive jurisdiction, enemy persons and property become liable to capture immediately upon the outbreak of war; and the subjects and public and private property of one belligerent found within the jurisdiction of the other at the commencement of the war, according to the strict theory of hostile relations, become liable to detention or seizure.

The exercise of the undoubted right of one belligerent to seize the subjects of the other so found in his territory, has been limited and modified both by municipal laws and regulations, and by the usage of nations, confirmed by a long series of treaties. But the existence of the right is clearly proved by the means that have been found necessary to limit it. <small>Enemy persons.</small>

By Magna Charta it was provided that merchants

belonging to the country of the enemy shall, at the outbreak of war, be attached without harm of body or goods till the King or his Chief Justiciary be informed how our merchants are treated in the country with which we are at war; and if ours be secure in that country they shall be secure in ours. And by the Statute of Staples, 27 Edward III., foreigners were granted a warning of forty days by proclamation in which to depart the realm with their goods on the outbreak of war.

Similar laws and regulations have been made by other states at various times, moderating the harshness of the ancient rule.

From the seventeenth century it has been usual to insert stipulations in nearly all commercial treaties, that in case of war between the contracting parties a reasonable time (six months to a year) shall be granted mutually to each other's subjects to withdraw with their property.

A still milder usage has grown up in more recent times, and is enshrined in a great number of treaties, subjects of either belligerent being allowed to remain unmolested during the war in the dominions of the other, so long as they behave peaceably, commit no offences against the laws, and make no attempt to communicate with their own country or with its ships. This was the course adopted both during the Crimean and Franco-Prussian Wars.

The right to stay is not yet, perhaps, so clearly established as the right to retire, but it may be said that enemy subjects are entitled to one or other of these rights, and cannot now be detained as prisoners of war on the outbreak of hostilities.

The last example of the exercise of the right in its ancient rigour was in 1803, at the beginning of the war between Great Britain and France, when Napoleon ordered the arrest of all Englishmen in France between the ages of sixteen and sixty. His action has been generally condemned. It was, in fact, a gross breach of faith according to modern views, and it is improbable that any attempt will be made in the future to revive the obsolete severity of the strict rule.

With regard to enemy property, both public and private, the old rule was res hostiles res nullius, and it was liable to seizure wherever seizure could be effected. This right was formerly exercised with much rigour, but it has gradually given way to milder usage, until, like the right of detaining enemy subjects just noticed, it has become almost non-existent. It was, in fact, the indulgence granted to enemy subjects, necessarily extending to their property, which has tended to the immunity of enemy property within the jurisdiction; but this immunity is not so pronounced as that extended to the persons of enemy subjects. As Hall says, "Although seizure would always now be looked upon with extreme disfavour, it would be unsafe to declare that it is not generally within the bare rights of war."

Enemy property.

The milder practice has been due to policy rather than to principle. For example, the exemption of debts from confiscation is due to the fact that a state by confiscating debts due to enemy subjects will probably compel its own subjects to pay them twice over, viz. to itself, and after the war to the original creditor.[1] There is only one species of debt which is absolutely safe from confiscation— a debt due from the Government of one belligerent to private citizens of the other belligerent.[2] All other debts, public and private, are theoretically liable to confiscation, and a belligerent is strictly entitled to seize every kind of personal property belonging to enemy subjects found within his territory.

The ancient English practice of seizing and condemning as "droits of admiralty" the property of the enemy found in English ports at the commencement of war, illustrates

[1] Wolff v. Oxholm. 6, Maul. and Sel. 92.
[2] The Silesian Loan. Cf. *supra*, p. 59.

the former rigour of the rule. But in recent times a usage has grown up for belligerents to allow enemy merchant ships six weeks in which to quit their respective ports. Of course when war has once commenced, ships entering the territorial waters of an enemy are strictly liable to capture and condemnation. Exemption has been on occasion accorded in the case of enemy vessels driven in by stress of weather, from motives of pure generosity.[1] But there is no rule of international any more than of municipal law to compel generosity, and any such vessel may be made lawful prize just as she might be on the high sea.

[1] In 1746 an English man-of-war was driven into Havana and offered to surrender. She was not only allowed to refit, but to proceed on her voyage with a passport protecting her as far as the Bermudas. Such generosity as this appears to be misplaced. To allow a ship of war to go free is to neglect an opportunity of diminishing the enemy's fighting force. "It is magnificent, but it is not war," the first duty of a belligerent state being that which it owes to itself.

CHAPTER III

ENEMY CHARACTER

THE old-fashioned barbarous belligerent "plan" was, of course, that "he should take who had the power," without inquiring too minutely into the character of what was taken. That a strange ship was not a friend or an ally was often quite enough to make her fair game for the glorious but piratical old sea-dogs of the sixteenth century.

Refinements as to enemy character undreamt of in those days owe their origin to the conception of neutrality, which till the eighteenth century was vague and almost non-existent, and their development to the creation and growth of the Law of Neutrality within the last hundred and fifty years.

Enemy character may attach to persons, to property, or to territory and its produce, and is in every case ultimately determined by the application of one broad leading general principle.

Where a person of whatever nationality, or his property, or a tract of territory, becomes connected with the enemy state in such a manner as to be a source, directly or indirectly, of strength and assistance to that state, such person, property, or territory must be regarded as being subject to or belonging to the enemy, and acquires an enemy character. *The general principle.*

Enemy character as attaching to persons and their property may arise from permanent allegiance to, and residence within the territory of, the adverse belligerent, in which case it is complete; or it may be of a partial and temporary nature, limited to certain intents and purposes, arising from such particular circumstances as having possessions in enemy territory, or maintaining a house of commerce there, from personal residence there, or from particular modes of traffic, such as sailing under the enemy's flag or passport.

In this manner a belligerent's own subject or a neutral subject may acquire an enemy character depending upon a kind of implied temporary allegiance to the enemy state; but as soon as he chooses to terminate his hostile allegiance he terminates his hostile character.

<small>Enemy Character not co-extensive with Nationality.</small>
To put it briefly, enemy character does not coincide with national character. A subject of the adverse belligerent may by the Rules of War be in the position of a neutral subject, or a neutral subject in the position of an enemy subject, the one test being in all cases not nationality but domicil.

How persons and property are affected by a residential or commercial domicil in time of war is explained more fully below, and it will be seen that property may acquire a hostile character from other causes than the hostile domicil residential or commercial of its owner, and that the hostility of territory depends upon its being within the *de facto* control of the enemy, thus illustrating the broad general principle already stated.

1. *Hostile Persons.*

<small>Domicil.</small>
The primary test of the legal position of an individual in respect of belligerent operations is domicil and not nationality. There are two kinds of domicil, residential and
<small>Residential.</small> commercial. The former of these affects an individual in his private and personal relations, and as regards his property and contracts, both in time of peace and in time of war. In the eye of the law he can never be without some residential domicil, which has been well described as "the central station of a man's fortunes."

A commercial domicil, on the other hand, does not affect a man's person but only his property, and that only in time of war. Ordinary or residential domicil (which will hereafter in these pages be termed simply domicil) may be defined as " the relation of an individual to a particular state which arises from his residence within its limits, as a member of its community." A man may be said to acquire a *civil* status by his domicil, and a *political* status by his nationality, which is not affected by his place of residence. Commercial.

Residential Domicil.

Domicil may be acquired in two ways—" by origin," or " by choice." A domicil of origin is that of every individual at his birth, *i. e.* that of his father, or, if posthumous or illegitimate, that of his mother, and during his legal infancy the domicil of the child changes with that of his parent, or, if he be an orphan, of his guardian. Of origin.

When a man becomes *sui juris*, he may change his domicil of origin by actual removal to a new place of residence, coupled with an animus manendi, or intention to stay there indefinitely. He thereby acquires a " domicil by choice," but unless and until he makes this positive change his old domicil of origin continues; and, in the event of the domicil by choice being terminated at any time, the domicil of origin revives and continues until a new domicil by choice is duly acquired. By choice.

Thus a man never entirely loses his domicil of origin during his life. At the most it is only dormant, and is always ready to revive on the termination of a domicil by choice. It follows that the latter may be more easily abandoned than is possible in the case of domicil of origin, which can only be superseded by the substitution of a domicil by choice completely established and evidenced by an intention to give up the old domicil, actual removal to a new country, and an intention to stay there indefinitely. And it must be noted that there are some circumstances incompatible with such an intention; *e. g.* where a person is involuntarily detained in a country, or is liable to be removed from it by the orders of a superior. There is also the fiction of exterritoriality, which renders the acquisition of a foreign domicil by princes and diplomatic agents in a foreign country impossible.

It is domicil, then, which at the commencement of war determines the status of every individual with reference to it; and if war breaks out between countries A and B, a subject of A domiciled in B becomes in person and property an enemy as regards A in all respects save one. He cannot be compelled to serve against his own country in the war, this being inconsistent with his native allegiance.

This principle has been reinforced by treaties between some states, stipulating that in case of war between them subjects of the one country domiciled in the other shall not be compelled to serve for national or political objects, but only by way of police for the maintenance of internal order. This, however, does not apply to subjects of one state in the permanent, civil, or military employ of another. Such persons are so closely identified with the state in whose service they are, that they are enemies of its enemies for every purpose.

It is always open to a man to change his domicil, but he is presumed to have retained throughout the war the domicil that he had at its commencement until he proves the contrary. If a man changes his domicil with a view to the commencement of the war, or during its continuance, the burden of proof is upon him to show that the change was made in good faith, and with no fraudulent purpose or intention of returning.

It is quite clear that a man who has an enemy domicil at the beginning of a war cannot be allowed to change it to a neutral one *flagrante bello*, intending to resume the previous domicil at the end of the war, as all belligerent rights of capture might be thereby defeated.

2. *Hostile Property.*

The enemy character of an individual as such is not of

great importance so long as he keeps his person out of the sphere of belligerent operations. Its chief importance is that it is one of the circumstances which determine the liability of ships and property captured at sea during the war.

A. The first and most general circumstance to impress a hostile character upon property is the enemy character of its owner, arising from his domicil. His property is regarded as being "attendant on him," and partakes of his enemy character. *Enemy character of owner.*

The following cases illustrate the application in England and the United States of the general principles as to domicil already stated, and the manner in which it determines the enemy character of persons, and consequently of their property. *Cases.*

The "Indian Chief." (3, C. Rob. 12.)

During the war between England and Holland this vessel, which belonged to an American citizen domiciled in England, made a voyage from London to Madeira and other places, eventually taking in a cargo at Batavia, which belonged to Holland. In 1797, on her return to England, she was arrested for illegal trading with the enemy. Before that date, however, her owner had left this country for good, and had returned to the United States. Sir William Scott held that by *bonâ fide* quitting the country *sine animo revertendi*, her owner had terminated his English domicil, and consequently the ship was not liable to condemnation.

The "Nayade." (4, C. Rob. 251.)

This ship was captured on a voyage from Lisbon to Bordeaux in 1802, England being at war with France, and Portugal being her ally. The cargo belonged to a Prussian merchant resident in Lisbon, and was condemned by Sir William Scott for illegal trading with the enemy on the part of an ally, the owner's domicil being Portuguese.

II

The " Ocean." (5, C. Rob. 90.)

A British merchant, settled at Flushing, on the imminent approach of hostilities in 1803, dissolved his partnership and took other measures with a view to return to England. He was, however, prevented by the forcible detention of all British subjects who happened to be within the territories of the enemy at the outbreak of the war. Sir William Scott held him entitled to restitution of his property which had been captured as enemy property. His enemy domicil terminated and his British domicil of origin revived when he made up his mind, and actively endeavoured, to leave the hostile territory, *sine animo revertendi*.

The " Venus." (8 Cranch, 280.)

This ship, together with her cargo, belonged to certain American citizens settled in England, and engaged in commerce there. She sailed from an English port after the outbreak of the war between Great Britain and the United States in 1812. She was captured by an American privateer, and condemned by an American court, the hostile domicil of her owners rendering her enemy property.

Hostile commercial domicil of owner.

B. The next circumstance which may affect property with a hostile character is the commercial domicil of its owner.

A man has a commercial domicil in any country in which he owns or is partner in a commercial establishment. It follows that he may possess more than one such domicil, co-existing and utterly unconnected with his ordinary legal domicil.

Commercial domicil does not affect a man's personal status, but it imparts an enemy character to the property which he possesses connected with a commercial establishment in an enemy country; and the character of every commercial transaction is tested with reference to the establishment where it originated.

Two illustrations will make this perfectly clear.

The "Portland." (3 C. Rob. 41.)

During the war between England and France in 1800, this vessel was seized on the ground that part of the cargo belonged to an enemy subject, and was therefore enemy property. It belonged to a neutral (a German) who had two houses of business, one in enemy and one in neutral territory, the transaction in this case being connected with the latter. It was contended that having a house of trade in the enemy's country made him an enemy subject, and gave an enemy character to all his transactions. Sir William Scott held that there was no case or principle to support such a proposition, and the cargo was released.

The " Jonge Klassina." (5 C. Rob. 297.)

Great Britain and Holland being at war in 1804, a merchant having two houses of business, one at Birmingham and the other at Amsterdam, obtained a royal licence to import goods as a Birmingham merchant from Holland. He then proceeded to export goods from his Dutch house to his English house, and a cargo was captured. It was held that where a man has mercantile concerns in two countries, and acts as a merchant in both, the character of each of his transactions is determined by the place where it originated. In this case the transaction was clearly Dutch, and, not being protected by the royal licence (cf. the *Hoop*, supra, p. 87), confiscation of the goods was decreed.

C. There are other circumstances which may give property an enemy character irrespective of the domicil or commercial domicil of its owner. *(Other circumstances impressing enemy character upon property.)*

These circumstances, all implying some association with the interests of the enemy, may be arranged under three heads.

(1) The origin or local position of the property.

(2) The character of the trade in which the property is embarked.

(3) The mode in which the trade is conducted.

(1) *The origin or local position of the property.*

Origin or local position.

Land and movable property locally situated in an enemy country, and belonging to a neutral, acquire an enemy character without regard to the status of their owner. All persons not otherwise enemies, whether subjects, subjects of an ally, or neutral subjects, are, so far as they are holders of enemy soil, taken to have incorporated themselves with the enemy state. Within the limits of the enemy territory such property can, of course, only be endangered by the invasion of the adverse belligerent; but if the produce of the land or the movable property be exported beyond those limits its hostile origin renders it liable to capture by the enemy.

Enemy character imposed by a commercial domicil, as already described, is an illustration of this rule. But the rule is of wider application, and extends to impart a hostile character to property, the owner of which cannot be said to have a hostile commercial domicil.

The "Phœnix." (5, C. Rob. 20.)

During war between Great Britain and Holland in 1803, this vessel was captured on a voyage from Surinam to Holland. The cargo was claimed in the English court by certain persons resident in Germany, as being the produce of their estates in Surinam, a Dutch settlement in South America.

Sir William Scott held that, being the produce of the claimant's own plantation in an enemy colony, the cargo must be condemned.

Bentzon v. *Boyle.* (9, Cranch, 191.)

This is the well-known case of the "Thirty hogsheads of sugar." During the war which broke out between Great Britain and the United States in 1812, the plaintiff, a Dane, exported sugar, the produce of his estate in Santa Cruz, in a British ship to London. Santa Cruz originally belonged to Denmark, but had been taken possession of by British forces. The ship was captured by a United

States cruiser, and the cargo condemned. Condemnation was affirmed on appeal, the plaintiff in respect of land belonging to him in Santa Cruz being bound by whatever the fate of the latter might be. At the time of the capture it was British, and its produce was therefore hostile.

(The converse of this doctrine is rejected by Great Britain and the United States. Property originally hostile does not acquire a friendly character by the fact of the place from which it comes ceasing to be enemy soil. Cf. the *Boedes Lust*, supra, p. 60.)

(2) *The character of the trade in which the property is embarked.*

(*a*) A cargo belonging to a neutral subject, whether in a neutral or an enemy ship, has an enemy character, and may be seized by a belligerent, if it consists of contraband intended for the use of the other belligerent. If the contraband is laden on a neutral ship, the enemy character extends in certain circumstances to the ship as well, in which case it will also be liable to confiscation. (See Part III. chap. v.) Trade in which embarked.
(*a*) Contraband.

(*b*) A ship owned by a neutral acquires an enemy character by wilfully acting as a despatch-boat or transport for the enemy, despatches and persons in the military or naval service of the enemy being regarded as "analogues of contraband." (See Part III. chap. v.) (*b*) Analogues of contraband.

(*c*) A neutral ship by engaging in time of war in a colonial or coasting trade closed to foreigners in time of peace adds to the force and resources of one belligerent, and practically becomes enrolled in its mercantile marine. Both ship and cargo are therefore hostile, and are liable to capture and confiscation by the other belligerent. (*c*) Breach of Rule of 1756.

(This is the celebrated "Rule of 1756," for a fuller discussion of which, together with its application to continuous voyages, see Part III. chap. vii.)

(*d*) The original character of both ship and cargo is

(d) Fraudulent assignments of enemy ships or cargoes to Neutrals.

liable to be altered by assignment. Therefore, in order to prevent the protection of belligerent ships and cargoes from hostile capture by means of fraudulent assignments, all sales and transfers of ships at sea during the war are scrutinized with great jealousy by prize courts.

The assignment of an enemy ship or her cargo *in transitu* made up to the outbreak of war is generally held valid; but if such an assignment be effected during the war, or in contemplation of a war to the knowledge of the assignee, it is regarded as invalid both by English and American courts.

The assignment of an enemy ship to a neutral not *in transitu*, but in an enemy port, even if made *flagrante bello*, is valid, provided that the assignor retains no interest in the ship, and that it is in all respects a *bonâ-fide* transaction. A neutral cargo consigned to an enemy is *in transitu* regarded as the property of the consignee, and this rule is subject to no modification by the parties as it is in time of peace; but an enemy cargo consigned to a neutral is deemed by English and American courts to be, whilst *in transitu*, the property of the consignor, unless evidence is given that the consignee is the real owner, and is bound to accept the cargo, and that the consignor has no claim upon it save the right of stoppage *in transitu* in the event of the insolvency of the consignee.

As between the parties to the Declaration of Paris, enemy cargoes other than contraband may now be protected simply by shipping them on neutral bottoms; but it is still necessary to guard against the fraudulent assignment of enemy ships and of enemy cargoes on enemy bottoms.

Mode in which trade is conducted. Under enemy protection.

(3) *The mode of conducting the trade in which the property is embarked.*

(*a*) A ship owned by a neutral acquires an enemy character, which extends to her cargo, if she sails under the enemy flag, or holds a pass or licence from the enemy.

Both ship and cargo become liable to confiscation, but the English practice has been to release the cargo if it has been laden in time of peace.

The same rule holds good in the case of a ship owned by a neutral but manned by an enemy crew, commanded by an enemy master, and employed in the trade of the enemy.[1]

(*b*) A ship owned by a neutral acquires an enemy character, which may extend to her cargo, if she attempts to commit any breach of blockade. (See Part III. chap. vi.) Breach of Blockade.

(*c*) If a neutral places his ship under enemy convoy, or (according to the British doctrine) loads his goods upon an armed enemy vessel, he must be taken to display an intention to resist search by the adverse belligerent, and identifies his interests with those of the enemy so closely as to impart an enemy character to the ship or cargo, as the case may be. (See Part III. chap. viii.) Under enemy convoy.

3. *Hostile Territory.*

All territory that comes under the effective control of the enemy during the war acquires a temporary enemy character, although its national character and that of its inhabitants is not changed until military occupation has ripened into permanent conquest. Thus a portion of a state's own territory, *e. g.* an island colony, may become hostile if occupied by its enemy during the war, and the consequences attendant upon enemy character with regard to trading and property ensue. Effective enemy control.

This doctrine is fully accepted by English and American

---

[1] It is perhaps unnecessary to point out that the Declaration of Paris, which decides the fate of enemy and neutral goods captured at sea, has nothing whatever to do with the determination of enemy or neutral *character*. If a cargo *primâ facie* neutral as belonging to a neutral subject is affected by other circumstances (*e. g.* the above rule) with an enemy character, the Declaration will apply to it in that character, and its *primâ facie* neutrality will not avail to save it from condemnation.

courts, and may be illustrated by the "case of the thirty hogsheads of sugar" cited above.

<small>Territory of a Confederacy.</small> It is possible that a territory may be subject to a dual sovereignty, and so may appear to occupy an equivocal position in time of war, *i.e.* it may appear to possess at the same time both a belligerent and a neutral character. This is the case of territory belonging to the members of a confederacy. It may be neutral in respect of the confederacy and belligerent in respect of its immediate owner, the members of a confederacy having a separate power of making peace and war subject to the interests of the confederacy. (Cf. Part I. p. 39.)

During the existence of the Germanic Confederation, 1815—1866, this difficulty arose as regards Austrian and Prussian territory.

But it is now well settled that the status of such territory is to be determined in accordance with the doctrine already stated, and its belligerent or neutral character will depend upon the character of the state which exercises *permanent military control* within it.

<small>Egypt.</small> The present position of Egypt is somewhat striking. It is, strictly, a semi-sovereign state, being under the suzerainty of the Porte. It is under the rule of the Khedive, an hereditary Viceroy, who is as regards his suzerain almost or practically independent. Yet he is at the same time entirely dependent upon the good-will and support of the British Government for the maintenance of his authority. He has resident English advisers (whose advice, moreover, cannot be disregarded), his army has been created and is to a large extent officered by Englishmen, and there is a strong garrison of English troops in the country. What would be the position of Egypt if England were involved in war? It is no doubt a delicate question, but on principle it is difficult to avoid the conclusion that the enemy of England would be justified in regarding Egypt as enemy soil. This, of course, does not

include the Suez Canal, which was neutralized by convention between England and France in 1887, a convention which secured the adhesion of the other Great Powers and the ratification of the Sultan in 1888.

If the English proposals for the neutralization of the whole country in 1887 had been accepted, the present anomalous condition of Egypt would have been avoided.

CHAPTER IV

THE CONDUCT OF WAR

It is this portion of the subject to which the title "the rules of war" is in its narrowest sense usually applied; and it consists, briefly, of rules regulating the conduct of warfare by belligerent forces ashore and afloat. These rules determine the characteristics of lawful combatants, both military and naval, and the nature and extent of lawful hostile operations by land and sea.

They prescribe, in fact, *who* may fight, and *how* they must fight, or, perhaps more accurately, how they must *not* fight; for the rules as to the conduct of warfare are mainly of a negative nature, being restrictions now more or less generally accepted upon that primitive "right of devastation" which is the expression of the barbarous instincts of wild beasts and savage races.

The fundamental principle. The one fundamental idea upon which these rules are based is that there is a limit to the right of using violence in warfare. And the measure of violence permissible is that amount only which is strictly necessary to overcome the resistance of the enemy, and reduce him to terms at the least possible cost of suffering and loss. (Cf. p. 73.)

The rules now to be considered form a series of isolated applications of this leading principle rather than a body of connected and coherent legal principles. "Springing originally from limitations upon a right (*i.e.* the right to use violence), which in its extreme form constitutes a denial of all other rights, and developed through the action of practical and sentimental considerations, the law of war cannot be expected to show a substructure of large principles, like those which underlie the law governing the relations of peace. . . . It is, as a matter of fact, made up of a number of usages which in the main are somewhat arbitrary, which are not always very consistent with one another, and which do not therefore very readily lend themselves to general statements."—*Hall*.

It is inexpedient to keep hostilities by land and sea absolutely distinct, as many rules apply equally to both kinds of warfare. The most convenient course is, first, to define and describe military and naval combatants, and then to state a series of rules relating to the conduct of belligerent operations in general, thus paving the way for a separate account of the special incidents and consequences of "military occupation" and "maritime capture."

The rules are distributed under nine headings in the present and succeeding chapters.

I. *The Combatants by whom the war is conducted.*

Although all the subjects of one belligerent become enemies of all the subjects of the adverse belligerent, they are not liable to be killed or taken as prisoners of war so long as they do not actively engage in hostilities. The right of violence is limited by the reasonable necessities of war, and on this doctrine is founded the immunity of non-combatants. {Combatants and Non-combatants.}

This immunity is accorded on the tacit understanding that the distinction between the two classes of combatants and non-combatants shall be maintained in good faith, and it is forfeited by a non-combatant who commits any hostile act.

Combatants must be open enemies, known and knowable, and non-combatants must be harmless. As soon as an individual ceases to be harmless, he ceases to be a non-combatant, and must be reckoned a combatant; and unless he bears the distinguishing marks of an open combatant, he puts himself outside the laws of war, and is, if captured, liable to be shot as a bandit instead of detained as a prisoner of war.[1] The exceptional circumstances of a *levée en masse* are considered below.

Of course the immunity of non-combatants is never an absolute one. They have to take their chance of injuries to person and property resulting from legitimate belligerent operations directed against the armed forces of their state, such as the bombardment of a fortified town.

Old men, women, and children, and perhaps ministers of religion, are always regarded as non-combatants, although they may on occasion, *e. g.* a siege, be capable of rendering effective service to their country.

Combatants whilst resisting or capable of resistance, in other words, whilst it is lawful to attack them, may be killed, and may at all times be captured and detained as prisoners of war.

A. *Military Combatants.*

Regulars and Irregulars.
Hostilities on land are carried on by regular or irregular troops. If the regular army, which is maintained expressly for warlike purposes, is insufficient, the assistance of irregulars may be necessary.

Regular troops are permanently organized bodies of men acting under the authority of their state, and wearing external marks in the way of uniform not easy to destroy

---

[1] Certain auxiliaries who accompany armies, but wear no uniform, are entitled to rank as combatants, and, if captured, to be made prisoners of war. Messengers, guides, contractors, newspaper correspondents, vivandiers, balloonists, and sutlers furnish examples of this class of non-combatant.

THE CONDUCT OF WAR 109

or conceal, and recognizable by the enemy in the field.¹ Troops exhibiting these characteristics are combatants proper, and as such will always be treated by the enemy.

The status of less formally organized bodies of men who carry out belligerent operations is a question upon which states are not agreed, and was the point which brought the Brussels Conference to a deadlock in 1874. The Brussels Conference.

That conference met, on the invitation of the Russian Emperor, to consider the Russian "Project," which was practically a codification of the laws and customs of war.

The British Government only sent a delegate on receiving a distinct assurance that no question relating directly or indirectly to maritime operations or naval warfare would be discussed. Even the delegate sent was only a military officer unintrusted with plenipotentiary powers, and he had no authority to pledge the British Government in any way, his sole duty being to report the proceedings of the Conference to the Foreign Office at home. The United States sent no delegate at all.

It was considered by many powers whose standing armies are small, that the great military powers sought to prevent resistance being offered by the civil population to an invader, and the Draft Declaration was not generally accepted. It was expressly repudiated by Lord Derby, speaking for Great Britain, as being calculated "to facilitate aggressive wars, and to paralyze the patriotic resistance of an invaded people." Irregulars and *levée en masse*.

It is, however, of very great authority, and expresses the general sense of the concert of nations upon most of the points with which it deals;² and many of its rules find

---

¹ In England, therefore, the volunteers as well as the militia and standing army are, for the purposes of International Law, "regular troops."

² These include lawful weapons and stratagems, sieges and bombardments, spies, prisoners of war, bearers of flags of truce,

a place in the manuals of war now generally issued by governments for the instruction of their officers in the field.

On the whole, it seems that the distinction drawn by Articles 9 and 10 of the Declaration between small bodies of irregular troops and the whole population of a district making a *levée en masse* is well-founded, and these Articles, so far as they go, may be said to express the rules on this subject as generally understood and tacitly accepted at the present day.

Article 9. Irregulars.

Under Article 9, small bodies of irregulars are lawful combatants if they act under a responsible leader, wear external irremovable badges, carry on open warfare, and respect the usages of war.

Article 10. Levée en masse.

Under Article 10, the inhabitants of territory *not yet occupied by the enemy*, may on the enemy's approach make a *levée en masse*, and are lawful combatants if they respect the usages of war. This Article, coupled with the first eight Articles, which deal with the military authority of an invader over the hostile territory actually occupied by him, would render a *levée en masse* unlawful when once occupation has been effected. On the ground that this would place a premium on the treacherous invasion of weak powers by strong, the Declaration was successfully resisted by the smaller military powers at the Brussels Conference.

In accordance with the principle of Article 9, all uncommissioned volunteers such as guerilla troops are unlawful combatants, and if captured they may be treated not as prisoners of war, but as criminals.

The French francs-tireurs in Franco-Prussian War.

The French francs-tireurs in the Franco-Prussian War, who simply wore the national blouse, a removable badge,

---

capitulations, sick and wounded, armistices, and belligerents interned in neutral territory.

and a cap, were undoubtedly unlawful combatants, inasmuch as they could easily resume a civilian, non-combatant character at will. As members of a *levée en masse* (where, the whole population being combatants, no sort of uniform is required) they would have been lawful combatants, but the francs-tireurs took part in the war long before there was anything approaching the nature of a *levée en masse* in France.

It is true that a law was passed by the French Assembly in August 1870, under which citizens rising spontaneously in defence of the territory were considered to form part of the National Guard, provided they wore one at least of the distinctive marks of that corps. If this law was meant to authorize a *levée en masse*, provisions as to uniform were unnecessary, and the law itself was in fact unnecessary, no authority being required. And if intended to apply to small bodies of irregulars, its provisions as to uniform were inadequate according to the generally accepted laws of war, which probably no state will deny are correctly expressed in Article 9 of the Draft Declaration of Brussels.

No state can by its municipal law override the laws of war so as to confer privileges on its subjects which are unshared by the subjects of other states. The harsh treatment of the francs-tireurs by the Prussians has been condemned, but neither their state authorization nor their military character were sufficiently well-founded to entitle them to be considered lawful combatants.

B. *Naval Combatants.*

The first and most important instrument of maritime warfare is a state's regular navy, composed of vessels of various kinds owned and commissioned by the state. These are all lawful combatants. Public vessels.

The actual combatants are of course the officers and crew, but it is necessary to class naval combatants according to the character of the ship on which they serve, and therefore what is said of the ship will include without mention the officers and crew.

Vessels hired and commissioned by the state are public vessels and lawful combatants. Fast ocean-liners whose speed enables them to defy enemy ships of war will no doubt chiefly figure in this class in the naval warfare of the future, but it also includes every kind of hired transport used to further belligerent operations.

Privateers. A privateer is a private vessel commissioned by the state, by the issue of a letter of marque to its owner, to carry on all hostilities by sea permissible according to the laws of war. She continues under the control of her private owner, and her crew are under the same discipline as the crew of a merchant ship.

Formerly a state issued letters of marque to its own subjects and those of neutral states as well, a proceeding which enabled powers not possessed of a large standing navy to create a temporary maritime force if involved in war. If a privateersman accepted letters of marque from both belligerents he was regarded as a pirate, and became the "common enemy of mankind," liable to be seized by the ship and tried by the tribunals of any country.

Privateering has, however, ceased to be a question of the first importance. The Declaration of Paris, providing, *inter alia*, that "privateering is and remains abolished," is binding upon all states except the United States, Spain, Mexico, and Venezuela; and therefore, except in a war in which any one of these four states is engaged, a privateer is now an unlawful combatant. The change in the character of fighting ships and of the whole conditions of naval warfare will probably render privateers, even if lawful, less effective combatants in the future than they have been in the past.

THE CONDUCT OF WAR 113

The creation of a volunteer navy on the outbreak of war is not prohibited by the Declaration of Paris. *Volunteer cruisers.*

A volunteer cruiser is a vessel lent by her private owner to the state. Her officers are commissioned, and her crew subject to the naval discipline of a ship of war. She is therefore immediately under state control, and only resembles a privateer in that prizes taken by her belong to her owner.

In 1870 Prussia proposed the creation of a volunteer navy. The owners of the vessels were to furnish the crews and officers, and to receive a large premium on the destruction of French vessels of war, Prussia having declared her intention of exempting enemy private vessels from capture. The crews were to be under naval discipline, and the officers to have temporary commissions and wear naval uniform. The English Law officers, on considering the protest of the French Government, gave it as their opinion that such volunteers were to be distinguished from privateers, and that their employment was not an evasion of the Declaration of Paris. From that opinion, it may be observed, Phillimore decidedly dissents. A similar course was proposed by Russia in 1878, on war with Great Britain appearing imminent. It seems to follow, *a fortiori*, that if a patriotic ship-owner, without thought of private gain, lends his vessel to the state, such a volunteer cruiser, like an organized volunteer regiment on shore, is a lawful combatant.

An ordinary merchant vessel without any commission only becomes a lawful combatant in self-defence, and if she succeeds in capturing and bringing in her assailant, the latter will be condemned as lawful prize. *Merchant vessels.*

II. *Lawful Weapons.*

The object of war is to disable the enemy at the least cost of suffering and death to his subjects. All weapons, therefore, which add to the cruelty of warfare without

1

conducing to its termination must be considered unlawful. It follows that no weapon is unlawful merely because of the amount of suffering it entails. If that amount of suffering has a proportionate effect in more speedily reducing the enemy to submission, the weapon is perfectly lawful.

<small>Destructiveness not the test of illegality.</small>

On this principle rests the legality of such weapons of wholesale destruction as the ironclad's ram, torpedoes, and mines; and weapons such as the two latter, which are otherwise legitimate, are not rendered unlawful by reason of their secrecy or concealment from the enemy, that being the real source of their efficacy.

The use of particular weapons, or kinds of weapons, has been condemned at different periods from early times. The cross-bow, for example, was stigmatized by the Lateran Council in 1139 A.D. as "artem illam mortiferam et Deo odibilem," and many princes in consequence ceased to arm their soldiers with that weapon. The use of poison or poisoned weapons has been proscribed amongst civilized nations since the time of the Romans. It was, moreover, considered at one time to be contrary to the rules of military honour and etiquette to employ unusual implements of war. On this ground, hollow shot, red-hot shot, and chain-shot have all at various times been objected to. Red-hot shot was employed in the wars of Frederick the Great, but at the beginning of this century Great Britain indignantly denied the French accusation of employing red-hot shot in a naval battle, and it was then clearly considered an unlawful weapon.

<small>Cross-bow.</small>

<small>Poisoned weapons.</small>

<small>Red-hot shot.</small>

<small>Musketeers.</small>

Musketeers were originally refused quarter. The Chevalier Bayard held the introduction of fire-arms to be an unfair innovation on the rules of war, and ordered all musketeers who fell into his hands to be slain without mercy.

<small>Bayonet.</small>

The bayonet at first naturally shared the detestation

in which the musket was held, and therefore did not come into general use until the legitimacy of fire-arms came to be recognized.

The practice of loading cannon with "langrel" or "langridge," composed of nails, knife-blades, bits of old iron, etc., which makes horrible wounds, and only increases suffering without proportionately diminishing resistance, is now, in accordance with the principle stated above, universally condemned.

Langrel.

By the Declaration of St. Petersburg in 1868, to which most of the European powers were parties, it was agreed to renounce the use of projectiles weighing less than 400 grammes (about 14 oz.) if of an explosive nature or charged with fulminating or other inflammable substances.

Declaration of St. Petersburg.

It was generally agreed at the Brussels Conference that unlawful weapons now comprise, as stated in Articles 12 and 13 of the Draft Declaration—

Unlawful weapons at the present day.

1. Poison or poisoned weapons.
2. Arms, projectiles, or substances which may cause unnecessary suffering, such as langridge.
3. Projectiles prohibited by the Declaration of St. Petersburg.

III. *Devastation.*

In former times it was the common practice to devastate the enemy's country, not with any direct military object, but to wantonly inflict as much pain and distress on his subjects as possible. This practice was regarded both by Grotius and Wolff, and even by the humane Vattel, as a lawful "independent means of attack."

During the seventeenth and eighteenth centuries, however, the principle that the suffering inflicted on the enemy must not be wanton or disproportionate to the advantages gained thereby was gathering strength, and devastation came to be regarded as only justifiable when forming an incident of some strategical object. At the

A direct military object necessary.

present day the measure of permissible devastation is to be found in the strict necessities of war; and it is only lawful when it forms a necessary part of some offensive or defensive belligerent operation. To destroy standing crops, for example, with a view to reducing a district by depriving it of immediate sustenance, is a legitimate military measure, but to root up vineyards and olive-trees, and thereby desolate the country for some years, is the reverse.

Devastation of territory.

The right of self-preservation in the face of imminent danger outweighs every other principle, but where there is no question of self-preservation, or where no immediate military object is served, devastation is mere wanton barbarity, and as such contrary to the modern rules of war.

Bombardment of towns.

The bombardment of a fortified town directed against the houses of the inhabitants as well as against the fortifications, is considered by some writers to be an unworthy survival from the dark ages, and a regrettable exception to the general rule.[1] It is undoubtedly a cruel measure, but such writers have been led away by the peculiar horrors incident to a siege, and forget that the cruelty of a measure does not *per se* make it illegitimate, if it tends to hasten proportionately the reduction of the enemy. It seems almost idle to contend, that this is not the usual and probable effect of a bombardment which extends to the town as well as to the forts. The shelling of a strongly fortified place might be a long and tedious operation, but the sufferings of the townspeople will hasten the surrender of the garrison; and this cannot be represented as putting compulsion upon combatants by an attack upon non-

---

[1] In the Franco-Prussian War, the Prussians shelled the town of Strasburg for two days, and wrecked its public buildings in order to induce its surrender; failing which, they commenced regular siege operations. They pursued a similar policy at other places during the war.

THE CONDUCT OF WAR

combatants, because, if the contrary practice obtained, and the town were held sacred, it would amount to permitting non-combatants to strengthen the hands of combatants against the enemy.

The inhabitants of fortified towns must, in case of a siege, be considered to have temporarily lost their non-combatant character by reason of their close association with the garrison. So far from the enemy having any guarantee that the distinction between combatant and non-combatant classes is being strictly preserved within the town (and on this the immunity of non-combatants depends), it is quite certain that every inhabitant is doing his utmost to aid and strengthen the garrison; and the enemy can therefore, in his own interest, make no distinctions, and is justified in directing his bombardment against the town as well as the forts.

The reaction that followed the horrors of the Franco-Prussian War led to the meeting of the Brussels Conference. The object of that Conference admittedly was to make the laws of war not only more certain and stable, but also more humane. Yet the provisions of the Draft Declaration do not prohibit the bombardment of a defended town;[1] and it must be recognized by even the most humane, that a belligerent cannot be expected to court repulse or defeat by fighting as it were with his hands partly tied. A successful bombardment may end in two ways—either the town surrenders without the combatants coming to close quarters at all, or it is carried by storm through the breaches made by the bombardment.

The storming of a bombarded town.

---

[1] According to the Draft Declaration, undefended towns and villages must not be bombarded; but if an unfortified place is defended the commander of the attacking force must, except in the case of a surprise, warn the authorities before bombarding it. In this case public buildings should be spared as much as possible, provided that they are not used for military purposes (Articles 15—17).

It is the horrible scene of massacre and plunder that has commonly followed the storming of a bombarded town, and not the actual bombardment itself, which constitutes the true objection to this military measure.

The Duke of Wellington. As regards massacre, the Duke of Wellington, most humane of commanders, said—"I believe it has always been understood that the defenders of a fortress stormed have no right to quarter;" and as to plunder he said, after the storming of San Sebastian—"It has fallen to my lot to take many towns by storm; and I am concerned to add, that I never saw or heard of one so taken by any troops that it was not plundered."

Much has been written of the storming of Ciudad Rodrigo and Badajoz, and of the horrible scenes enacted in those places, and other and more recent instances of savage excess could no doubt be given; but it is sufficient to record, that in the earlier half of the nineteenth century, the giving up of a town and its inhabitants to the fury of the troops which stormed it was permitted by the usages of war.

It is true that rough soldiers in the heat of victory are not to be restrained by mere rules constructed by publicists or diplomatists in time of peace and quiet, and that Article 18 of the Brussels Declaration, providing that "a town taken by storm shall not be given up to the victorious troops to plunder," may not of itself be of much value, but it is evidence of the prevalence of a milder spirit, the existence of which will insure a milder practice in the future.

Milder spirit now prevalent.

To put a garrison to the sword, unless they had violated the laws of war, would now constitute a gross breach of the modern law of quarter, and there seems to be little danger of the recurrence of such a hideous outrage in civilized war at the present time.

CHAPTER V

THE CONDUCT OF WAR (*continued*)

IV. *Stratagems.*

Certain devices for deceiving the enemy are lawful, provided they do not involve any breach of good faith, express or implied. Such a breach is simply treachery. A stratagem must not amount to treachery.

"No deceit is allowable when an express or implied engagement exists that the truth shall be acted or spoken."—*Maine.*

For example, certain flags constitute a tacit guarantee of the existence of certain states of affairs, and in that sense they are understood by both sides. The fraudulent use of a flag of truce, or of a Red-Cross hospital flag, or of signals of distress, is therefore not a lawful stratagem, but a gross act of perfidy.

In 1783, the *Sybille*, a French frigate of 38 guns, by flying signals of distress, enticed the British ship *Hussar* of 20 guns to approach, intending to rake and board her. The *Hussar*, however, succeeded in capturing the *Sybille*, and her captain publicly broke the French captain's sword for his perfidy.

To fly signals of distress is an implied guarantee of security to the succourer, whether friend or foe, and the fraudulent abuse of such signals seems to be an act of peculiar treachery.

One form of treachery common in ancient and mediæval

THE LAW OF WAR

Assassination. and even later times, was the assassination of some statesman or general who happened to be the chief pillar of the enemy's strength. The *modus operandi* was to send an assassin in disguise to the General's tent, or to accept the services of some traitor within the enemy's camp.

There were brilliant exceptions to this practice, even in early times, as evidenced by the famous story of Fabricius, who warned Pyrrhus against his treacherous physician.

So late in civilized times as 1806, a Frenchman proposed to Fox, then Foreign Secretary, a scheme for the assassination of Napoleon. Fox arrested the would-be assassin, and immediately sent warning to M. Talleyrand, the French Foreign Minister. Fox's action, which was universally approved at the time, reflects the modern civilized view as to treacherous methods of warfare.

The Brussels Conference. The essence of a lawful stratagem is that there must be no fraud and no disguise. The Brussels Conference prohibited the abuse of the flag of truce, the national flag, or the military insignia, or uniform of the enemy, as well as the distinctive badges of the Geneva Convention.

Military surprises. A military surprise carried out by combatants in the regular guise of combatants is perfectly lawful, it being the enemy's business to guard against any such attack. An attempt by a handful of cavalry to capture or kill the enemy's General by night is a lawful military surprise. They are not assassins, and if captured, can only be detained as prisoners of war.

Publicists from Vattel to Sir Henry Maine have held it more glorious to win a victory by a lawful stratagem involving little bloodshed, than by the carnage of a pitched battle; and to do so is to carry out the great rule of war—to reduce the enemy to terms with as little suffering as possible.

False information. To deceive the enemy by spreading false information is perfectly legitimate. He must judge of the character of the information he acquires, and acts upon it at his peril.

On the same principle, a feigned offer of betrayal made to the enemy for the purpose of drawing him into an ambush would appear to be a lawful stratagem. The enemy acts upon such an offer at his peril, the person from whom it emanates being under no engagement, express or implied, to act or speak truly in making it. Such a stratagem would, in the opinion of some writers, be chiefly justifiable if carried out in answer to an actual attempt by the enemy to suborn treachery, but, in any case, many fair-minded men would probably agree that it lies unpleasantly near the borderlands of fraud. The important point, however, is that it is not unlawful. *[Feigned offer of treachery.]*

One more lawful stratagem should perhaps be mentioned, and that is the sailing of a ship under false colours. A ship of war may approach an enemy under false colours, but must hoist her own colours before she fires. On getting within range she usually fires an "affirming" gun, or a *coup de semonce*, across the other ship's bows, warning her to heave to. This is merely a preliminary to search, or, if the other vessel shows fight, to hostilities, and therefore some authorities maintain that the true colours need not be hoisted until after the affirming gun has been fired. The general opinion is that she must hoist her national colours before she fires at all. *[Sailing under false colours.]*

As already pointed out, a fraudulent use of signals of distress as a means of approach is not legitimate sailing under false colours, but an act of treachery.

V. *Spies.*

A spy is an individual who enters the enemy's lines secretly or in disguise, or upon false pretences, with the object of acquiring information. *[Secrecy, disguise, or false pretence.]*

The case of an officer in uniform reconnoitring in the immediate neighbourhood of the enemy's position is very different. If captured he becomes a prisoner of war, whereas a spy is liable to be hanged or shot after trial by court-martial.

<small>Case of Major André.</small> In the case of Major André, the character of spy was extended to include persons who enter the enemy's lines secretly or in disguise to convey messages or despatches, or to seduce officers or troops from their duty.

In 1780 Major André, an English officer, was captured while taking a secret message from General Sir Henry Clinton to General Benedict Arnold, who had undertaken to surrender a fortress on the river Hudson to the English forces. Unfortunately he had discarded his uniform and was in plain clothes; and this fact seems to have led to his condemnation by a board of American officers. He was hanged as a spy. It is well known that Washington would gladly have spared his life if the English Government had consented to give up the traitor Arnold, who fled to England. This case excited universal sympathy, and forty years afterwards the remains of Major André were exhumed by the consent of the President and Congress, and interred in Westminster Abbey.

<small>Definition by Brussels Conference.</small> It is to be observed that this wide extension of the character of spy was not adopted by the Brussels Conference. Article 19 of the Draft Declaration defines spies as persons " who, acting secretly or under false pretences, collect or try to collect information in districts occupied by the enemy with the intention of communicating it to the opposing force."

Questions of ethics must not be confounded with questions of law. Whatever be the propriety of employing spies or suborning treachery in the enemy's camp, these measures are not contrary to the rules of war.

Vattel significantly remarks, " Although generals practise such acts, they do not afterwards boast of them."

The employment of spies is, then, a legitimate military

measure, and is one which has been resorted to in warfare from time immemorial. But the service of a spy is generally regarded as a dishonourable one, and it is therefore never a matter of duty or compulsion. A spy volunteers his services for a reward, and is paid in proportion to his risk. He is only liable to be treated as a spy if he is captured *flagrante delicto*. If he succeeds in rejoining the army which employs him, after performing his service, and is subsequently captured by the enemy, he cannot, although known to have been a spy, be treated otherwise than as a prisoner of war. These rules as to his liability to punishment were adopted by the Brussels Conference (Articles 20 and 21). *Liabilities of spies.*

An absurd claim was made by the Germans in 1870 to treat persons in balloons as spies. Even if such persons are seeking for information for the use of the enemy, they exhibit none of the characteristics of a spy (secrecy, disguise, or false pretence), and are entitled if captured to be treated as prisoners of war. They are clearly on the same footing as a military officer carrying despatches or collecting information openly, and their immunity from the penalties attaching to spies was affirmed by the Brussels Conference (Article 22). *Persons in balloons.*

At that Conference it was sought to establish a distinction between the patriotic spy, who takes his life in his hand purely in his country's service, and the mercenary spy who does so for gain. The latter is often a traitor as well, if, as is not uncommon, he is acting against his own country in its enemy's service. It is this description of spy which has brought the word into universal odium and contempt. But there is no real dishonour attaching to the service of a patriotic spy. King Alfred won not the blame but the praise of posterity by spying in the Danish camp disguised as a minstrel. The Brussels Conference, however, would admit no distinctions, and the refusal was *Patriotic and mercenary spies.*

well-founded, because an army is equally endangered by the presence of a spy in its midst, whatever may be the motives which inspire the latter.

VI. *Quarter.*

Unknown in early and mediæval warfare.

The motto of ancient and mediæval warfare was 'Væ Victis." The conquerors treated the vanquished with revolting barbarity. The dead were stripped and mutilated, and the living were put to the sword. These were the common incidents of warfare recorded in Greek and Roman history. Even the heroes of chivalry hung the commandants of captured towns, and butchered the garrisons and inhabitants.

Death, or at the best slavery, was the only prospect of the prisoner, and wholesale slaughter of the vanquished continued to be the rule rather than the exception late into the Middle Ages. The English gave no quarter at Crecy, and the severities of Edward III. and Henry V. towards their "rebel" French subjects are familiar to everybody. Gradually, however, the maxim, " Qui merci prie merci doit avoir," came into vogue, and even to meet with some sort of observance. Quarter began to be recognized as the due of the vanquished, but it was often refused them upon the smallest provocation and the slightest pretexts.

Gradual recognition of right to quarter.

By the end of the seventeenth century, however, any general declaration by a belligerent of an intention to deny quarter to the enemy was regarded as barbarous and intolerable, and quarter to enemies who had done nothing to forfeit it became an established usage of war. With the advance of humanity and civilization, opinion as to the conduct sufficient to forfeit the right of defeated enemies to quarter underwent great changes. Some actions which would formerly have deprived them of quarter have come to be regarded as redounding to their honour and glory.

It was formerly the practice, for example, to give up to

indiscriminate slaughter the garrison of a stormed fortress, and even of a weak place which resisted a superior force. But, bearing in mind the fact that the commandant of a garrison who abandons or delivers up his post, except under pressure of the utmost necessity, is by the municipal law of most countries liable to be tried and shot, it is now considered that, if there still remains the smallest possibility of success, the besieged are justified in holding out to the last extremity; and, as has been already seen, the attitude of modern civilization towards a gallant resistance, even if it be hopeless, is such that the practice of slaughtering the garrison is never likely to recur in civilized warfare.

The Brussels Conference prohibited both the murder of an antagonist who, having laid down his arms, or having no longer the means of defending himself, has surrendered at discretion, and also the general declaration that no quarter will be given. Brussels Conference.

Thus the right of the vanquished to quarter is now recognized as one of peculiar sanctity, and is only forfeited under the following exceptional circumstances. Quarter forfeited.

(i.) In case of absolute necessity the right of self-preservation is paramount, but the necessity must be "instant, absolute, and overwhelming." Necessity.

A small force cut off in a savage and hostile country, and encumbered with a large number of prisoners, might be justified by necessity in killing the latter if their own lives would be endangered by their release; whereas in a civilized country such prisoners could be released upon parole and no such case of necessity would arise.

(ii.) Persons who violate the laws of war may be refused quarter. If a belligerent employs savage native troops in civilized warfare, the latter are liable to be refused quarter if, as is not unlikely, they violate the laws of war. Chatham's scathing denunciation of the alliance of civilized Persons who violate the laws of war.

arms with the scalping-knife of the savage is in accordance with modern views as to the employment of such allies as the North American Indians, Circassians, or Bashi-Bazouks against civilized troops.

Savage troops. In warfare against uncivilized races friendly savages are commonly employed against the enemy. In such a case an exact observance of the rules of war is impossible; yet the civilized belligerent must certainly be held morally responsible for the conduct of his savage allies, and must not permit them to refuse quarter to the enemy unless the latter commit wanton barbarities. (Cf. Part II. chap. i.)

Troops of whatever race or colour are entitled to be dealt with according to the laws of war, so long as they respect and observe those rules.

Reprisal (iii.) By way of penal reprisal or retaliation, quarter may be denied to an enemy whose troops have denied it without sufficient cause. This exception differs from and goes beyond the denial of quarter to persons who violate the laws of war. In that case the guilty are punished for their misdeeds; in this the innocent may in an extreme *only in cases of utmost necessity.* case be punished for the misdeeds of the guilty. It is clearly a kind of "protective retribution," to which recourse can only be had in the very last resort, to compel fair play at the hands of an enemy who wantonly and persistently disregards the rules of war.

If retaliation is resorted to except to meet a case of flagrant outrage, the enemy will probably reply with still greater severities. It will then defeat its own object, and only increase the barbarity of warfare.

In modern civilized warfare any nation refusing quarter to its enemies, whether upon the ground of necessity or upon any other of the grounds mentioned above, would be called strictly to account by the general concert of powers.

That collective body will not permit any of its members, strong or weak, to lightly violate the laws of war; and the increasing tendency towards concerted action upon the part of the powers constitutes the real strength and true sanction of those laws.

VII. *Prisoners of War.*

Captured enemies in early times were either butchered or enslaved. The Roman *servus* was a prisoner captured in war and "saved" from slaughter. The practice of en- *Slavery.*
slaving instead of killing prisoners increased as time went on, the mercy of the conqueror finding a strong ally in his desire of gain; and later, as a natural development of this practice, arose the custom of permitting a captured enemy to buy his ransom. To enslave men of kindred race, of equal civilization, of the same colour and religion, was repugnant to ideas of Christianity, and slavery to this extent accordingly fell into decay. There were occasional instances, and as late as 1685 many a sturdy West-countryman, who had taken part in Monmouth's rebellion, and escaped the Bloody Assize, was sold as a slave and shipped off to the plantations. It must not, however, be forgotten, that in this latest and extreme case the prisoners of war were also legally traitors and rebels, and, though many circumstances combine to enlist the sympathy of posterity in their favour, they had incurred the legal penalty of death for treason.

The custom of ransom, which superseded slavery, paved *Ransom.*
the way for, and has in its turn been practically superseded by, the modern exchange of prisoners. Just as a scale or tariff for the ransom of prisoners according to their rank and importance used to be fixed by cartel at the outbreak of war, or as occasion arose during its continuance, so in modern warfare an exchange of prisoners is negotiated *Exchange.*
under a cartel, and a scale of value agreed upon under which prisoners are exchanged number for number, rank for rank, or so many of inferior for one of superior rank.

The last instance of ransom was in 1780, under a cartel

agreed to by England and France, but the practice cannot be regarded as entirely obsolete, as the convenience of particular belligerents might revive it at any moment. It is not a less humane or commendable practice than that of exchange, but the question is entirely one of convenience, and convenience points to exchange as being the most simple, speedy, and efficient method of disposing of prisoners of war.

<small>Exchange voluntary.</small>

There is no obligation upon a belligerent to accept a proposal for exchange of prisoners, if not advantageous to himself. Each belligerent has a right to detain his prisoners until the end of the war, and an exchange may conceivably be of much greater advantage to his opponent than to himself. A thousand trained soldiers restored to a small military power would probably far exceed in proportion the value of a corresponding number restored to a great military power with unlimited resources at its command.

<small>Equality of value in exchange.</small>

If, however, an exchange is agreed to, equality of value must be as nearly as possible maintained, and non-efficients cannot be exchanged for efficients. In 1810 England proposed an exchange of English for French prisoners only. France had three times as many Spanish as English prisoners, and demanded three Frenchmen for one Englishman and two Spaniards, on the plausible ground that the latter were allies and ranked *pari passu*. It was not perhaps very flattering to the pride of our Spanish allies to have to contend that their soldiers were not of the same quality as the English and French, but it was the fact, and the contention could not be gainsaid. The negotiations ultimately fell through.

Having briefly traced the development by which the captured enemy, originally liable to death or slavery, has become through the medium of ransom and exchange the modern prisoner of war, it remains to consider what persons may be made prisoners of war, how they must be treated whilst in captivity, and in what manner otherwise than by ransom or exchange they may regain their liberty.

The rules upon these subjects as generally accepted are comprised in Articles 23—34 of the Draft Declaration of the Brussels Conference, and are, briefly, to the following effect. *Brussels Conference.*

All lawful combatants, on surrender or capture, become prisoners of war, as also do such non-combatants as guides, messengers, newspaper correspondents, balloonists, telegraphists, vivandiers, and contractors, who are present with the army, and so closely associated with it as to be rendering it direct service. *Who may be made prisoners of war.*

Surgeons and chaplains are protected by the Geneva Convention, but in a war where one of the belligerents was not a party to that Convention, it would be within strict belligerent right on both sides to detain surgeons and chaplains as prisoners of war in the absence of any agreement to the contrary. Such agreements, however, were so common before the Geneva Convention that the present immunity of surgeons and chaplains may be pronounced to be absolute.

Important public servants, such as ministers or diplomatic agents, may be seized in any place where acts of war are lawful and detained as prisoners of war. This rule has been unquestioned since 1744, when during war between Great Britain and France the Maréchal de Belleisle was seized in Hanoverian territory on his way to Berlin, and was sent as a prisoner of war to England.

Sailors in merchant ships are a source of strength to the enemy, forming a naval reserve which can be called into commission at any time. In order to cripple the enemy's resources they may therefore be made prisoners of war.

Certain persons by their own actions forfeit their right to be treated as prisoners of war. These are unlawful

K

combatants, such as guerillas, deserters, and other traitors captured amongst the enemy's troops, spies caught *flagrante delicto*, and enemies who are retaken after having broken their parole. Such persons are liable to suffer the penalty of death.

Treatment of prisoners of war. Prisoners of war are not criminals, and must not be treated as such. In the sixteenth century they used to be sent to the galleys, and have at various times been confined on board hulks and in common gaols. They must now, however, only be subjected to sufficient restraint to prevent their escape. They are usually disarmed, and interned in some fortress or camp under military discipline away from the seat of war. They enjoy a large measure of liberty, and may only be punished for breach of discipline or an attempt to escape.

Their food and clothing must be provided by the state who holds them captive, and they are sometimes given a money allowance as well.[1] This was done in the Franco-Prussian War. In return they may be compelled to do work, suitable to their rank and position, not directly connected with any warlike operations against their country. And if the captor does not require any work of them, they may be permitted to work subject to regulations for their own private profit.

Release. A prisoner of war regains his liberty at the end of the war, when all the prisoners on both sides are released; but he may also regain it during the continuance of hostilities

---

[1] The cost of their support is generally made the subject of an agreement between the belligerents either during the hostilities or at the negotiations for peace.

Fugitive combatants who take refuge in neutral territory practically become prisoners of war, it being the neutral state's duty to intern them away from the seat of the war, and provide for their support until peace is concluded, when of course it is reimbursed for the expense it has incurred. (Brussels Conference, Articles 53—56 of the Declaration.) Cf. Part III. chap. i.

by ransom or exchange, by a successful flight, or by release on parole.

Whilst attempting an escape a prisoner may be lawfully shot, but if he is recaptured unhurt he can only be punished by imprisonment sufficiently close to prevent any repetition of the attempt. *Escape.*

A prisoner may be released on pledging his parole, or word of honour (unless forbidden to do so by the municipal law of his own country), not to render active service to his country again during the existing war. The pledge can only be given by a commissioned officer either for himself or troops under his command; and officers so long as a superior is within reach can only give their word with his permission. Such an agreement is *primâ facie* binding on the prisoner's Government, but if the latter refuse to confirm it the prisoner must in honour return into captivity. *Parole.*

A captor is not bound to offer to release his prisoner on parole, nor is the latter bound to give his parole if that offer be made. It is a voluntary arrangement on both sides. A prisoner returning to his country on parole is only precluded from active service in the field; he may therefore raise and drill recruits or find administrative, civil, or diplomatic employment away from the actual seat of the war. His parole terminates with the return of peace, and also during the war, if he is included in an exchange of prisoners. If he violates his parole, and is recaptured by the enemy before the end of the war, he is not entitled to quarter and may be shot as a bandit.

VIII. *Hostages.*

The custom of giving security by means of hostages, which was common in ancient and mediæval warfare, has now become almost obsolete. In comparatively modern times hostages have been seized to secure the payment of contributions and the compliance with requisitions, to *When exacted.*

insure the fulfilment of treaties and conventions,[1] by way of guarantee against marauding by the inhabitants of an occupied country, and by way of collateral security when a vessel is released on a ransom-bill.

The practice of taking hostages was resorted to occasionally by the Prussians in the Franco-Prussian War. They are treated in all respects as prisoners of war, but are generally subjected to somewhat closer surveillance.

American Instructions. The rules as to hostages, so far as any may now be said to exist, are summed up in the "Instructions for the Government of the armies of the United States in the field," as follows:—

> Article 54. A hostage is a person accepted as a pledge for the fulfilment of an agreement concluded between belligerents during the war, or in consequence of a war.
>
> Article 55. If a hostage is accepted, he is treated like a prisoner of war, according to rank and condition, as circumstances may admit.

IX. *Sick and Wounded.*

It is not sufficient that a belligerent should abstain from treating the enemy's sick and wounded with cruelty, as was common in ancient times. He must not even treat them with neglect.

Geneva Convention, 1864. Under the articles of the Geneva Convention of 1864, it is his clear and positive duty, if he wins the day, to collect and tend the enemy's sick and wounded in the field no less than his own. Whilst in hospital the wounded are regarded as neutralized, and if on recovery they are permanently disabled and rendered unfit for further military service they must be sent to their homes. Otherwise they become prisoners of war.

---

[1] After the Peace of Aix-la-Chapelle in 1748, Lords Cathcart and Sussex remained on parole as hostages in Paris until Cape Breton in North America should be restored to France.

Ambulances and military hospitals, and the medical staff and chaplains and other persons employed in them, are neutralized. Such hospitals must be marked by a distinctive flag as well as by their national flag, and such individuals must wear a distinctive arm-badge, the flag and badge both consisting of a red cross on a white ground.

It is clear that the Geneva red cross must be used in the most abundant good faith. To cover a weak spot in a military position from the enemy's fire by the use of the red cross flag, or to permit a spy to acquire information by wearing the arm-badge, would be acts of supreme treachery. Every belligerent therefore is entitled to take such reasonable precaution as he may deem necessary to prevent any such abuse.

It is believed that the only countries which have not yet adopted the Convention are Portugal, Brazil, Mexico, Columbia, Costa Rica, Uruguay, and Venezuela. It is consequently binding upon almost the whole of the civilized world, including Persia and Japan.

Its provisions were adopted *en bloc* by Article 35 of the Draft Declaration of the Brussels Conference; and they are at the present day regarded as of overwhelming authority. Brussels Conference.

In 1868 a second Conference met at Geneva with a view to framing a supplementary convention. This consists of fifteen Articles, partly explaining the provisions of the original Convention, and partly making provisions as to hospital ships, etc., applicable to the peculiar conditions of maritime warfare. Geneva Convention, 1868.

This Convention was signed by most of the signatories of the original Convention and by other states in addition, but it has never been formally ratified. It was adopted provisionally by France and Prussia in the Franco-Prussian War, and although it has not the binding authority of the original Convention, is of very considerable importance.

CHAPTER VI

MILITARY OCCUPATION AND PRIZE

Liability of enemy property.

IN ancient times, wherever enemy property was accessible, it was liable to seizure. "Res hostiles res nullius." This rule has been considerably modified and restricted by modern usage.

Public.

1. *Public Property.*

The territory of a state (which is not, strictly, its "property") can only be permanently acquired by its enemy by absolute conquest. It may, however, be held temporarily during the war by a military occupation. All property held by the state on the footing of a private owner, its ships, naval and military stores, buildings, etc., may within its own territory be seized, and in certain cases its movable property may be permanently retained by an invading enemy. Beyond its own limits the property of the state is liable to seizure on the high sea, and, in theory at least, in places within the jurisdiction of the enemy. (Cf. chap. ii. of this Part.)

Private.

2. *Private Property.*

The private property of enemy subjects must necessarily be situate in one of the following places—in their own country, in that of a neutral, in that of the enemy, or upon the high sea.

In their own country until invaded, and in a neutral country, such property is obviously safe, and in the country of the enemy it now enjoys a practical immunity. (Cf. chap. ii. of this Part.)

It only remains, therefore, in order to complete the account of the liability of enemy property, public and private, to describe the incidents of military occupation and maritime capture or "prize."

A. *Military Occupation.*

Military occupation must be carefully distinguished from conquest, which alone can confer upon the conqueror full rights of sovereignty over the conquered territory and its inhabitants.

<small>Military occupation.</small>

Military occupation at the most can only be said to give the invader certain limited partial and temporary rights of sovereignty. Until conquest the sovereign rights of the original owner of the territory remain intact, and are merely suspended during the occupation by the enemy.

<small>To be distinguished from conquest.</small>

It is, therefore, more logical to place the rights of occupation, as Hall does, upon "the broad foundation of simple military necessity" than upon what may be termed a substitutive right of sovereignty. A military invader has the right to do whatever acts may be necessary within his enemy's territory in order to bring him to terms.

The essentials of conquest are actual possession and intention and ability to retain such possession evidenced by some formal act of annexation or incorporation. Conquest is completed and confirmed by the recognition of foreign states, by treaty, or by uninterrupted enjoyment for a considerable number of years. A general treaty of peace based upon the principle *uti possidetis* tacitly confirms a conquest, or it may do so expressly by a clause ceding the conquered territory to the victorious state.

<small>Conquest.</small>

The effects of conquest are, generally, to give the conqueror full rights of sovereignty over the conquered territory and its inhabitants, and, retroactively, to legalize all acts of ownership or other invalid acts done by the

<small>Effects of conquest.</small>

invader in excess of his right as mere military occupant. Municipal laws, unless and until altered by the conqueror, remain unchanged, and all private rights of property are unaffected. The inhabitants may elect to leave the country, but if they remain their allegiance is transferred to the new sovereign. The political laws and constitution of the new sovereign, where differing fundamentally in principle from those of the former sovereign, must necessarily replace the latter; and the new sovereign succeeds to all state property, whether corporeal or incorporeal.

<small>Military occupation.</small> The only essential of military occupation is actual and exclusive possession.

<small>Brussels Conference.</small> The military authority of an invader over the hostile territory is the subject of the first eight Articles of the Draft Declaration of the Brussels Conference. By Article 1, "a territory is considered as occupied when it is actually placed under the authority of the hostile army. The occupation only extends to those territories where this authority is established and can be exercised."

<small>It must be effective.</small> In other words, occupation in order to confer rights must be *effective*. This principle is now very generally accepted, but in practice it has been customary for invaders to declare large tracts of territory occupied by small flying columns regardless of any resistance still being offered by the inhabitants.

On entering France in 1870, the Crown Prince of Prussia proclaimed that the establishment of a single post in any French canton would constitute a military occupation of the whole of that canton. The average area of a French canton is seventy-two square miles! Such abuses are unlikely to recur in the future, and it is probable that only territory effectually held or covered by the enemy will be considered subject to the rights of military occupation. If a territory can be "occupied" by a small flying column or by a mere declaration that it is occupied, it is clear that under Article 10 of the Draft Declaration a *levée en masse* might always be prevented, or at least rendered unlawful. (Cf. p. 110.)

Military occupation does not create sovereignty, but only a special temporary administrative authority. It does not confer proprietary rights, but only certain rights of control and appropriation. Military occupation is in fact inchoate conquest, and its effects while it exists are, except as regards property rights, very similar to those of conquest. This may be illustrated by the case of the "Thirty hogsheads of sugar" (cf. p. 100, *supra*), which shows how closely an occupied territory is during occupation associated with the interests of the occupant. {Effects of military occupation.}

The occupant administers the government of the occupied territory, secures public order, collects and applies taxes, and generally discharges all the administrative and executive functions of the temporarily displaced government. He has a strict right of making changes in the municipal law, but unless the occupation is confirmed as a conquest at the end of the war, all such changes cease with the occupation. It is by common consent considered to be the duty of the occupant to allow the ordinary administration of the national laws to continue with as few changes as possible, although his strict right to even proclaim martial law in case of necessity is generally admitted. {Rights of the occupant.}

With regard to public property in the occupied territory the occupant has the following rights. {Public property.}

He may use public land and buildings, or he may let them and appropriate the rents and profits. He cannot alienate such land and buildings so as to confer a good title, but a subsequent confirmation of the occupation as a conquest would probably make the title complete. Similarly, if the original owner attempted to alienate occupied {Immovable.}

territory during the occupation the title could, on principle, only be completed by the restoration of the territory at the end of the war.

Movable. Ships of war, warlike stores and materials, treasure, telegraphs, and similar movable property belonging to the state vest in the occupant with firm possession, and he can give an absolute title to any purchaser.

Incorporeal. The publicists differ as to whether he can also exact payment of debts due to the state and give a valid discharge. The legality of Napoleon's action in appropriating the private debts of the Elector of Hesse Cassel was subsequently affirmed by the German Universities; but his occupation had then ripened by lapse of time into conquest. This precedent, therefore, is no clear authority that an invader whilst merely occupant may lawfully seize debts owing to the state or individuals. The contrary view is, in fact, held by Sir R. Phillimore, and is consequently entitled to considerable respect. This subject is again referred to in chapter vii. of this Part.

Public property exempt from seizure. Certain public property has by usage acquired a sanctity which renders it safe from seizure by an invader.

State archives and historical records, for example, are now held sacred by all civilized countries, and so are charitable, educational, religious, and scientific institutions. Public buildings and monuments are safe from wanton destruction, and museums, libraries, and picture galleries and their contents may now be said to enjoy a recognized immunity from spoliation. Public property which belongs not to the state but to civil administrative bodies, such as parishes, districts, or communes, or to religious, charitable, or similar institutions, must be treated as private property; and seizure, destruction of, or wilful damage to such establishments, historical monuments, or works of art or science, must be prosecuted by the competent authorities. (Brussels Conference, Article 8.)

Before 1800 Napoleon had despoiled the small Italian states of most of their marvellous art treasures, which were transferred to the Louvre. These were all subsequently restored, under pressure from England, upon the initiative of Lord Castlereagh, and the English view as to the sanctity of works of art now meets with almost universal assent.

Public vessels engaged in scientific discovery are usually accorded an immunity from capture or attack, so long as they maintain a strictly non-combatant character.

With regard to private property, lands and houses, being immovable, are exempt from seizure, and their fate is attendant upon that of the whole territory of which they form a part. *Private property. Immovable.*

Private movable property[1] was, however, always at the mercy of the invader, and liable to pillage or destruction; *Movable.*

[1] It has been seen in chapter iii. of this Part, that a neutral subject domiciled in an enemy country acquires an enemy character which extends to his property; and that, apart from domicil, neutral property may acquire such a character by being locally situated in the enemy's country. Such neutral persons or property, therefore, are subject to all the consequences of lawful hostilities, loss or injury by bombardment, the payment of contributions, and the like. *Neutral property in enemy country.*

But neutral property only *temporarily* situated in the enemy country acquires no hostile character, and though the belligerent's necessity may justify his seizing or making use of it, the neutral is entitled to compensation.

The belligerent right, which is termed the jus angariae, is not viewed with much favour by most writers on International Law. *Angary.*

During the Franco-Prussian War six British vessels were sunk in the Seine by Prussian troops in order to prevent French gunboats proceeding up the river and interfering with Prussian military operations. Although the Prussians appear to have used unnecessary violence on this occasion, the British Government did not deny that they were acting within their rights, and made no complaint upon full compensation being paid, including the value of the ships and their cargoes, with interest, and the expenses of the seamen home.

and it only came to be spared when the invader saw that such a course was for his own advantage. Wholesale pillage undermines the discipline of troops, and to destroy the crops of the country is to cut off supplies from the invading force as well as from the inhabitants. Therefore it became customary, as early as the Thirty Years' War, to allow the inhabitants to buy off pillage by the payment of a ransom to the invader, or by furnishing him with fixed amounts of provisions, or other things requisite for his campaign. This custom developed into the practice of levying contributions and requisitions from the inhabitants; and subject to their paying the former and supplying the latter, their private property is safe.

<small>Contributions and requisitions.</small>

Contributions and requisitions are dealt with in Articles 40-42 of the Draft Declaration of the Brussels Conference.

Contributions are payments of money in excess of the ordinary taxes, and may only be levied by the Commander-in-Chief. Requisitions consist in the supply of food or transport, or articles of immediate use for the troops, or personal service, such as acting as a guide, blacksmith, or driver in the army. Hostages are sometimes taken to secure the payment or supply of contributions or requisitions. The latter may be exacted by the commander of any detached body of troops, either with or without payment. Article 42 of the Draft Declaration provides that for every requisition an indemnity shall be granted or a receipt given. But the discussion at the Conference showed clearly that payment could only be arranged for in the treaty of peace at the end of war, when, if the invader does not pay, a government may, if it sees fit, reimburse its subjects who have supplied requisitions to the enemy. The "*bons de réquisition*," or receipts given by the invader, facilitate such a course, though their primary object is to protect holders from having to supply an unreasonable quantity of requisitions during the occupation. Private property on land, therefore, is only exempt from seizure because a more excellent substitute for seizure has been found; and writers who argue that private property at sea should be exempt from capture *because it is exempt on land*, and that pillage should be abolished at sea *as it has been on land*, are at once confuted by the well-established usage of contributions and requisitions, which are simply pillage in a mitigated form. Private property not absolutely exempt.

Further, it may be said that, apart from contributions and requisitions, private property is not absolutely exempt from seizure or destruction.

Military necessity may require the razing of houses to the ground or the destruction of crops. Acts of hostility and other offences against the invader on the part of individuals or communities in the occupied territory are most effectually punished and repetition prevented by the seizure or destruction of their private property. Lastly, private property has always been, and always must be, liable to seizure as "booty" on the field of battle, or when a town which refuses to capitulate is carried by assault. Military necessity. Offences against invader. Booty.

Booty may be defined as property seized by a belligerent on land, and includes not only arms and munitions in the hands of the enemy, but also all property that can be appropriated. In other words, it includes both public and private property. It vests in the state, but is commonly divided among the captors upon principles laid down by each state's own municipal law.

In England neither the Admiralty nor the ordinary courts had any original jurisdiction as to booty, but under an Act of 1840 the High Court of Admiralty was given jurisdiction to proceed as in cases of prize of war in all questions of booty. Division of booty.

THE LAW OF WAR

English practice. The principle of division is identical with that laid down by the Naval Prize Act 1864 as regards naval prize, **Captors.** and booty is now divided amongst the actual captors, joint-captors if any, and the Commander-in-Chief.

Joint captors. Joint capture may be by way of association or co-operation.

Troops strictly associated with the captors, and under the immediate control of the same commander, although not actually present or assisting at the capture, are joint-**By association.** captors by association. This was the case of Colonel Keating's regiment as regards the Banda and Kirwee Booty, and their claim to share in the distribution was upheld. The rule is practically the same as that laid down by David, "As his part is that goeth down to the battle, so shall his part be that tarrieth by the stuff: they shall part alike" (1 Sam. xxx. 24).

Troops affording direct and immediate assistance in the field at the time of capture are joint-captors by **By co-operation.** co-operation. The limits of time and place are drawn strictly, and services rendered some time before the capture, or at a considerable distance from the place of capture, would be insufficient to constitute joint capture by co-operation.

The Commander-in-Chief. The Commander-in-Chief, in order to share, must be in the field, though not necessarily present with the division which effected the capture.

These principles were definitely laid down in a learned and elaborate judgment by Dr. Lushington in the case of the Banda and Kirwee Booty taken by General Whitlock's forces in the Indian Mutiny.

Termination of military occupation. When military occupation comes to an end, the legal state of things previously existing is restored, and by a legal fiction derived from Roman Law, called Post-liminium, is deemed to have been in continuous existence during the occupation.

The result is, that acts done once and for all by the invader within his competence during the occupation hold good, as, for example, a distribution of booty. Such acts cannot be undone. And all acts of a continuing nature or effect, such as judicial or administrative acts, hold good during the occupation, but become inoperative from the moment of the restoration of the old government, as, for example, a punishment for an act which is not criminal by the national law.[1] Acts done by an invader in excess of his right as military occupant, *e.g.* an alienation of territory, are simply null and void.

Postliminium is said to apply to both persons and things. To territory and private immovable property, and to every other kind of property that may not lawfully be seized, postliminium undoubtedly does apply. But property, whether public or private, that has been lawfully taken, such as treasure or booty, is not subject to postliminium. As this follows directly from the rule that acts done once and for all within an invader's competence hold good, it would be unnecessary to state it, but for the fact that the effects of postliminium have sometimes been erroneously claimed for recapture whilst hostilities are still going on, whereas they differ considerably. If movable property is recaptured on land within twenty-four hours of its capture, it reverts to the original owner; otherwise it vests in the recaptor, subject amongst most nations to restoration to the owner on the payment of military salvage.

Similarly, as will appear below, there is no postliminium

Postliminium.

---

[1] In 1870 the Prussians, by right of military occupation, sold 15,000 oaks in French forests. When peace was made the French Government refused to allow the contractors to finish cutting the timber that still remained uncut, the contracts being annulled from the date of the restoration of the French Government.

as regards lawful prize, though there may be recapture.[1]

Lawful prize. B. *Maritime Capture or Prize.*

Lawful prize includes enemy property captured on the high sea or in territorial waters belonging either to the captor [2] or to the enemy, and property of neutrals captured and confiscated for breach of blockade or as contraband of war.

When an enemy ship carries an enemy cargo the case is quite clear, and both may be seized and condemned as lawful prize; but when an enemy ship carries a neutral cargo, or a neutral ship an enemy cargo, a conflict of belligerent and neutral interests arises, just as in the case of carriage of contraband and breach of blockade.

The history of the practice of maritime capture as affecting neutral property associated with enemy property, being so intimately connected with neutral rights and duties, may be more conveniently reserved for discussion in Part III.

Dismissing for the moment the enemy or neutral character of the ship or its cargo, and assuming the mere fact of capture without entering into its legality, it is important **When is capture complete?** to determine at what moment the capture becomes complete. Upon this will depend the mutual rights of a neutral purchaser, or the recaptor and the original owner in case of recapture. The principle is clear enough. The captor must have actually seized the prize, and there must be an intention and a reasonable probability on his part of retaining it. The rules embodying this principle, and

---

[1] If recapture takes place before capture is complete, its effects may be said to resemble those of postliminium (cf. p. 146, *infra*). But postliminium proper knows nothing of the payment of salvage.

[2] Immunity has been on occasions accorded out of generosity to enemy vessels driven into territorial waters by stress of weather. (Cf. chap. ii. of this Part,—footnote on p. 92.)

adopted in practice, have varied at different periods. "Although all nations agree that to change the property by capture a firm and secure possession is necessary, yet the practice of nations is so various that it seems difficult to collect a general rule as to what constitutes such firm and secure possession, which might properly be asserted to be the Law of Nations."—*Phillimore.*

The moment of actual capture, when the prize hauls down her flag, has sometimes been considered sufficient, but in general practice down to the seventeenth century twenty-four hours' possession was required to complete the captor's title. *Practice to capture.*

From that time it became the practice, supported by the opinion of Bynkershoek, Wolff, Vattel, and other eminent eighteenth-century publicists, to require prizes to be brought *infra præsidia* into a place of safe keeping.

By modern usage, however, the title of the original owner is not barred either as against a neutral purchaser from the captor, or as against a recaptor, until the prize has been brought in for adjudication, and condemned by a competent Prize Court.

The "Flad Oyen." (1 C. Rob. 135.)

During war between Great Britain and France a French privateer captured the *Flad Oyen*, a British vessel, in 1799, and carried her into a Norwegian port, where she was condemned by the French consul and subsequently sold. On being recaptured by a British cruiser, her original owner applied for restitution.

Sir William Scott held that condemnation by a competent Prize Court was necessary to transfer property in the prize to the captor, and that a Prize Court held in neutral territory was not a competent Prize Court. An order was therefore made for restitution.

The captor may lose possession of the prize, either

L

before or after the capture is complete, by abandoning it, by its escape, or by its recapture.

Recapture. In the case of recapture the practice of nations has varied considerably, their views as to its effects necessarily depending upon their view as to the moment when capture becomes complete.

Original owner's title against recaptor. If any broad general principle can be stated it is this:— If recapture takes place before the capture has become complete the property reverts to its original owner, subject to the payment by him of military salvage to the recaptor. If the capture has become complete the property vests *primâ facie* in the recaptor, who is, however, generally compelled by his municipal law to restore it to the original owner upon the payment of salvage. There are some exceptions. If a belligerent captures neutral property, and it is recaptured by the other belligerent, the latter usually restores it without payment of salvage, on the presumption that the court of the captor would not have condemned it. Allies act upon a system of reciprocity; one ally condemns or restores the ships of another ally which it recaptures according to the latter's action under similar circumstances.

The Consolato del Mare prescribed that a prize, if recaptured before being taken into a place of safety, should be restored to the owner on payment of salvage; otherwise it belonged wholly to the recaptor. This was also the rule stated by Grotius and Bynkershoek.

Coming to modern practice, the English rule has been, and now under the Naval Prize Act 1864 is, to restore a recaptured prize to the owner on payment of one-eighth of its value by way of salvage, unless the ship has been fitted out by the enemy as a man-of-war, in which case she is the lawful prize of the recaptors.

The United States rule is to restore the vessel to the

owner on payment of salvage, if she is recaptured before condemnation by a competent court.

The English rule is clearly more favourable to the owner than that of the United States, because the English owner's title is, notwithstanding condemnation, never lost as against the recaptor unless the vessel has been fitted out as an armed ship; whereas the American owner's title as against the recaptor is gone if the prize has been condemned by a competent court.

If, however, the prize has been duly condemned and sold to a neutral purchaser by the captors, the neutral title will necessarily prevail as against either original owners or recaptors both in English and American courts. This follows from the doctrine laid down in the *Flad Oyen*. Condemnation enables the captor to give a neutral purchaser a good title.

<small>Neutral purchaser's title against recaptor or original owner.</small>

The French rule is to restore to the owner a prize recaptured by a public vessel within twenty-four hours of its capture on payment of one-thirtieth of its value as salvage. If recapture takes place after twenty-four hours the salvage is one-tenth. In the case of recapture effected by privateers the rules are different.

The practice of other nations is in general terms to restore recaptured prizes on payment of salvage, the rate varying according to the length of time the property has been in the possession of the enemy.[1]

If a vessel made prize by the enemy is recaptured before being taken *infra præsidia* she is not uncommonly allowed to proceed upon her voyage, but she is strictly liable to be brought in at once for adjudication. The recaptor does not of course lose his right to salvage by allowing the vessel to continue her voyage.

[1] Vessels recaptured from pirates after whatever length of time are always restored to the owner on payment of salvage, the maxim being "Pirate ne peut changer domain."

Under the Naval Prize Act the recaptors may proceed to adjudication on the return of the vessel to a port of the United Kingdom, and if she does not do so within six months, they can recover salvage in the Court of Admiralty.

Prize Courts. At the commencement of war each belligerent erects a Prize Court to determine questions of capture and prize, the court of the captor being the only competent court for this purpose.

The substantive law administered by all Prize Courts is International not municipal law, except in so far as the latter is identical with or declaratory of the former.[1] Their procedure is determined, as procedure always is, by the *lex loci*, and varies in different countries. That of the English Prize Court is regulated by the Naval Prize Act, 1864.

Functions. The chief functions of Prize Courts are to decree condemnation or restitution according as property has been rightfully or wrongfully captured, to determine all consequent questions of freight, costs, damages, and expenses, and to punish the crew either of captor or prize in case of misbehaviour.

Condemnation vests the property in the prize in the captors. In England prize-money is distributed amongst the captors, joint captors (if any), and the Admiral in command on the station; and what has been said above as to joint-capture in case of booty holds good with reference to prize.

Prizes must be brought in. The general rule that all prizes must be brought in for adjudication, which owed its origin to the fact that in

---

[1] A Prize Court "ought to administer a consistent law upon certain and known principles, impartially applied to all states and to their subjects," a law "one and the same everywhere founded and applied, so far as human infirmity will permit, upon the principles of immutable right and eternal justice."—*Phillimore*.

early times the state claimed a share of their value, now exists chiefly for the benefit of neutrals. It is the duty of the Prize Court to protect and restore neutral property which, though it may happen to be associated with enemy property, is untainted with an enemy character.

The captor may, however, be short of hands, or weather or other circumstances may prevent him from sending in the prize. In such a case he has two alternatives—to destroy her or release her under a ransom-bill. *If it is impossible,*

Where both ship and cargo have a hostile character her destruction is not a harsh measure, for the captor only destroys what would otherwise become his own property. In two wars destruction has been adopted as a deliberate policy: by the United States against Great Britain in 1812—1814, and by the Confederate States in the American Civil War. In the latter case all the Confederate ports were blockaded, and they could not have sent in prizes if they had wanted to. *destruction.*

But where the cargo, or a portion of it, is neutral property, destruction can only be justified in exceptional circumstances, on the ground of military necessity, if the Declaration of Paris has any binding value. It is impossible to reconcile a policy of systematic destruction applied to neutral cargoes with the provision of the Declaration of Paris, protecting neutral goods in enemy ships, except contraband.[1]

[1] During the Franco-Prussian War the *Vorwaerts*, a German vessel, was captured by a French cruiser and burnt, the captor not having the means of taking the prize into port. An application for compensation by an English firm, to whom the cargo belonged, was refused by the Conseil d'État, it being held that the Declaration of Paris did not give neutrals any right of indemnity against losses arising from lawful capture or from acts of war accompanying or succeeding such a capture. This decision was followed in the case of the *Ludwig*, in which the facts were similar.

Ransom-bills.

The other course is to release the prize under a ransom-bill, which is a contract by her master binding upon her owners to pay a certain ransom. A hostage is also left with the captor by way of collateral security. The prize is exempt from further capture by ships of the captor's country or its allies on her voyage home. This practice is regulated by municipal law of individual countries; it is wholly forbidden by that of Russia, Sweden, Denmark, and other states. Citizens of the United States are allowed to enter into such contracts in all cases, and English subjects under the provisions of the Naval Prize Act.

Enemy property exempt from capture.

In conclusion, certain enemy property may be mentioned which is, or may be, exempt from capture at sea.

Fishing-boats are generally spared, but their immunity is not absolute. Like that of non-combatants, it depends upon their harmlessness, and if used for noxious purposes they may be captured. Ships engaged in scientific discovery are exempt from capture so long as they abstain from hostilities. In 1766 the French Government granted Captain Cook immunity from capture on these terms, a precedent of generosity which has since been followed. Enemy vessels on their way to a belligerent port at the outbreak of war are sometimes allowed to land their cargo, and granted a safe pass home. This is a selfish and unjust belligerent practice. The belligerent spares an enemy vessel conveying supplies to himself, but exercises his strict right to capture one carrying a cargo to a neutral port.[1] This practice was, however, adopted by England

---

[1] "Equity appears certainly to demand that, if a belligerent for his own convenience spares enemy's ships laden with cargoes destined to him, he shall not put neutrals to inconvenience who have not had an opportunity of sending their goods in vessels which are free from liability to capture."—*Hall*.

and France at the outbreak of the Crimean War, by France in 1870, and by Russia in 1877.

Lastly, since 1856 enemy goods, except contraband, are exempt from capture on neutral ships when the belligerents are states who are bound by the Declaration of Paris.

CHAPTER VII

INTERCOURSE BETWEEN BELLIGERENTS. THE TERMINATION OF WAR

Intercourse between belligerents.

NON-HOSTILE intercourse between belligerents before the war is brought to a definite termination takes place either by way of a temporary cessation of hostilities or a partial waiver of hostile rights.

Cessation of hostilities.

A temporary cessation of hostilities may be general and extend to all combatants on both sides, or it may extend to particular armies, or smaller detached bodies of troops, or merely to individuals. A cessation of hostilities affecting bodies of troops takes place under suspensions of arms, truces, and armistices, whilst individuals may be temporarily protected by flags of truce, passports, or safe-conducts.

A belligerent partially waives his hostile rights by entering into a cartel agreement with the enemy, by accepting a capitulation, or granting a safeguard or a licence to trade. A cessation of hostilities is described as a truce, an armistice, or a suspension of arms according to its duration, local extent, and object.

Suspension of arms.

If the cessation agreed upon is only for a very short period, at a particular place, or for a temporary military object, such as a parley between the opposing commanders, or the burial of the dead, it is usually termed a suspension of arms. Agreements having such a temporary and local effect may be entered into by officers holding detached commands, and are binding upon all the forces under their immediate control.

There is no clear or authoritative distinction between a truce and an armistice; but, for convenience' sake, a general cessation of hostilities binding all the forces of both belligerents may be described as a truce, and an armistice as a partial or restricted truce. *Truce.*

A truce is not equivalent to a peace. It does not terminate the war, but merely suspends all acts of war whilst it lasts. It can only be concluded by the Commander-in-Chief, and only by him as a state act. There must therefore be a ratification on each side by the sovereign power of the state to validate a general truce.

The duration of the truce being fixed by the parties, all hostilities on both sides are suspended during that period, but the *status quo ante* at the seat of the war must not be altered. Away from the immediate theatre of operations each belligerent may continue to throw up fortifications, build ships, raise levies, and manufacture arms and munitions of war, the general principle being that each belligerent is permitted to do during the truce any acts which the enemy could not prevent if hostilities were still being carried on.

The object of a truce is in general not military but political. It enables the belligerents to treat as to the terms upon which they will both be willing to enter into a treaty of peace and thereby end the war. The recent Chino-Japanese War was brought to a conclusion by this kind of preliminary truce.

An armistice is a truce of a restricted character, limited as to the forces and the local area to which it applies. It stands midway between a truce and a mere suspension of arms. A general or admiral in command of an army or a fleet can enter into an armistice binding the combatants *Armistice.*

under his command, subject to ratification by the supreme authority of the state. As in the case of a truce, the *status quo ante* must not be altered, and it is usual to specify what acts are permitted and what are forbidden during the armistice in the agreement by which it is concluded.

In case of siege. This is especially necessary in the case of an armistice between the commander of a fortified town and the army investing it. As a matter of theory both sides must refrain from doing acts which the other could have hindered or prevented, had no armistice been concluded.

The besiegers, for example, must not erect fresh batteries nor the besieged receive succours. But the French view that both sides may do any military acts within their lines in the absence of express stipulation to the contrary is more practicable, and prevents secret abuse of the armistice. The insertion of stipulations expressly prohibiting certain acts would no doubt sufficiently preserve the *status quo ante*, or at all events prevent it from being unfairly changed in favour of one of the parties.

Revictualling a besieged place is a necessary incident of such an armistice, and is not a change of the *status quo ante*. If revictualling were not allowed the effect of an armistice would be to reduce the besieged place by famine. But, in order that the town may not be strengthened by an excessive importation of provisions, it is usual for the besieger to specify the amount and superintend the supply.

The commencement and termination of any cessation of hostilities are usually definitely arranged by the commanding officers on either side. But if there is no express agreement as to its duration, the armistice binds both parties from the date it is concluded, and may be terminated by either belligerent on giving due warning to the enemy, according to the provisions contained in the armistice.

Troops at a considerable distance are not bound by the armistice until they are officially notified of its existence, but prisoners or property captured by them in ignorance after the conclusion of the truce or armistice are usually restored.

By Articles 51 and 52 of the Declaration of the Brussels Conference, the violation of the armistice by one side gives the other the right to terminate it, but a violation by private individuals acting on their own account only gives the right to demand their punishment, and an indemnity for any losses which may have been suffered.

An individual may be temporarily protected from hostilities by a flag of truce, a passport, or a safe-conduct.

A flag of truce is used when a belligerent wishes to enter into negotiations with the enemy. The person charged with the mission presents himself for admission accompanied by a drummer or bugler and a person bearing a white flag. The bearers of a flag of truce are inviolable, but they cannot insist upon admission into the enemy's lines, as the latter cannot be compelled to enter into negotiations against his will. Flag of truce.

The troops from which a flag of truce is sent halt and cease firing; and, if the enemy is willing to receive it, his troops do the same. If not, a signal to that effect is made, and the bearers of the flag must retire. If they persist in advancing they may then be fired upon, but to fire upon them in the first instance without any previous signal, in order to turn them back, is a grave offence against the rules of war.

A flag of truce must be used in the fullest good faith, and if one is displayed during an engagement the enemy is not bound to immediately cease firing and signal his refusal to receive the bearer. The flag must not be used to "gain a breathing space" during the progress of an engagement, and, until victory is actually assured, a belligerent is justified in disregarding a flag of truce displayed by his enemy in the battle.

If a deserter returns to the lines from which he has deserted as the bearer of a flag of truce it affords him no protection, and he may be seized and dealt with as a traitor.

When the bearer of a flag of truce is admitted, precautions may be taken to prevent his acquiring knowledge of the enemy's position. He may accordingly be blindfolded and prevented from holding intercourse with any person except the commander.

Any attempt to obtain military information surreptitiously under the cover of a flag of truce exposes its bearer to be treated as a spy.

These principles have been endorsed by the Brussels Conference (Articles 43—45), and their authority is now hardly open to doubt.

Passport. A passport is a written permission given by a belligerent government to a subject of the enemy whom it allows to pass freely without any restrictions in territory belonging to it or under its control.

Safe-conduct. A safe-conduct is a written permission given by a belligerent government or one of its naval or military commanders, enabling an enemy subject to go to a particular place for a particular object.

For obvious reasons neither a passport nor safe-conduct is transferable. They may be granted for a certain time only and revoked for sufficient cause, the grantee being allowed to withdraw in safety. If detained beyond the prescribed limit of time by illness or *force majeur*, he is still entitled to protection, but if he voluntarily exceeds limits of time or place he becomes subject to the ordinary laws of war, or to penalties if such are imposed under the *lex loci*.[1]

A partial waiver of hostile rights takes place in case of cartels, capitulations, safe-guards, and licences to trade.

Partial waiver of hostile rights.

A cartel is a form of convention regulating the mode of certain forms of non-hostile intercourse permitted between belligerents. Arrangements as to exchange of prisoners, or postal and telegraphic communication, are carried out in this way. The waiver of hostile rights takes place with reference to the cartel ships which negotiate the exchange of prisoners. These ships sail under a safe-conduct from the enemy, which protects them both going and returning, whether they have prisoners on board or not. They are unarmed vessels, and forfeit protection if they abuse it by trading, attempting to gain information, or otherwise departing from their non-combatant character.

Cartel.

A capitulation is an agreement under which an armed force surrenders upon conditions. Officers in superior or detached commands are assumed to be invested with powers of capitulation extending only to the immediate question of the fate of the fortress or place surrendered, and that of its garrison and inhabitants. For any excess or abuse of these powers a commanding officer is of course accountable to his own state. Stipulations "affecting the political constitution or administration of a country or place, or making engagements with respect to its future independence," cannot be entered into even by a Commander-in-Chief without special powers or subsequent ratification by his government.

Capitulation.

The conditions upon which capitulations are made vary according to circumstances. The greater power the surrendering force has of prolonging its resistance, the more

---

[1] *E.g.* an Act of Congress, 1790, exposed any civilian violating a passport or safe-conduct to imprisonment not exceeding three years or a fine.

favourable terms it is enabled to secure. The most honourable form of capitulation is "marching out with all the honours of war," colours flying and drums beating. All the terms of the surrender are in every case strictly defined in the articles of capitulation.

Small detached bodies of men, or individuals, cut off from the main army, and falling into the enemy's hands in a place distant from any succour, may surrender at their discretion. Being unable to receive their sovereign's commands or enjoy his protection, they may with honour provide for their own safety, and their state is bound to respect the agreement of surrender which they have entered into.

Safe-guard. A safe-guard is a protection to person or property accorded by commanding officers of belligerent forces. It may be either an order in writing or a guard of soldiers. Their chief use is for the protection of property when a place has been carried by assault, and it is desirable to preserve churches, libraries, museums, and such buildings from spoliation.

The guard is posted upon the property to be protected, and any violation is punished by the military law of most nations with great severity. In the British and American armies the conviction of this offence upon active service exposes the offender to the penalty of death, and in other circumstances, to cashiering or imprisonment.

Licence to trade. A general or special licence to trade may be granted by a belligerent state to the subjects of its enemy exempting them from the ordinary consequences of war.

A general licence is a permission to all enemy subjects to trade with a particular place or in particular articles.

A special licence is a permission to an individual to carry on a particular trade specified in the licence.

A licence to trade is not usually construed very strictly by the grantor, who issues it for his own advantage, but if it is obtained by misrepresentation or *suppressio veri*, it will be held void.

There is a legal as well as a moral necessity that there shall be no unnecessary continuation of the horrors of war. The termination of war.

As soon as an invader has obtained or secured his rights, or has redressed the injury which he has suffered, or has otherwise fulfilled whatever may be its precise object, the war must come to an end.

A war may be terminated by a mere *de facto* cessation of hostilities, by the conquest and unconditional submission of one of the belligerents, or by the conclusion of a formal treaty of peace. It is very seldom that a war comes to an end by a mere cessation of hostilities. The only unequivocal instance of such an event appears to be in the case of the war between Sweden and Poland, which had this kind of tacit and informal termination in 1716. Cessation of hostilities.

The inconvenience of such a state of affairs explains its rarity. The original subject of the quarrel remains still in dispute; blood has been spilt and treasure wasted to no purpose, and it is probable that a fresh war will follow in the future, when either of the belligerents has recruited its strength sufficiently to again take up the ancient quarrel.

In addition to this the inconvenience affects neutral states even more than the belligerents, because, after the last interchange of active hostilities, an interval, greater or less according to circumstances, but in any case of some considerable extent, must necessarily follow, during which the rights and obligations of neutral states will be uncertain. It is unlikely that such a state of things would now be tolerated, and neutral states would probably bring pressure to bear on the belligerents in order to bring them to terms, and thereby put a formal end to the war.

As soon as a mere cessation of hostilities has tacitly developed into a termination of war—supposing such a case to occur—the effect would be to restore generally the relations and incidents inherent to a state of peace unaccompanied by any of the special results which flow from a formal treaty of peace.

Conquest. Termination of war by the complete conquest of one of the belligerents is no longer possible in modern times. In former ages there were, no doubt, instances of a kingdom or a tribe completely absorbing or blotting out its neighbour by seizing the latter's territory and killing and enslaving its population. Modern civilization makes this impossible, and in speaking of conquest as putting an end to war, only a partial conquest, affecting some portion of the territory belonging to the "conquered" state, is meant. Such a conquest develops out of a preceding military occupation, and the general effects of conquest apart from treaty have been already described. It is clear, however, that a conqueror desirous of retaining the conquered territory is seldom content to suffer his occupation to develop into conquest by lapse of time, or to rely upon the generalities of International Law. Being in a position to enforce his wishes, he gets his conquest confirmed and its consequences defined by a formal contract with the conquered state. Thus it happens that, even in case of conquest, the normal termination of war consists in a treaty of peace.

Treaty of peace.

Overtures for peace are made by one of the belligerents, or in some cases a neutral state offers its friendly services to both parties.

The treaty which then terminates the war may adopt as its basis the rule " *uti possidetis,*" or the *status quo ante bellum,* or a combination of these two principles.

In other words, it may vest territory and property held by either belligerent at the end of the war in him absolutely; it may restore territory and certain kinds of property (always excepting lawful prize or booty) seized during the war to the original owner; or it may establish a new state of affairs by partly confirming conquest and possession, and partly providing for restoration.

In default of any express provision to the contrary in the treaty, the doctrine of *uti possidetis* prevails.

The general effect of the treaty is to restore the normal relations of peace, such as intercourse and commerce between the belligerent states. These relations are governed by the ordinary "Rules of Peace," and require no further mention. But the termination of war has in addition certain special effects with reference to acts done before the commencement, or during the continuation, or after the conclusion of hostilities, which must be described in this chapter. Effects of treaty of peace.

The first obvious consequence of a treaty of peace is that all hostilities must cease from the date of its conclusion, unless some other date is fixed by the treaty itself. The treaty is not of course actually binding until ratified by the parties to it, but its signature is the date for the termination of hostilities. This rule is founded both on convenience and reason, because the treaty amounts at least to an armistice in the unlikely event of ratification being refused. If the armed forces of belligerent states which have shown their willingness to come to terms should continue hostilities up to the moment of formal ratification, that moment would in most cases probably never arrive. Cessation of hostilities.

When hostilities extend to distant regions with which immediate communication is impossible, it has been usual to fix some future date for their termination. The extension of telegraphs of late years is likely to make such a provision less necessary in the future, especially as cruisers and other vessels on the high seas are in more immediate communication with their base of operations than they were in the days of canvas and wooden walls.

It is not necessary that the war should end upon the

M

same day in all the places where it has been carried on. The treaty may provide different dates for the cessation of hostilities at different places, according to the difficulty of making the combatants in each district or on each naval station acquainted with the establishment of peace, the one requirement being that the knowledge of the combatants as to the cessation of hostilities must be derived from an *authentic* source. A military or naval officer is not held to have such knowledge except by communication from his own government. A hard-and-fast rule of this kind is necessary in order to prevent a cessation of hostilities being brought about, perhaps at a critical time, by the circulation of intentionally deceptive information. But it is a rule which, as applied by the French Court in the case of the *Swineherd*, operates with considerable harshness.

<small>Cessation dates from authentic knowledge.</small>

Of the two factors constituting a termination of war in a distant place, the knowledge of the combatant that peace has been made is unquestionably of far more importance than the precise day fixed by the treaty for the cessation of hostilities. That date is merely given as a margin of time in order that the knowledge may be acquired. Therefore, if authentic information of the peace arrives before the date fixed by the treaty, hostilities must cease from the date when the knowledge was acquired, and not from the date contained in the treaty. If, however, the information comes from some unauthentic source an officer is justified in continuing hostilities, though he may have the best reason to believe that his own country and the enemy are no longer at war.

The "Swineherd," 1802.

This was an English vessel captured by a French privateer before the date fixed by the Treaty of Amiens for the termination of hostilities between Great Britain and France in the Indian seas. The French vessel had been informed by three other ships, one Portuguese, another Arab, and the third an English vessel which she had captured, that peace had been concluded; and there was a copy of the official English announcement of peace on board the *Swineherd*. She was nevertheless condemned by the French Prize Court in accordance with the strict letter of the rule already laid down.

The capture and condemnation in such a case were *primâ facie* lawful and correct; but where a vessel has been captured after the captor has received information of the conclusion of peace, acquired from an unauthentic source, justice and good faith seem to demand that, if that information subsequently turns out to have been correct, the vessel ought to be restored. It is certain that, in case of a capture made in ignorance after the time limited by the treaty, restoration would be decreed; and if constructive knowledge of the peace renders a capture void, *a fortiori* actual knowledge, derived from whatever source, should produce the same effect, the capture in both cases really being made in time of peace. This contention has not as yet been supported in practice, and it is possible that the increased facility of communication may prevent the occurrence of any case similar to the *Swineherd* in the future.

The position of public property and contracts, and private rights and property at the end of the war may be made clear by a consideration of the effects of the treaty of peace upon acts done before, during, or after the hostilities. {Other effects of treaty of peace.}

1. *Acts done before the war.*

The statement of the effects, permanent or temporary, of the outbreak of war upon then existing contracts, public and private, has already shown directly or by implication how such contracts are affected by the termination of war. (Cf. chapter ii. of this Part.) {Acts done before the war.}

A short recapitulation may perhaps be given in the present place. Of treaties affected by the war, some whose operation is merely suspended revive *ipso facto* on the return of peace, while others only revive by express stipulation contained in the treaty of peace. The termination of hostilities restores generally all private rights and remedies. Private contracts with some exceptions are merely suspended during the war, and unless fulfilment has been rendered impossible by belligerent operations, must be fulfilled on the conclusion of peace. During the war " non jus tollitur sed juris executio," and the return of peace re-opens the law-courts for the enforcement of private claims of every kind.

2. *Acts done during the war.*

<small>Acts done during the war.</small>

The effect of a treaty of peace is to amnesty all offences committed during the war and connected with it. This immunity of offenders from civil and criminal process rests upon the expediency of burying the occurrences of the war in as complete and speedy oblivion as possible. It only extends to offences such as violation of the rules of war, or maintaining treasonable relations with the enemy—

<small>Amnesty.</small>

offences, in short, connected with the war, and not to ordinary offences recognized as crimes by the law of the country to which the offender belongs. This act of oblivion is always implied and understood as being one of the necessary consequences of the termination of war; so, although it is usual for a treaty of peace to contain an express amnesty clause, it is unnecessary, except for the purpose of protecting subjects who, having had treasonable relations with the enemy, would not be protected from their own government by a merely implied amnesty.

<small>Acts affecting property.</small>

Acts done during the war affecting public and private property are of great importance with regard to their after-effects. Such acts are all those which are incident to a conquest, a military occupation, or other warlike operation by which the enemy's property can be affected. With regard to the immovable property of the enemy, both public and private, the only good title is that of conquest or cession under a treaty of peace. A conquest may be confirmed by express mention in the treaty, or without mention at all if the treaty is based upon the principle of *uti possidetis*. Therefore in the absence of a *de facto* conquest, and in the absence of express cession by a treaty not based upon the above-mentioned principle, the termination of hostilities restores immovable property, public and private, to the original owners. This is one of the effects of the legal fiction called Postliminium, described in chapter vi.

<small>Immovable property.</small>

Where a treaty is based on the *status quo ante bellum*, all immovable property is restored as a matter of course without express mention. But in all cases where restoration takes place, the territory and buildings upon it are handed over in the condition in which they happen to be at the end of the war, and there is no obligation upon a state to make good the damage to fortresses dismantled or territory ravaged in the course of a military occupation by its forces. Such damage is the result of legitimate acts of war; but to destroy fortifications or crops after the cessation of hostilities, out of mere hatred and malice, would be an act of perfidy, from which in its own interest, if on no higher ground, every civilized state is bound to refrain. The offending state would of course have to make good wanton damage of this description.

There is one distinction to be drawn between the fate of public and that of private immovable property. If the former is restored the latter is also. But if the former passes into the enemy's hands by conquest or cession, it does not follow that the latter shares its fate. As has been seen, one state can acquire the territory of another expressly or tacitly—in the case of conquest—but the private property of the individual in the soil can in no case be tacitly taken from him, and it reverts to him at the end of the war, unless there is express stipulation to the contrary in the treaty of peace.

A landowner in a conquered or ceded country is required to make an election of nationality, and if he elects to retain his old nationality, must retire from the territory within a given time. He is, however, in some cases allowed to retain his landed property in the ceded territory—a privilege which was conceded to the natives of Alsace and Lorraine by the Treaty of Frankfort.

<small>Movable property.</small>

With regard to all movable property, public and private, the rule of *uti possidetis* holds good, and all such property vests in its actual possessor at the end of the war, unless there is any express provision to the contrary in the treaty of peace. Thus all lawful booty and prize taken on land or sea during the war vests in the captor, and his possession is undisturbed by the conclusion of peace. All movable property lawfully appropriated in accordance with the rules of war during a conquest or occupation continues in the possession of the appropriator; and, conversely, all movables left in the hands of their original owners remain their property at the end of the war, notwithstanding the conquest of the territory where they are situated.

<small>Incorporeal property.</small>

It remains to consider whether a belligerent can appropriate his enemy's public and private incorporeal property, which in modern times far exceeds movable property in value and extent. There have been many instances of confiscation of debts between the celebrated exercise of the rights of conquest by Alexander the Great, recorded by Quintilian,[1] and the case of the Elector of Hesse Cassel—the last remarkable historical example.

---

[1] On conquering Thebes Alexander presented to his allies, the Thessalians, a debt of 100 talents, which they owed to the Thebans.

In 1806 Napoleon confiscated the private property of the Elector, including a debt due from Count Hahn Hahn, to whom he gave a release in full on part payment. The legality of the confiscation and discharge were affirmed by the German Universities, to whom the matter was subsequently remitted. At first Napoleon was only a military occupant, but between 1806 and 1813 the occupation was consolidated into conquest, and therefore his acts, invalid as occupant, became valid *ex post facto* in virtue of conquest. (Cf. p. 135.)

Debts due to the enemy state or to its subjects, whether from the belligerent state itself or from any of its subjects, cannot now be confiscated at all. The tendency in modern opinion and practice against the confiscation of the debts which a belligerent itself owes to the enemy is so strong, that it is correct to say that such confiscation is now impossible. (Cf. p. 91.)

The only question remaining is whether a belligerent can receive payment, and give a valid discharge, of debts owed to the enemy by third persons and states, and to this extent confiscate its enemy's debts. The answer seems to be that debts due to the enemy cannot be confiscated by a mere military occupant, but only by a conqueror and perhaps—but not certainly—by a *de facto* intermediate government, if established, as in the case of Hesse Cassel.

Hall, adopting the opinion of Phillimore, puts the case against confiscation very clearly. "Incorporeal things can only be occupied by actual possession of the subject to which they adhere. When territory is occupied there are incorporeal rights, such as servitudes, which go with it because they are inherent in the land. But the seizure of instruments or documents representing debts has not an analogous effect. They are not the subject to which the incorporeal right adheres; they are merely the evidence that the right exists, or, so to speak, the title-deeds of the obligee. The right itself arises out of the purely personal relations between the creditor and the debtor; it inheres in the creditor. It is only consequently when a belligerent is entitled to stand in the place of his enemy for all purposes, that is to say, *it is only when complete conquest has been made*, and the identity of the conquered state has been lost in that of the victor, that the latter can stand in its place as a creditor, and gather in the debts which are owing to it."

3. *Acts done after the conclusion of peace.*

<small>Acts done after the war is over.</small>

All acts of war done after the conclusion of peace, or after the time fixed for the cessation of hostilities, are, whether done in knowledge or in ignorance of the existence of peace, null and void. The effects of such acts must be, so far as is possible, undone by the state responsible for the doers of them, and compensation given for the harm suffered through such effects as cannot be undone.

Such acts as the destruction of buildings or crops in an occupied country, or the capture of a ship after the time fixed for cessation of hostilities, alluded to above, fall under this category.

The British doctrine, as stated by Sir William Scott in the *Mentor* (1, C. Rob. 179), is, that in such a case compensation may be recovered by an injured party from the officer by whose act injury has been caused; and that if the officer acted through ignorance, his own government ought to indemnify him.

PART III
THE LAW OF NEUTRALITY

CHAPTER I

THE RIGHTS AND DUTIES OF NEUTRAL STATES

WHEN war breaks out between two or more powers, the normal rights of all non-combatant or neutral states as against each other remain unaffected, and are affected as against the belligerent powers only to such an extent as is necessitated by the existence of war.

It follows that the outbreak of war, rather than creating new neutral rights, only emphasizes certain existing rights of neutral states; the effect of war being to invest neutral powers with duties rather than with rights.

A neutral power has, however, two rights incident to a state of war. The first of these is a right to be informed of the existence of the war, because without such knowledge no liability for breach of neutral duties can arise. The other is a right to recognize, under certain conditions, a revolted colony or province as a belligerent power, or even as a new state. *Two neutral rights resulting from war.*

The outbreak of hostilities between two powers is likely to lead to the infringement of certain of the normal rights of neutral states. These rights, though remaining the same as in peace, acquire a greater prominence in time of war, and have to be guarded with a correspondingly increased watchfulness. Such rights are principally those which arise out of the sovereignty of a state, namely, its rights over its territory and ships. *Neutral rights of sovereignty.*

THE LAW OF WAR

Ships.
With regard to ships, the public vessels of a neutral state are inviolable, as also at the present time are its private ships, subject to the laws relating to breach of blockade, contraband, and search.

Territory.
Neutral territory, which includes the sea for a distance of three miles from low-water mark on the shore, is inviolable. Any act of hostility committed by a belligerent within its limits constitutes a violation of the neutrality of the state to which the territory belongs.

As a necessary consequence of the doctrine of territorial sovereignty, a neutral state has a theoretical right to the inviolability of its territory, and belligerents are under a corresponding duty to abstain from violation.

Neutral duty rather than right.
In actual practice, however, the importance of the neutral right is entirely swallowed up in the well-established duty on the part of the neutral state of protecting and enforcing that right, a duty which well illustrates the subordination of neutral to belligerent interests in the development of the rules of war.

If a ship is captured in violation of neutrality, the neutral government is bound to enforce her restoration, or pay compensation to the injured belligerent. To this rule there is only one exception.[1] If a belligerent attacked in neutral territory elects to defend himself, he is in *pari delicto*, and releases the neutral state from liability in respect of the violation of territory.

The "General Armstrong," 1814.

In this case an American privateer was captured after a conflict in the harbour of Fayal in Portugal by a British cruiser. The United States claimed compen-

---

[1] There was formerly one other exception according to Bynkershoek. He stated that a belligerent cruiser might complete a chase commenced on the high sea by a capture effected in neutral waters *dum ferret opus*. This doctrine was confined to the Dutch, and is entirely contrary to all modern practice and opinion.

THE RIGHTS AND DUTIES OF NEUTRAL STATES 173

sation from the Portuguese Government, and the matter was subsequently referred for arbitration in 1851 to Louis Napoleon, then President of the French Republic. He held that as the captain of the privateer had not applied at the outset to the neutral state, but had used force to repel the aggression, he had himself disregarded the neutrality of the territory, and had released Portugal from all obligation to protect him, and all responsibility for the violation of its territory.

The practical result is that a neutral state, rather than enjoying a right to the inviolability of its territory, is subject to a duty of taking care that its territory is not violated by either of the belligerents. The right exists; but, inasmuch as the neutral state can be compelled to enforce it by whichever belligerent is damaged by its breach, it exists for the benefit of the belligerent rather than for that of the neutral.

This duty on the part of the neutral state to enforce its own right is simply part and parcel of its duty of strict impartiality towards both belligerents. It must not, by waiving that right, enable one belligerent to carry on hostile operations in neutral territory to the prejudice of the other belligerent.

This will appear abundantly plain in dealing with the use of neutral territory for the passage of the belligerent troops, or the fitting out of expeditions, and the employment of neutral ports as a base of operations and supplies.

Among other rights belonging to a neutral state in virtue of its territorial sovereignty is the important right of hospitality or asylum. The conditions under which this right may be exercised vary in land and sea warfare. *Right of asylum.*

It is almost unnecessary to say that this right does not justify the reception within its territory by a neutral of a belligerent armed force contemplating a descent upon the territory of the other belligerent. To countenance an *Land warfare.*

active hostile expedition in such a manner would constitute a gross breach of neutrality; but a neutral state has the right to extend its hospitality to a beaten army or detachment, or to individual fugitives taking refuge from the pursuit of the enemy in its territory. The general practice has been to disarm and intern such fugitives, and keep them at the cost of their government until the conclusion of peace. This practice was confirmed by the Brussels Conference in its Draft Declaration (Articles 53—56). The neutral's duty of friendliness to both belligerents is supposed to be thereby satisfied, but it is clear that the practice strengthens the hands of the belligerent, who is saved the trouble and expense of keeping and guarding the fugitives as prisoners of war, and works to the detriment of the other belligerent, who is bound to pay for their keep, although deprived of their services until the end of the war.

There is one other possible course which would perhaps be fairer to both belligerents, and certainly less burdensome to the neutral state. This would be for the latter to restore fugitives to their country on their government giving an undertaking not to employ them again during the continuance of hostilities. Any fugitive having been restored on such terms, and taking further part in the war, would on falling into the enemy's hands be exposed to the penalties for breach of parole. This would be an ample guarantee for the execution of the undertaking given by their government. This course has, however, not hitherto been adopted in warfare.

If a belligerent brings prisoners of war into neutral territory they become *ipso facto* free, except in the case of prisoners of war on board a public vessel anchoring in neutral waters.[1] This merely follows from the territorial

[1] In 1588 several hundred Turkish and Barbary captives escaped from one of the galleys of the Spanish Armada which was wrecked

THE RIGHTS AND DUTIES OF NEUTRAL STATES 175

sovereignty of neutral and the exterritorial character which attaches to a public vessel. A neutral sovereign cannot allow subjects of a state with which he is in amity to remain deprived of freedom within his territory. If he were to permit this he would be aiding the hostile operations of one of the belligerents, and acquiescing in a violation of his own territorial sovereignty.

With regard to a neutral state's right of hospitality in sea warfare, the general rule is that a belligerent may bring prizes into neutral waters, unless especially prohibited from so doing. A prize under the command of a commissioned officer is a public vessel (cf. the *Sitka*, footnote below), and the ordinary rule as to the admission of public vessels in territorial waters in time of peace holds good. This rule has, however, been qualified by a practice which has sprung up during the present century. It is now usual for a neutral state to restrain belligerents from bringing prizes into its ports except under stress of weather, or in case of supplies running short, and then only for as short a time as necessity demands. This course was adopted by Great Britain and France in the American Civil War.

Sea warfare.

---

near Calais. They were claimed by the Spanish ambassador, but the Council of the King decided that in touching the shores of France they had regained their liberty, and they were sent to Constantinople. If instead of being wrecked the galley had merely put into Calais, the French authorities could not of course have interfered with the captives.

Thus in the case of the *Sitka* (1855), a Russian ship captured by a British cruiser entered San Francisco with a prize crew on board. Two Russian prisoners of war took out writs of habeas corpus, and the commander accordingly put out to sea. His action was upheld by the American Law officers, on complaint being made by Russia. The United States clearly had no jurisdiction over a public vessel in their territorial waters, and no right of hospitality to exercise for the benefit of prisoners of war on board such a vessel.

Under the general rule a prize may not only be brought into a neutral port, but may also be kept there until duly condemned by a Prize Court sitting in the belligerent's own territory. This clearly amounts to a permission to make military use of neutral territory, and is only justified in that it is granted impartially to both belligerents.

On the whole it seems likely that the practice of excluding the prizes of both sides, except in cases of necessity, will be adhered to in future. Such a course is, in fact, almost a necessary corollary of the strict rules which either already regulate, or are likely to regulate, the admission of belligerent public vessels other than prizes into neutral waters and ports in time of war. These rules as to recruitment, coaling, and such matters are discussed in detail in chapter iii.

Speaking generally, it may be said that just as a neutral state's right of "inviolability of territory" is overshadowed by its duty of impartiality, which compels it to protect and enforce that right, so is its right of hospitality overshadowed by the duty of preventing its territory or ports from being made a theatre of warlike operations by either of the belligerents.

Other neutral rights.

Many of the books mention other rights enjoyed by neutral states in time of war, such as the right to continue diplomatic intercourse with both belligerents. Rights of this kind are clearly independent of the existence of war. They are the ordinary rights of one state against another with which it is at amity. They belong, in fact, to peace, not to war, and the rules which relate to them are the "Rules of Peace." Therefore they require no discussion, and find no appropriate place, in a book which deals with the "Rules of War" alone.

The Law of Neutrality, as already indicated, is chiefly concerned with the duties, not with the rights, of neutral states. These duties may be distributed into three wide classes—duties of abstention, duties of prevention, and duties of sufferance. *Neutral duties.*

Duties of the first class relate solely to acts done by the state itself in its corporate capacity, in other words, state-acts done by its government. *Classified.*

The second class comprises certain duties binding upon a neutral government either in regard to its own conduct or in regard to the conduct of its subjects or other persons within its jurisdiction.

Duties of the third class are connected solely with the conduct of the belligerents who have the right to interfere in certain ways with the interests of neutral subjects in the prosecution of the war.

The remaining portion of this book is concerned with the examination and description of these three classes of neutral duty. They may be briefly summarized as follows:—

I. The government of a neutral state must abstain from the following acts:— *Duties of abstention.*

(i.) Furnishing either belligerent with troops, arms, warlike materials, ships of war, or money.

(ii.) Allowing passage of forces of either belligerent over its territory.

(iii.) Deciding in its courts upon the validity of captures made by either belligerent.

(iv.) Acquiring during the war any conquest made by either belligerent.

II. A. The government of a neutral state must restrain the conduct of its subjects in the following respects:— *Duties of prevention.*

(i.) Pecuniary gifts or gratuitous loans to either belligerent.

(ii.) Enlistment within its jurisdiction in the forces of either belligerent.

B. The government of a neutral state must prevent

the following violations of its neutrality by all persons within its territorial jurisdiction:—

(i.) The issue of commissions by persons acting for either belligerent within the jurisdiction.

(ii.) The fitting out within the jurisdiction of hostile expeditions on behalf of either belligerent.

(iii.) The use of its ports by the ships of either belligerent as a base of operations and supplies.

<small>Duties of sufferance.</small>

III. The government of a neutral state must suffer certain interferences with the trade of its subjects by permitting both belligerents to exercise the following rights:—

(i.) The right to prevent carriage of contraband.

(ii.) The right to prevent breach of blockade.

(iii.) The right to capture enemy ships carrying neutral goods.

(iv.) The right of search.

CHAPTER II

DUTIES OF ABSTENTION

IT is possible to write with comparative certainty of neutral duties of this class, although very few questions have arisen with regard to them in modern practice. The very nature of the acts which they prohibit is directly opposed to the spirit of modern neutrality; and the absence of any attempt in recent times to maintain contrary doctrines, which may have been accepted in the days when the principle of neutrality was almost or entirely unknown, seems to indicate a general recognition among the Powers of their duty to abstain from these acts as being incompatible with the character of neutrality.

Some writers of authority, such as Kent, Wheaton, Halleck, and Bluntschli, still assert the existence of a "qualified neutrality" arising out of antecedent engagements by which a neutral state has bound itself to one of the belligerent states to furnish a limited succour or to extend certain privileges in case of war. It is, however, clear that such an engagement does not bind any third party; and the other belligerent state is not obliged to recognize an agreement by which a state undertakes to do acts of war and at the same time claims the immunity of a neutral. *Qualified neutrality.*

There now exists but one species of neutrality, of a *Strict neutrality.*

strict and absolute character, consisting not merely in impartial treatment of both belligerents, but in a combination of such impartial conduct with an entire abstinence from any participation in the war. To quote Phillimore, " the neutral is justly and happily designated by the Latin expression *in bello medius*. It is of the essence of his character that he so retain this central position as to incline to neither belligerent." This view is upheld both by the mass of learned opinion and by the practice of nations recorded in modern history.

It is therefore the duty of a neutral state to abstain from rendering either belligerent military, naval, pecuniary, or other assistance, however limited in extent, and even though under a treaty concluded before the outbreak of the war.

Duties of abstention may be distributed under four headings.

Troops, arms, ships, and money.

1. A neutral state must not furnish either belligerent with troops, arms, and warlike materials, ships of war, or money.

Troops.

In the eighteenth century and earlier times it was not unusual for a neutral state to furnish troops for a belligerent under a treaty made before the war. For example, in 1727 Hesse Cassel agreed to provide England with 12,000 men whenever they were required.

The last instance of a neutral state supplying a belligerent with troops was in 1788, during the war between Sweden and Russia, when Denmark, in accordance with a treaty to that effect, furnished Russia with troops. Great Britain, Prussia, and Holland interposed to compel their recall. The Danish Government declared themselves to be at peace and amity with Sweden, and maintained that the latter had no cause of complaint so long as the troops did not exceed the number stipulated for in the treaty. Sweden protested against the doctrines of the Danish

Government as contrary to the law of nations, but in order to prevent war, accepted their declaration of friendliness.

Somewhat analogous to the supplying of troops in former times was the practice regarding levies in neutral states. A neutral state, even in the absence of a treaty, not infrequently permitted a belligerent to raise troops within the neutral territory. Both Bynkershoek and Vattel were of opinion that soldiers could be bought just like any other munitions of war, but treaties were usually entered into for this purpose, *e. g.* the treaty between England and Sweden in 1656 authorizing either state to raise levies within the territory of the other. *Levies.*

No such treaty has been concluded in recent times, and the practice has only been resorted to on one occasion, in 1876, when a number of Russian volunteers were enrolled in Russia for the Servian service.

There can be no doubt that at the present time it would be considered a flagrant violation of neutrality for a neutral state to supply troops to a belligerent, or to permit him to raise levies in the neutral territory, even under a treaty.

A neutral state must not sell arms or other munitions of war, or ships of war, to either belligerent. A government is not a trading corporation, and therefore any such sale is tantamount to assisting one of the belligerents and a violation of neutrality. *Arms.*

The rule seems obvious and necessary; yet, if the doctrine propounded by the United States Government in 1870 meets with acceptance in the future, an easy means of evading it will have been established.

During the Franco-Prussian War a sale of surplus guns, rifles, and other arms took place at New York. Large quantities were bought by French agents, taken on board French ships direct from the arsenal, and paid for through the French consul. The contention of the United States was that it was a sale to private individuals, the precise destination of the articles sold not being disclosed. This was a mere quibble. If a neutral state during war sells a large quantity of munitions of war it seems idle to pretend that it does not know that the purchaser intends them for one of the belligerents.

Ships of war.

A better precedent with regard to the sale of ships of war was set by Sweden in 1825.

During the war between Spain and her colonies the Swedish Government offered six frigates for sale to Spain, who refused to buy. Three of them were subsequently sold to an English mercantile firm, acting, as it turned out, on behalf of the recognized Mexican agent in England. Upon learning this the Spanish Government demanded the rescission of the contract, a demand which, after some negotiation, was complied with by the Swedish Government, notwithstanding the fact that the ships had in this case been sold in absolute ignorance of their ultimate destination.

Money.

Lastly, a neutral state must abstain from lending money to either belligerent, or from guaranteeing or promoting any such loan.

A state loan to a belligerent stands upon a different footing to a private loan negotiated by subjects of a neutral state. In dealing with duties of prevention in the next chapter, it will be seen that a neutral state is under no duty to prevent the negotiation of such a loan by its subjects, that being an ordinary commercial transaction, and the state not being responsible for the commercial acts of its subjects.

The authorities who deal with this subject, though differing in opinion as to the legality of a private loan, are all agreed that a gift or loan of money by a neutral state to a belligerent amounts to a direct subvention, and is, therefore, a violation of neutrality—a proposition not likely to be ever contested.

2. A neutral state must not permit passage of forces belonging to either belligerent over its territory. *Passage of forces over territory.*

This rule cannot be stated with the same confidence as the preceding one. Publicists are still divided in opinion as to whether such permission constitutes a breach of neutrality or not.

Down to the end of the eighteenth century the doctrine that a neutral state might lawfully make this concession was undisputed, and passage was granted as a matter of course.[1]

In 1815 the Federal Council gave the Allies permission to cross Switzerland, but as the Council was practically acting under duress the precedent is of little authority. Since that date there has been no example of a similar neutral concession, nor has any belligerent directly asserted a jus passagii innoxii.

Modern practice, on the contrary, has tended in the opposite direction. In 1870 the Swiss Federal Council forbade any person capable of bearing arms to pass across Swiss territory from one belligerent country to the other. And when the Germans, after the battle of Sedan, applied to the Belgian Government for leave to transport their wounded on Belgian railways their request was refused. This latter was an indirect attempt to gain passage across neutral territory for facilitating warlike operations. Belgium was in a position to afford the Germans great assistance by relieving them of the encumbrance of their

---

[1] In *Hamlet*, Act IV. scene iv., the scene being a plain in Denmark, Fortinbras of Norway at the head of his forces says—

"Go, captain, from me greet the Danish king;
Tell him, that, by his licence, Fortinbras
Craves the conveyance of a promis'd march
Over his kingdom."

wounded, and the ostensible plea of humanity which supported the German request increased the difficulty of the Belgian Government in refusing it. Had it been granted, however, it would have amounted to more than a mere grant of innocent passage over territory, and would, in fact, have constituted a grave breach of Belgian neutrality.

With regard to the opinion of writers, Vattel said that passage over territory might be granted by a neutral state to one of two belligerents under a treaty; otherwise, if granted to one, it must be granted impartially to the other belligerent also. This view has been accepted by other great writers, including Kent and Phillimore, but the opinion of nearly all the more recent authorities is adverse to the grant of such passage to either belligerent under any circumstances whatever.

It may therefore fairly be urged, that the rule supported by the latest practice and opinion, and the one most in accordance with the general principles of neutrality, is the rule, stated above, that a neutral state must not permit passage of belligerent forces over its territory.

It is difficult to see how such passage in time of war can be "innocent." Even if it is not granted for the purpose of immediate attack (when it would be a clear breach of neutrality) it directly or indirectly furthers some warlike object, and amounts *pro tanto* to a participation in the hostilities. It is, therefore, entirely opposed to the spirit of modern neutrality. Fortunately, as Hall points out, the simplification of the map of Europe, which has been affected by the formation of the German Empire, has notably diminished the possible occasions upon which the question is likely to arise.

If a belligerent endeavoured to assert a right of passage against the will of the neutral state it would be a simple violation of neutral territory, for which it would be the duty of the neutral state to call the belligerent to account in accordance with its "duty of prevention" described in the next chapter.

Territory for the purposes of this rule does not include territorial waters. *Passage over territorial waters.*

The neutral's right of asylum extends to receiving public vessels of both belligerents within its territorial waters, unless it expressly excludes them (cf. last chapter, p. 175). So long, therefore, as a neutral state exercises this right, belligerent public vessels necessarily have an implied right of innocent passage over the neutral territorial waters; and such a passage will not vitiate captures subsequently made by a belligerent man-of-war on the high seas, or within its own territorial waters. But if the passage is not innocent, e. g. if it has been forbidden by the neutral state, all captures made subsequently by the offending vessel will be vitiated. The law was very clearly stated by Sir William Scott in the two following cases:—

The " Twee Gebroeder." (3, C. Rob. 336.)

This was a Dutch vessel captured by an English cruiser in 1801 on the high sea after passing through Prussian territorial waters, Prussia then being neutral. She was condemned by Sir W. Scott, who laid down the rule that the mere passage of a ship over waters claimed as neutral territory would not invalidate an ulterior capture, unless the passage was an unpermitted one over territory where permission was regularly required, or one under permission obtained on false representation.

The " Twee Gebroeder." (3, C. Rob. 162.)

This was another Dutch vessel of the same name captured in 1800 on the high sea by the boats of an English cruiser, at the time anchored in neutral territorial waters. Sir W. Scott ordered her restoration. This was clearly not a case of innocent passage, but owing to the close connection between the ship of war and her boats, was an act of war originating in neutral territory, which Prussia, the owner of the territory, was in duty bound to resent.

The conclusion is, that a neutral state is under no duty either to permit or to prohibit the passage of belligerent war vessels over its territorial waters. In this matter it is at liberty to act in whatever way it may consider most conducive to the preservation of its strict neutrality.

Decision of questions of prize.
3. A neutral state must not decide in its courts upon the validity of captures made by either belligerent unless in violation of its own neutrality.

The court of the captor is, in general, the only competent court to adjudicate upon questions of prize. If, however, a prize is captured in neutral territorial waters, or by a privateer illegally equipped in neutral territory, or otherwise in violation of neutrality, the neutral state may inquire into the capture and restore the prize to its original owner, even though it has been transferred in the meanwhile to a *bonâ-fide* purchaser. But if the prize has been converted into a commissioned ship of war before coming into the neutral jurisdiction it acquires the ordinary exterritorial character of a public vessel, and the neutral state cannot interfere. The British Government acted upon this well-settled rule of International Law in refusing to detain the *Alabama* on her entering various British ports and again coming within British jurisdiction during the American Civil War. (See chapter iv. of this part.)

Acquisition of conquests.
4. A neutral state must not acquire during the war any conquest made by either belligerent.

This rule is found upon two considerations.

The title of a belligerent to conquered territory is not complete until confirmed by lapse of time, or, as is more usual, by treaty. During the war, therefore, he has no interest to convey; and, if he had, a neutral state by purchasing it would relieve him of the trouble and expense of maintaining the conquest, and enable him to withdraw troops from the territory for employment elsewhere. This would be a direct assistance to one belligerent at the expense of the other, and, consequently, a breach of neutrality.

CHAPTER III

DUTIES OF PREVENTION

THE duties of a neutral government with regard to its own state acts having been discussed, the neutral duties to be next considered are the "duties of prevention," which relate to the conduct of a neutral state's own subjects, or that of subjects of either belligerent or of other persons within the neutral territory. The doctrine of territorial sovereignty requires that the responsibility of a neutral state for the acts of its subjects or of other individuals should be limited by the extent of its territorial jurisdiction.

<small>Limited by a state's territorial jurisdiction.</small>

In this matter principle is strongly reinforced by expediency. It clearly is no concern of the neutral state to interfere with the conduct of foreigners beyond the limits of its territory; and with regard to the conduct of its own subjects beyond those limits, expediency as well as principle demands that a neutral state should be relieved of responsibility for such acts as carriage of contraband, breach of blockade, or enlistment abroad, which in most cases it would probably be unable to prevent. It is therefore the duty of a neutral government to prevent the abuse of its territory by its own subjects or other persons, and for every act amounting to a violation of its neutrality committed within its territory it is consequently responsible.

DUTIES OF PREVENTION 189

It is not possible to keep the acts of a neutral's own subjects entirely separate from those of belligerent subjects, because both may be implicated in the same violation of neutral territory. By maintaining the distinction, however, so far as possible, a neutral state's duties of prevention may be presented to the reader more clearly and systematically, according as they relate to acts done by the neutral's own subjects, acts done by subjects of either belligerent, or acts in which both neutral and belligerent subjects participate.

I. A neutral government must prevent its subjects from making gifts of money or gratuitous loans to either belligerent. *Gifts of money and gratuitous loans.*

This rule does not extend to prevent the raising of a loan for interest on behalf of a belligerent in a neutral country.

In 1792 and 1793 subscriptions were set on foot in England for the assistance of Poland, and no prohibitive action was taken by the Government. *1792.*

In 1823, however, when it was proposed to aid Greece against Turkey by a public subscription, the Law officers of the English Crown gave it as their opinion, that voluntary subscriptions by subjects of a neutral state for the use of one of two belligerents are inconsistent with their country's neutrality, and if carried to any considerable extent may afford a just ground of complaint on the part of the other belligerent. They were also of opinion that a loan for interest is a legitimate commercial transaction, though a gratuitous contribution afforded without interest, or with merely nominal interest, under colour of a loan, is an infringement of neutrality which may expose the individuals concerned to a criminal prosecution. *1823.*

In 1873 the question was again raised with regard to subscriptions started in England on behalf of the Spanish pretender, Don Carlos. Mr. Gladstone, in the House of *1873.*

Commons, denounced such subscriptions as likely to create a misapprehension abroad of the true state of opinion in England. He adopted the former opinion of the Law officers, that the character of the transaction depended largely upon the proportions it assumed, and said that the Government would be prepared in a proper case to vindicate the general principle of the common law requiring British subjects to respect the peace of the dominions of a power with which her Majesty is at amity.

It seems only reasonable that a small subscription raised by a few insignificant persons should not be held sufficient to compromise the neutrality of their country, and that a state, to use Hall's expression, should not be "expected to take precautions against the commission of microscopic injuries" by its subjects.

The rule, as broadly stated above, applies to some general movement towards assisting a belligerent which a neutral government may reasonably be expected to prevent, and not to small "hole and corner" subscriptions of which it may possibly be unaware.

Loan for interest.

The raising of a belligerent loan for interest in a neutral country has become so firmly established in modern practice that it hardly needs defence or explanation.

The explanation is a simple matter. Money is an article of commerce; and the belligerent buys money in a neutral market precisely in the same way that he buys any other article of commerce.

The authority of the English Law officers has already been quoted, and the view of the United States was put with equal clearness by Mr. Webster in 1842. Replying to a complaint made by Mexico in regard to a loan by American citizens to the Texan insurgents, he said, "As to advances and loans made by individuals to the Government of Texas, the Mexican Government hardly needs to be informed that there is nothing unlawful in this, so long as

Texas is at peace with the United States, and that these are things which no government undertakes to prevent."

In 1854 a Russian loan was floated in Berlin and Amsterdam. In 1862 money was raised in England for the Confederate States in America on the security of cotton; and in 1870, during the Franco-Prussian War, both the French Morgan Loan and part of the North German Confederation Loan were issued in England. *Examples.*

There are decisions of English and American courts which make the legality of such a loan depend upon the status of the power for whom it is raised. Loans raised for mere insurgents, or for an insurgent state or colony recognized as belligerent, but not as independent, have at various times been held to be illegal transactions. But it can scarcely now be disputed, that a purely commercial loan to a fully recognized belligerent independent state is a lawful enterprise for neutral subjects.

II. A neutral government must prevent its subjects from enlisting within the limits of its territorial jurisdiction in the service of either belligerent. *Enlistment.*

This rule is implied partly in the rule, already considered, that a neutral state must abstain from allowing either belligerent to make levies in the neutral territory, and partly in the rule, discussed below, concerning the issue of commissions by belligerents in neutral territory.

A neutral state must not permit its territory to become a recruiting-ground for either belligerent; but it incurs no responsibility for the actions of its subjects which, taking place outside the bounds of its territory, it is unable to prevent. Some states, however, either by their municipal law or by a proclamation issued at the commencement of a particular war, have prohibited their subjects, wherever they may be, from enlisting or participating in the hostilities, under various penalties. A neutral state does not thereby in theory increase its responsibility, the measure *Enlistment abroad.*

of its duty being international and not its own municipal law. Such laws as the United States Neutrality Act and the British Foreign Enlistment Act were passed, not for the benefit of foreign states, but for the protection of the states that passed them. They do not state principles of International Law, but merely provide the executive with an improved machinery for fulfilling the duties of International Law. The practical result of the Alabama Claims, however, was to show that a neutral state may affect its responsibility by the insufficiency of the powers conferred upon its executive by its municipal law.

Gideon Henfield. In 1793 occurred the case of Gideon Henfield, a citizen of the United States, who took service on board the *Citizen Genêt*, a French privateer fitted out in America. On putting into Philadelphia in charge of a prize taken from the English, he was indicted for a breach of the neutrality laws of the United States. The judge pointed out that Henfield had offended both against International Law and the municipal law of the United States, but owing to the strong feeling then existing in America against England the jury returned a verdict of not guilty.

American Act. This led to the passing of the United States Neutrality Act, 1794, which was afterwards superseded by the Act of 1818. By the latter Act a citizen of the United States is declared liable to fine and imprisonment if he accepts a commission from a foreign government at war with another government with whom the United States are at peace, or if he enlists or procures others to enlist in the service of such a foreign government.

English Act. The British Foreign Enlistment Act, 1870, superseding a previous Act of 1819, makes it an offence punishable with fine and imprisonment, with or without hard labour, for any British subject to enlist or induce others to enlist in the service of a foreign state at war with a power friendly to Great Britain, or to leave or induce others to leave her Majesty's dominions in order to so enlist. The Act also prescribes a similar penalty for any ship-owner or master who takes illegally enlisted persons on board, the ship being detainable as well.

These English and American statutes do not affect the rule of International Law already laid down, which requires neutral states to prevent the enlistment of their subjects only within their own jurisdiction.

It would of course be possible for two or more powers to extend their mutual responsibility on this head by means of a treaty, but no duty in excess of the requirements of International Law can be exacted from some one particular state on the mere ground of the strictness of its own municipal law.

III. A neutral government must prevent the issue of commissions by persons acting for either belligerent within the neutral territory.

Commissions.

Commissions can only be issued by the sovereign or his recognized representatives.

Every nation has at all times the right to prevent acts of sovereignty (such as the issue of commissions) being exercised within its territory by another nation, and in war every neutral power has the duty of preventing the exercise of such acts by one belligerent to the detriment of the other, this being simply one aspect of its broad general duty of impartially keeping its territory from violation by either belligerent.

In 1793, war having broken out between England and France, M. Genêt, the French minister accredited to the United States, on arriving at Charleston proceeded to issue commissions and letters of marque to American citizens. The latter then fitted out privateers principally manned by American crews (cf. the case of Gideon Henfield, p. 192), and commenced depredations upon British commerce. In this case the neutrality of the United

M. Genêt.

o

States was violated both by the belligerent subject who issued the commissions, and by its own citizens who accepted and acted upon them. Consequently, upon the remonstrance of the English Government the United States took measures for the restoration of prizes captured by privateers sailing under M. Genêt's commission, and demanded his recall.

In a somewhat analogous case in 1855, Mr. Crampton, the British minister at Washington, was dismissed by the United States Government for endeavouring to obtain recruits in America for the British army. This, however, was rather an indirect attempt to raise levies than an open issue of commissions by a belligerent subject in a neutral country.

Hostile expeditions.

IV. A neutral government must prevent a hostile expedition from being organized in and setting forth from the neutral territory to attack either belligerent.

Organization not armament the test.

The true test of what constitutes a "hostile expedition" is military organization, and not the possession of military arms and equipment. Indeed it is always probable that a hostile expedition, in order to baulk the vigilance of a neutral government, will leave the territory without arms or equipment, and arrange to pick up the latter at some place outside the neutral jurisdiction. But if a body of men is capable of acting as a military force immediately upon landing upon the shores or crossing the borders of the belligerent country, it constitutes, although unarmed, a hostile expedition. This is illustrated by the "Terceira affair,"

The Terceira affair.

which occurred in 1828. During civil war in Portugal a body of Portuguese troops took refuge in the neighbourhood of Portsmouth, and continued as an organized body of men under military officers. Later they embarked on four vessels ostensibly for Brazil, but in reality to make a descent upon Terceira, one of the Azores islands. The arms and equipment for this expedition were shipped from a different port. The English Government, suspecting the true destination of the vessels, sent a small squadron to Terceira to prevent the Portuguese troops from landing. This was done. The ships were practically captured in Portuguese waters and escorted back to Europe.

The action of the Government was approved by a majority in Parliament; but a protest in the House of Lords and a resolution moved in the House of Commons, condemned the capture at Terceira as a violation of the sovereignty of its owner, Portugal. This cannot be denied. The Government's method of interference, although intended for the benefit of Portugal, involved a violation of Portuguese sovereignty; but in principle it was perfectly right, as to the character of the expedition, in maintaining that an organized body of men, although unarmed, constitutes a hostile expedition.

Conversely, an unorganized body of men, even though it has arms within its reach, is not a hostile expedition within this rule.

In 1870, during the Franco-Prussian War, 1200 Frenchmen, unofficered and unorganized, left New York in two French ships for France. The vessels had also a cargo of 96,000 rifles and 11,000,000 rounds of ammunition. The United States Government, having permitted the departure of the vessels, maintained, quite correctly, in defence of their conduct, that the men were inefficient and useless for immediate military employment, and that the arms and ammunition were subjects of legitimate commerce; and that they had not, in fact, permitted the departure of a "hostile expedition" from United States territory.

The British Foreign Enlistment Act, 1870, provides penalties for aiding in the fitting out of any military expedition; and the United States Neutrality Act, 1818, prohibits any person from setting on foot a military

Municipal legislation.

expedition against a state with which the United States are at peace.

Action of the United States. It is to be regretted that the United States Government has seen fit on more than one occasion to disregard its duty of preventing hostile expeditions from setting forth from its territory, notwithstanding the powers conferred upon it by its Legislature (by the above-mentioned Act) of giving full effect to the rule of International Law.

1838. In 1838 a body of Canadian rebels invaded Canada from the United States. They were supplied with arms and artillery by a United States arsenal, and some of their preparations and acts of open hostility were carried on in the presence of a regiment of United States militia, which made no attempt to interfere.

1866. In 1866 the Fenians prepared to invade Canada from the United States. Their object was announced at public meetings, and their preparations were open and notorious. They carried out their intention without opposition from the United States authorities. On being driven back they were at first disarmed, and a prosecution commenced in the District Court of Buffalo. But the prosecution was dropped within six weeks, and the arms subsequently *1870.* restored. A similar supineness on the part of the United States Government attended two further Fenian incursions into Canada, both of which were repulsed, in 1870.

The conduct of the United States upon all these occasions amounted to direct complicity with raids on a friendly state.

1879. In 1879, however, the United States Government, fearing an incursion into American territory by a small body of Indians under the chief Sitting Bull, pointed out to the British Government that it was the duty of the latter to send a force to prevent any such hostile expedition from leaving British territory. This case does not exactly illustrate the neutral duty now being considered, but it is of some significance, as showing that the United States Government has now a keener perception of a state's duties in respect of its territory, and will no doubt be prepared in a future war to fulfil those duties as amply as it demands their fulfilment from other states.

Of far more importance, however, than the case of an organized body of men is the extension of a "hostile expedition" as constituted by a ship of war.

The British Foreign Enlistment Act may be dealt with most appropriately in this connection, and cases are given below which illustrate the manner in which effect has been given to its provisions not only in time of war but in time of peace. Action of Great Britain.

The old rule of International Law as to the construction and fitting out of a ship of war in neutral territory for export to either belligerent can be clearly stated. Hostile expedition constituted by a ship of war.

"There is nothing in the law of nations," said Mr. Justice Story, in the case of *La Santissima Trinidad*,[1]

---

[1] *La Santissima Trinidad.* (7, Wheaton, 283.)

This was a Spanish vessel captured during the war between Spain and her South American colonies by the *Independencia del Sud*, a cruiser commissioned by Buenos Ayres. She was condemned by a prize court of Buenos Ayres, but on a portion of her cargo coming within United States jurisdiction, restitution was claimed by the Spanish Consul on the ground that the *Independencia* had originally been fitted out in violation of United States neutrality, and had received a subsequent illegal augmentation of force in United States territory.

It appeared that the *Independencia* had been built in the United States, loaded with munitions of war, and sent to Buenos Ayres for sale if a suitable price could be obtained. This was ultimately arranged, and she was commissioned by the Buenos Ayres Government. The court held that this was no violation of United States neutrality, *the ship being merely contraband*, and liable to capture as such *in transitu*.

As to the augmentation of force, it appeared that the *Independencia* had put into Baltimore, and there enlisted certain persons to "that forbids our citizens from sending armed vessels as well as munitions of war to foreign ports for sale. It is a *commercial adventure which no nation is bound to prohibit.*"

The old rule. A ship of war was upon the same footing as contraband, a lawful article of commerce, but subject to the risk of capture by the other belligerent *in transitu;* and the neutral government was under no duty to interfere so long as nothing was done amounting to the sending out of a hostile expedition.[1]

A ship of war was held to constitute a hostile expedition if she sailed with a belligerent commission—conclusive evidence of hostile intent—or with an armament and fighting crew sufficient to enable her to inflict damage upon the enemy.

In other words, a neutral state was only expected to scrutinize the character of such a ship while within the neutral jurisdiction, and assumed no responsibility for

---

recruit her crew. In default of proof that such persons were subjects of Buenos Ayres, the court held that this recruitment constituted an illegal augmentation of force, and a violation both of the Law of Nations and of the United States neutrality laws, vitiating all subsequent captures made by the vessel during the cruise. The court therefore affirmed the decree of restitution which had been made by the District Court.

[1] The doctrine is stated thus by Dana in a note to Wheaton's *Elements:*—"The intent is all. . . . . Is the intent one to prepare an article of contraband merchandise to be sent to the market of a belligerent subject to the chances of capture and of the market? Or, on the other hand, is it to fit out a vessel which shall leave our port to cruise immediately or ultimately against the commerce of a friendly nation? The latter we are bound to prevent; the former the belligerent must."

It was the great difficulty of distinguishing between the *animus vendendi* and the *animus belligerandi*, which gave birth to the Three Rules of the Treaty of Washington, and the consequent restrictions by which Great Britain and the United States have bound themselves in excess of the requirements of International Law.

subsequent acts beyond those limits. This seems to be the true principle and a natural deduction from the doctrine of territorial sovereignty. But it has been considerably qualified as regards Great Britain and the United States by the results of the Alabama Claims, and international usage generally may be said to be undergoing a gradual change in the direction of restricting the supply of ships of war by neutral subjects to a belligerent. *A new practice.*

This change has been due to the action of the United States. As neutrals they were content with the ancient doctrine that a ship of war may be exported from a neutral country to a belligerent as contraband, unless she is clearly proved, *whilst still in neutral jurisdiction*, to constitute a hostile expedition. As belligerents they have demanded from neutral states a stricter vigilance and a wider responsibility. The practical result of the Treaty of Washington and the award of the Geneva Board of Arbitration is, very briefly, that so far as concerns Great Britain and the United States, a hostile expedition may be constituted *outside* neutral territory by the combination of elements which have issued separately from it, and which so issuing were in themselves perfectly innocent; and that for such a hostile expedition the neutral government is, in default of "due diligence," responsible. *Due to action of United States.*

By the Treaty of Washington, Great Britain and the United States have agreed that they will in future use due diligence to prevent the fitting out, arming, or equipping within the jurisdiction, or the departure from the jurisdiction, of any vessel which there is reasonable ground to believe is intended to cruise or carry on war against a friendly power. The question of due diligence is treated in the next chapter, but in the present place it will suffice to point out, that Great Britain and the United States have assumed a responsibility for acts which, unless a hostile intent is capable of clear proof within the jurisdiction, they are unable to prevent.

Municipal legislation.

As a result of the Alabama controversy, Great Britain passed a new Foreign Enlistment Act, which makes it an offence punishable by fine and imprisonment, with or without hard labour, to build, equip, or despatch a vessel with reasonable cause to believe it is intended for the service of a foreign state at war with a friendly power, or to issue a commission to or aid the warlike equipment of any such vessel, the latter, together with her equipment, being in addition liable to forfeiture.

Great Britain.

United States.

A very similar provision had already been made by the United States Neutrality Act, 1818, and many nations have since that date taken some action in the same direction, either by general legislation or by regulations laid down with reference to particular wars.

Other countries.

The laws of Austria, Italy, Denmark, Spain, and Portugal prohibit the procuring of vessels of war, arms, or ammunition for the service of a foreign power; and Holland has undertaken to prevent the equipment of vessels of war intended for the belligerent parties taking place in the ports of the Netherlands.

In 1861, on the outbreak of the American Civil War, France, by proclamation, prohibited French subjects from assisting in any way in the equipment or armament of a vessel of war or privateer of either of the two parties.

Special statutes or edicts relating to " foreign enlistment " have also been made or issued from time to time by Spain, Portugal, Holland, Denmark, and Sweden.

No nations, however, except Great Britain and the United States, have gone further than to prohibit the armament of a vessel fitted solely for fighting purposes. The British and American Acts apply to vessels of every kind.

Great Britain has shown a deep sense of its responsibility in the matter of hostile expeditions by the unflinching severity with which it has interpreted and carried out the provisions of the Foreign Enlistment Act (sections 8—13), which are more positive, precise, and stringent than the enactments of any other nation. *The British Foreign Enlistment Act.*

The " Gauntlet." (L. R. 4, P. C. 184.)

In 1870, during the Franco-Prussian War, a Prussian ship which had been captured by a French cruiser entered the Downs with a French prize crew on board, and somewhat damaged by heavy weather. The French Consul at Dover engaged the *Gauntlet*, an English tug-boat, to tow the prize to Dunkirk. The Judicial Committee of the Privy Council, reversing the decree of the Court of Admiralty, held that the owners of the *Gauntlet* had "despatched" a vessel within section 8 of the Foreign Enlistment Act, and the tug-boat was condemned as a forfeiture to the Crown.

The " International." (L. R. 3, Adm. and E. 321.)

During the same war an English company, having contracted to lay down cables on the French coast, embarked the telegraphic plant upon the *International*, a ship especially constructed for the purpose. The vessel was seized and detained by the Government under the Act, but was ultimately released on the ground that though the telegraph might be used for military purposes, the undertaking was primarily of a commercial character.

R. v. Sandoval. (56, L. T. 526. 3, *Times Rep.* 411, 436.)

In 1886 Colonel Sandoval, a foreigner residing in England, bought two Krupp guns and a quantity of ammunition in this country, and sent them to Antwerp, where they were put on board the *Justitia*, which vessel subsequently sailed to make an attack on Venezuela. Colonel Sandoval himself left the ship at Trinidad, and the *Justitia*, after being worsted by a Venezuelan man-of-war, retired to San Domingo, whence the crew were sent back to England. Colonel Sandoval was tried under section 8 of the Act for equipping and despatching the vessel, and under section 11 for fitting out and preparing a naval or military expedition against a friendly state. He was found guilty only under the latter section, and sentenced to imprisonment for one month, and to pay a fine of £500 and the costs of the prosecution.

This, it will be observed, was an extension of the application of the Act, Venezuela not being at war with any state friendly to Great Britain. But the object of the *Justitia* was to assist certain persons who were engaged in a rebellion against the Venezuelan Government, and the Act of 1819 had previously been held to apply to cases of vessels fitted out in aid of insurgents. (The case of the *Salvador*, R. *v.* Carlin, L. R. 3, P. C. 218.)

R. v. *Jameson*, 1896.

This, the most recent case under the Foreign Enlistment Act, was a case of a military hostile expedition, and not one of the building or despatch of a ship of war. But it may be properly discussed in this place as a further illustration of section 11 of the Act as applied in R. *v.* Sandoval. Since that case the Preamble of the Act has been repealed by the Statute Law Revision Act, 1893, and therefore the Act only applies to a state of war when expressly mentioned. Section 11 contains no such mention, and consequently operates without the existence of a state of war, the offence being simply constituted by preparing or fitting out a naval or military expedition against any friendly state.

At the end of December 1895, Dr. Jameson, the Administrator of the British South Africa Company, made an incursion into the territory of the South African Republic at the head of a force principally composed of men in the Company's service, many of whom had previously served in the recently disbanded Bechuanaland

Police. Dr. Jameson's object was to march to Johannesburg, where a revolution was being hatched against the South African Republic. He and his force were, however, surrounded by the Boers, and after a conflict, in which both sides suffered loss, surrendered on January 2, 1896. Johannesburg was disarmed, and no further fighting took place. The leading "Reformers," or prime movers in the rebellion, were arrested and tried in due course, whilst on January 19 Dr. Jameson and his entire force were given up to the British Government and sent to England for trial. As a result of the police-court proceedings at Bow Street, Dr. Jameson and five of his principal officers were committed for trial. The Grand Jury returned true bills on June 23 at the Central Criminal Court.

The prisoners were tried "at Bar" before a Court composed of Lord Russell of Killowen, L.C.J., Mr. Baron Pollock, and Mr. Justice Hawkins. The indictment contained twelve counts, all under section 11 of the Act, and the trial (which lasted seven days) resulted, on July 28, in a verdict of guilty against all the prisoners. The Court sentenced Dr. Jameson to fifteen months' imprisonment; Sir John Willoughby ten months; Major Robert White seven months; and Colonel Grey, Colonel Henry White, and Major the Hon. Charles Coventry five months each, all without hard labour. The above sentences were pronounced upon every count in the indictment, but the several terms of imprisonment were ordered to run concurrently.

The following general conclusions may be drawn :—

1. That International Law does not as yet prohibit the construction of a ship of war in neutral territory for sale to a belligerent, provided it is neither commissioned nor so manned as to be able to commit immediate hostilities on leaving the neutral territory.

2. That this rule no longer applies to Great Britain and

the United States *inter se*, the two nations having adopted a stricter usage by the Treaty of Washington.

3. That the rule is in course of becoming obsolete, there being a growing consensus of nations in favour of some usage more resembling that of Great Britain and the United States.

<small>Future usage.</small> This change is rendered inevitable by the changed conditions of naval warfare. A modern man-of-war is unquestionably something more than contraband. Three or four small vessels waiting a few miles off the neutral coast, with guns and ammunition, can convert it immediately into a powerful hostile expedition. It may be impossible for the neutral government to prove any *animus belligerandi* before the vessel sails, and it may not (according to the old rule) interfere with the *bonâ-fide* sale of a man-of-war. If the neutral government has not failed in its duty whilst the vessel is within its jurisdiction, the belligerent against whom the vessel has been fitted out will have no redress; and whether it obtains redress or not it will probably regard the neutral state with ill-will, and an international dispute and perhaps even war will follow. This is only what actually occurred in our Alabama controversy with the United States.

The remedy is, on paper, a simple one. It would be possible for the concert of states to agree to prohibit the sale of certain vessels to a belligerent state altogether, and for this purpose to agree upon some reasonable standard of the "due diligence" to be exercised in the discharge of this duty. Here again the changes in naval warfare would enable neutral governments to carry out this duty with greater ease and certainty than would formerly have been possible. The vessels fitted for modern naval warfare are more readily to be distinguished from ordinary merchant vessels in these days. They may be roughly divided into two classes—*armoured* vessels of every kind including all ships built primarily and obviously for warlike use, and mail steamers of large tonnage and high speed capable of being converted into fast cruisers.

An agreement to prohibit the sale to a belligerent of armoured vessels of every class and of merchant steamers exceeding a certain speed or tonnage[1] would simplify the law, diminish the occasions of international controversy, and add to the happiness and tranquillity of the world.

V. A neutral government must prevent its ports from being used as a base of operations and supplies by the ships of either belligerent. Use of ports.

In time of war, as in time of peace, public vessels may freely enter a foreign port in the absence of prohibition by the state to whom the port belongs. But if a neutral power chooses to close its ports to the public vessels of both belligerents, the latter can only enter under stress of weather or in case of absolute necessity. This practice has been already adopted by many states with reference to one class of belligerent public vessels, namely, prizes taken from the enemy (cf. chapter i. of this Part), and it is possible that, having regard to the strict impartiality expected from neutrals, it may be eventually extended to belligerent public vessels of every kind. The British regulations of 1862, described below, go far in this direction. At present, however, the rule is that, in the absence of prohibition, a belligerent man-of-war may enter a neutral port and make such repairs, and take in such coal and provisions as may be necessary to enable it to Present practice.

---

[1] A merchant steamer may be adapted for warlike use either by its speed alone, or by a combination of speed and tonnage, as in the case of the great ocean liners. Slow, unarmoured steamers of large tonnage would be of little use in naval warfare. The naval experts of all nations might be able to agree as to the measure of speed and tonnage, or of simple speed, which should be held to render a steamer of a warlike character, and at the same time to make it such as not to interfere with the ordinary ship-building industry of neutral countries in time of war.

navigate safely. Hospitality is lawful, but anything over and above this, amounting to an augmentation of force, is not. To permit a belligerent ship of war to receive such an illegal augmentation of force is a breach of neutrality, and vitiates all captures subsequently made by the ship which has received it. (Cf. *La Santissima Trinidad*, footnote p. 197.)

Coal.

Owing to the very modern development of steam, International Law does not as yet contain any authoritative rule as to the purchase of coal by a belligerent in neutral ports. During the American Civil War, Great Britain allowed ships of war to take in only so much coal in British ports as would suffice to carry them to the nearest port of their own country, and refused any second supply to the same vessel, without special permission, until after the expiration of three months.

These regulations enable a belligerent ship to navigate safely without adding to its fighting power, and prevent it from making the neutral port a base of operations by coaling there at frequent intervals.

The United States adopted similar regulations during the Franco-Prussian War, and the usage of the two countries is not unlikely to become general in the future.

The twenty-four hours' rule.

There is on principle no reason for limiting the stay of a belligerent ship in a neutral port, provided, of course, that she receives no augmentation of force there; but in the event of a ship belonging to the other belligerent appearing at the same port, restrictions become necessary in order to prevent a collision in neutral waters.

In 1759 Spain laid down the rule that the first of two vessels of war belonging to different belligerents to leave one of her ports should not be followed by the other until the expiration of twenty-four hours. At first this rule was only imposed upon privateers, the word of a captain of a ship of war that he would not commit hostilities being considered sufficient; but it has now been extended to all ships of war by most of the great states, including Great Britain, France, and the United States.

The "twenty-four hours' rule," as it is called, is not, however, sufficient of itself to prevent abuse of neutral ports. In 1861, the United States ship *Tuscarora* took advantage of the rule to practically blockade the Confederate cruiser *Nashville* in Southampton Water. The *Tuscarora* contrived always to start before the *Nashville*, when the latter attempted to sail, and returned before the twenty-four hours—during which the *Nashville* had to stay behind—had expired. A similar case occurred during 1862, at Gibraltar, where the Confederate ship *Sumter* was practically blockaded, at first by the *Tuscarora*, and afterwards by the *Ino* and *Kearsage*. This blockade was terminated by the sale of the *Sumter* to a British subject, and her subsequent escape to England. She was ultimately wrecked in attempting to run the blockade of Charleston. Accordingly, in 1862 Great Britain laid down the rule, that war vessels of either belligerent must not remain in British ports for more than twenty-four hours, except under stress of weather, or in order to effect necessary repairs, in either of which cases the ship must put to sea as soon as possible after the expiration of the twenty-four hours.

During the Franco-Prussian War this rule was again adopted by Great Britain, and also by the United States, and taken in conjunction with the old "twenty-four hours' rule," seems likely to be accepted in the future for the regulation of the hospitality accorded to belligerent cruisers in neutral ports. But it can never be a hard-and-fast rule of International Law, because, as Hall well observes, " the right of the neutral to vary his own port regulations can never be ousted. The rule can never be more than one to the enforcement of which a belligerent may trust in the absence of notice to the contrary."

<small>Supplement to the twenty-four hours' rule.</small>

CHAPTER IV

THE ALABAMA CLAIMS

ALTHOUGH the history of the Alabama Claims immediately concerns only Great Britain and the United States, some account of that celebrated controversy is necessary to illustrate and explain the principles adopted by those two states, as being the pioneers of a stricter international usage than has previously obtained with regard to the fitting out of ships of war in neutral countries, and the use of neutral ports in time of war.

During the American Civil War complaints were from time to time addressed by Mr. Adams, the United States minister in London, to the British Government with reference to vessels which were alleged to have been fitted out in England for the use of the Confederate States, or to have received an illegal augmentation of force in British ports, in violation of British neutrality.

After the excitement caused by the escape and subsequent career of the *Florida* and the *Alabama*, the British Government took proceedings to detain vessels built or building in England which were suspected of being destined for the use of the Confederate States. Amongst others two powerful steam rams, the *El Tousson* and *El Monassir*, built by Messrs. Laird at Birkenhead, on coming under the suspicion of the Government, were detained and placed under the charge of a Government

The El Tousson and El Monassir.

vessel in the Mersey, on October 31, 1863. The difficulty of proving the "intent," which converts the sale of a man-of-war into the fitting out of a hostile expedition, was such as to oblige the Government to ultimately purchase the vessels at a cost of £220,000, in order to prevent their departure from England.

The present sketch, however, only deals with the Alabama Claims, that is, with the claims made by the United States Government after the war with reference to vessels built and fitted out in England, which actually left or were alleged to have left this country for the use of the Confederate States, and vessels which received or were alleged to have received an illegal augmentation of force in British ports.

The *Florida* was a war-steamer built at Liverpool during the American Civil War. She was originally known as the *Oreto*, and stated to be destined for the Italian Government. During February 1862, the American minister communicated his suspicions to the British Government, but in the absence of sufficient evidence the vessel was allowed to clear for Palermo and Jamaica on March 4, with a cargo of spirits, wines, and groceries. On March 22 she sailed from the Mersey unarmed, with no warlike stores of any kind on board, and with a crew of 52 men, who were British with very few exceptions. On April 28 she arrived at the Bahamas, where, on the representation of the United States consul as to her suspicious character, she was, after considerable vacillation on the part of the authorities, seized on June 15. In spite of the report of Commander Hickley and other naval experts that she was fitted as a man-of-war, and clearly not built on the lines of a merchant vessel, in spite of the vessel's destination for the Confederate service being openly talked of in the port, and in spite of the statements of the crew of the ship herself, she was discharged by Sir John Lees in the Vice-

Admiralty Court, on the ground that she had shipped no munitions of war in the colony, and that there was no evidence of any attempt since her arrival in the colony to fit or equip her as a vessel of war, or of her having been transferred to a belligerent. The order of the British Government for her detention arrived too late, and on August 7 she sailed to Green Cay, where she was fitted out as a war vessel, her armament and equipment being brought out to her at that place by the *Prince Alfred* from Hartlepool. On September 4 she entered the port of Mobile, where, after eluding the blockading squadron, she remained four months. She then put to sea, and succeeded in committing extensive depredations upon Federal commerce, in which work she was assisted by her tenders the *Clarence*, the *Tacony*, and the *Archer*.

From time to time she sought the hospitality of British West Indian ports, where she was always treated as the commissioned cruiser of a belligerent power. Her longest stay in a British port was only nine days, but she was allowed to remain at Brest for four months at the end of 1863, and to refit in the government dockyard.

She was finally seized, in the absence of her captain and the greater part of her crew, by the United States ship *Wachusetts* in the harbour of Bahia, October 7, 1864, and carried off to sea. For this gross violation of neutral waters the United States had subsequently to make an ample apology to Brazil.

The *Alabama*.

The *Alabama* was a steam vessel of 900 tons and 300 horse-power, built by Messrs. Laird at Birkenhead, and launched May 15, 1862. She was known originally as "Number 290," but was evidently intended as a fighting ship. On June 23 Mr. Adams informed the Government that the vessel was about to sail in the service of the Confederate States. On the 30th the Law Officers advised that, assuming that information to be correct, proceedings should at once be taken under the Foreign Enlistment Act (of 1819). The Commissioners of Customs, acting upon the advice of their solicitor, then reported that the evidence was not strong enough to support a seizure, and dissuaded the Treasury from such a course. In spite of subsequent information communicated by the United States consul, and of sworn depositions setting forth the true nature and destination of the vessel, the Commissioners maintained this attitude, and it was not until Sir Robert Collier had expressed a strong opinion (in answer to the United States consul) that proceedings ought to be taken under the Foreign Enlistment Act, that the Law Officers, on being again consulted, recommended on July 29 the prompt detention of the vessel. Their opinion was not made known to the Commissioners of Customs until the 31st, and the *Alabama* had in the meanwhile escaped unarmed to sea by a stratagem. Coming out of dock on the night of the 28th, she was allowed by the authorities at Liverpool to proceed down the river on the morning of the 29th on pretence of a trial trip, picked up a crew from Liverpool off the Anglesey coast on the 30th, and steamed out to sea.

Her destination was the Azores, where she took in an armament and fighting crew brought out in two other vessels, the *Agrippina* and the *Bahama*, which left London and Liverpool respectively with a clearance for Demerara and Nassau in the Bahamas. She was then commissioned by Captain Semmes as a Confederate cruiser, and commenced depredations upon United States commerce, capturing many vessels between October and December. After having destroyed the United States ship of war *Hatteras*, she put into Jamaica on January 20, 1863, and stayed there for repairs until the 25th, the British authorities being of opinion that she was exempt from seizure as a commissioned ship of war.

Subsequently on putting into Saldanha Bay, in Cape Colony, for repairs, in answer to a protest made by the United States consul to the governor of the colony, the Law Officers of the Crown advised that the ship was exempt from the jurisdiction of the authorities at the Cape, and that, whatever her antecedents might have been, they were bound to treat her as a commissioned ship of war belonging to a belligerent power. On the same grounds she was allowed to put into other British ports on various occasions for coaling and repairs without molestation. Her tender, the *Tuscaloosa*, was, however, detained on her second appearance at the Cape, and handed over to the United States consul at the beginning of 1864.

The *Alabama* successfully continued her career of destruction until June 19, 1864, when in an engagement off Cherbourg she was sunk by the United States ironclad *Kearsage*.

The Shenandoah. The *Shenandoah* was originally a British merchant steamer known as the *Sea King*. She was bought by the Confederate Government at Madeira in October 1864 and transformed into a cruiser off that island, her equipment and the greater part of her crew, including some survivors from the *Alabama*, being brought out in the *Laurel*, which had cleared from Liverpool with a cargo marked machinery, but consisting in reality of arms and ammunition. The *Sea King*, re-named the *Shenandoah*, then proceeded to prey upon Federal commerce in the Southern Seas. In January 1865 she was allowed to coal and refit and take in supplies at Melbourne, and also to enlist recruits for her crew there, in spite of the remonstrance of the United States consul. This enabled her subsequently to capture several United States vessels in the Arctic seas before the fall of the Confederate Government came to her knowledge. On November 6, 1865, she finally surrendered to the British Government at Liverpool, and was handed over to the United States.

The history of these three vessels, the *Florida*, the *Alabama*, and the *Shenandoah*, has been given at some length, because it was in respect of them alone that the Geneva Arbitration found Great Britain to be liable.

The other vessels in respect of which the United States claimed unsuccessfully against Great Britain for breaches of neutral duty were the *Georgia*, the *Nashville*, the *Sumter*, the *Retribution*, the *Tallahassee*, and the *Chickamauga*. *Other claims.*

The *Georgia* was a steam vessel built on the Clyde, and left Greenock in April 1863 as the *Japan*. Off Ushant she was joined by another steamer, the *Alar*, from Newhaven, with arms and equipment, and was converted in the usual way into a Confederate cruiser. She did not, however, prove a success, and after having been received in various ports as a Confederate man-of-war, returned to Liverpool in May 1864, where she was dismantled and sold to an English subject. Mr. Adams, on behalf of the United States, refused to recognize this sale, and claimed the right to seize her on the high seas, which was in fact done off Lisbon not long afterwards. The English owner was referred by Lord Russell to the Prize Court of the captor. *The Georgia.*

The *Tallahassee* was a merchant steamer built in London, and subsequently converted into a Confederate cruiser, which destroyed many United States vessels during July and August 1864. *The Tallahassee.*

The circumstances under which the *Nashville* and the *Sumter* enjoyed the hospitality of British ports have been already described (p. 206). They were clearly not such as to fix Great Britain with any liability in respect of these vessels. *The Nashville and Sumter.*

Of the ships fitted out in England for the Confederate

States, Boyd's note to Wheaton gives the following

Summary. summary:—"The *Alabama* and the *Florida* were the only two vessels of war built in Great Britain for, and actually employed in, the service of the Confederates during the whole Civil War. Four others were intended to be built and equipped, but were arrested while in course of construction. Four merchant vessels, though not adapted for warlike purposes, were converted into vessels of war by having guns put on board, but out of the jurisdiction of the British Government."

The claims as to other vessels made by the United States were made in respect of illegal augmentation of force alone.

At the end of the war began a prolonged discussion between the two governments respecting claims for damage by the above-mentioned vessels, generically known as "The Alabama Claims."

The Johnson-Clarendon Convention. After a convention for their settlement had fallen through in 1868, the Johnson-Clarendon Convention (signed by the Earl of Clarendon and Mr. Reverdy Johnson) also came to nothing, being rejected by the United States Senate, April 13, 1869.

However, in 1871 a joint commission was appointed, each country being represented by five commissioners, to settle the fishery disputes, Alabama Claims, and other causes of difference between the two states. As a result of this

The Treaty of Washington. Commission the Treaty of Washington was signed May 8, 1871, providing *inter alia* for the decision by arbitration of the Alabama Claims, the Fishery Question, and the North-West Boundary Dispute. In particular, the Alabama Claims were referred to a tribunal of five Arbitrators, of whom two were to be selected by Great Britain and the United States, and the other three by foreign powers.

The Commissioners agreed upon certain rules (now famous as "the Three Rules of the Treaty of Washington")

to guide the Arbitrators in their decision of the matters in dispute. Article VI. of the Treaty provided as follows:—
"A Neutral Government is bound

> *First.* To use due diligence to prevent the fitting out, arming, or equipping within its jurisdiction of any vessel which it has reasonable ground to believe is intended to cruise or carry on war against a Power with which it is at peace, and also to use like diligence to prevent the departure from its jurisdiction of any vessel intended to cruise or carry on war as above, such vessel having been specially adapted, in whole or in part, within such jurisdiction, to warlike use. *[The Three Rules.]*
>
> *Secondly.* Not to permit or suffer either belligerent to make use of its ports or waters as the base of naval operations against the other, or for the purpose of the renewal or augmentation of military supplies or arms, or the recruitment of men.
>
> *Thirdly.* To exercise due diligence in its own ports and waters, and as to all persons within its jurisdiction, to prevent any violation of the foregoing obligations and duties."

Great Britain, while denying that the above rules contained a statement of the principles of International Law in force at the time when the matters in dispute occurred, agreed, in order to strengthen the friendly relations between the two countries, that the Arbitrators should settle those matters upon the assumption that Great Britain had undertaken to act upon the principles contained in those rules.

In other words, Great Britain consented to be tried by an *ex post facto* law, "an example of magnanimity," as Walker says, which is "hardly likely to secure extensive imitation." The British Government by acquiescing in these rules, which it had never previously acknowledged, and particularly by submitting its conduct to an undefined standard of due diligence, practically courted inevitable failure before the Geneva Board. It practically acknowledged its liability, and only left the Arbitrators to determine the extent of that liability and assess the damages. Hence, it is not the fact that the Board found Great Britain liable, but the method in which it determined the extent of her liability, that has brought the Geneva arbitration into discredit.

Great Britain and the United States also agreed by the Treaty of Washington, "to observe these rules as between themselves in future, and to bring them to the knowledge of other maritime powers, and to invite them to accede to them."

The mere fact that the authors of the rules have been unable to agree as to their interpretation has, however, prevented the suggested invitation ever being given.[1]

The Geneva Arbitration. The Tribunal of Arbitration met at Geneva in Switzerland on December 15, 1871. It was constituted as follows:—Count Frederic Sclopis (nominated by the King of Italy), president, M. Staempfli (nominated by the President of the Swiss Confederation), Vicomte d'Itajuba (nominated by the Emperor of Brazil), Mr. C. F. Adams (United States), Sir Alexander Cockburn (Great Britain).

The British and American cases were presented a few days later, and the Tribunal adjourned to the following June

[1] On March 21, 1873, Mr. Gladstone, as Prime Minister, stated in the House of Commons, that, in bringing these rules to the knowledge of other maritime powers, and inviting them to accede to the same, "you have a right to expect that we should take care that our recommendation of the three rules does not carry with it, in whole or in part, in substance or even in shadow, so far as we (the British Government) are concerned, the recitals of the Arbitrators as being of any authority in this matter." It has not yet been found possible to draft a note to meet the respective views of the two governments with reference to communicating the three rules to other maritime powers.

15th. The American case included claims for direct losses arising out of destruction of vessels and cargoes by insurgent cruisers, and the expense incurred in the pursuit of the latter, and for indirect losses in the way of transfer of trade from the American to the British flag, increased rates of marine insurance, and expenditure incurred by prolongation of the war. The enormous claim for indirect losses raised a storm of excitement in England; continuous correspondence on the subject ensued, and the Arbitration might even have fallen through, but that the Arbitrators cleared the way by a preliminary declaration that the indirect claims were invalid and contrary to International Law. The United States then withdrew them, and the Arbitration proceeded.

The final award was made September 14, 1872. It commenced with certain recitals detailing the principles of interpretation upon which the Arbitrators acted.

These were as follows :—

(1) The "due diligence" referred to in the above-mentioned rules ought to be exercised by neutral governments *in proportion to the risks* to which either belligerent may be exposed by their failure to fulfil their neutral duties.

Recitals of the Arbitrators.

(2) The circumstances out of which the Alabama Claims arose were such as to call for the exercise by the British Government of all possible solicitude for the observance of the rights and duties involved in Great Britain's declaration of neutrality of May 13, 1861.

(3) The effects of a violation of neutrality through the construction, equipment, and armament of a vessel are not done away with by the subsequent grant of a commission to it by the belligerent power, and the ultimate step towards completing the offence is no ground for the absolution of the offender; nor can the consummation of his fraud become the means of establishing his innocence.

(4) The exterritoriality accorded to a warship has been admitted into the Law of Nations not as an absolute right but solely as a matter of courtesy, and therefore can never be appealed to for the protection of acts done in violation of neutrality.

(5) The absence of a previous notice is not a failure in any consideration required by the Law of Nations, where a vessel carries with it its own condemnation.

(6) Supplies of coal must be connected with special circumstances of time, person, or place, in order to give them a character inconsistent with the second of the "three rules."

The Award. The terms of the Award may be briefly summarized as follows:—

(1) With respect to the *Alabama*, four of the Arbitrators[1] held that Great Britain was liable under the first and third rules on the ground that, nothwithstanding the warnings given her, she had omitted to take timely and effective measures of prevention; that the measures taken for the pursuit and arrest of the vessel were so imperfect as to lead to no result; that the vessel was afterwards on several occasions freely admitted into British and Colonial ports instead of being proceeded against as she ought to have been; and that the British Government could not justify its want of due diligence on the plea of the insufficiency of the legal means of action which it possessed.

(2) With respect to the *Florida*, the Arbitrators, by four voices to one (Sir A. Cockburn), held that Great Britain was liable under all three rules, owing to the circumstances of her original construction and outfit, her treatment by the colonial authorities at Nassau, her issue from that port, her enlistment of men, her supplies, her armament at

[1] Sir A. Cockburn also agreed as to the fact of Great Britain's liability with regard to the *Alabama*, but on grounds differing from those of the other Arbitrators.

Green Cay, and her subsequent admission into British ports.

(3) With respect to the *Shenandoah*, the Arbitrators held unanimously that Great Britain had not failed in her duties under the first rule, but by a majority of three voices to two (Sir A. Cockburn and Vicomte d'Itajuba), that she was liable under the second and third rules for all acts of the vessel after leaving Melbourne on February 18, 1865, on the ground of the negligence of the authorities, and the illegal augmentation of force in that port.

(4) With regard to the *Tuscaloosa* (tender to the *Alabama*), and the *Clarence*, *Tacony*, and *Archer* (tenders to the *Florida*), the Arbitrators held that liability for these vessels was included in the liability for the vessels to which they were attached.

(5) With regard to all the other vessels in respect of which claims were made, the Arbitrators held that Great Britain had failed in no neutral duty, and was free from liability.

(6) With regard to the expenses incident to the pursuit of the cruisers, the Arbitrators held, by a majority of three voices to two, that these costs were not distinguishable from the general expenses of the war, and should not be awarded.

(7) With regard to damages in respect of prospective earnings, the Arbitrators held unanimously that these should not be awarded, as depending upon future and uncertain contingencies.

(8) The Arbitrators by four voices to one (Sir A. Cockburn) awarded the United States 15,500,000 dollars in gold as indemnity.

Sir Alexander Cockburn refused to sign the Award, and published an elaborate dissenting opinion, containing a masterly and exhaustive examination of the laws of neutrality.

Having regard to the history and termination of this controversy, it is impossible to conceal the fact that not only has the Geneva Award no claim to rank as an authoritative source of International Law,[1] but it has even tended to throw some measure of discredit upon arbitration as a means of settling international disputes of any considerable magnitude.

The Award is of no authority,

That the Award is of no authority is self-evident, for the "three rules," although binding upon Great Britain and the United States, as set forth in the treaty, have not as yet been adopted by any other state, owing to the fact that Great Britain and the United States have been unable to agree as to the form in which they should be recommended for adoption. The reason for this inability to agree is equally self-evident. The rules themselves contain no definition of the standard of "due diligence" required from neutral states, and the principle of interpretation contained in the recitals of the Arbitrators is too loose and dangerous to be accepted by Great Britain, and has indeed been condemned by the writers and politicians of most countries.

But has caused distrust in arbitration,

Apart from the fact of the enormously excessive damages given,[2] the Award was not particularly unfavourable to England, seeing that the United States out of all their many claims only succeeded with reference to two vessels and partially as to a third. There is, therefore,

[1] Even had the Arbitrators been able to agree and to deliver a unanimous award, the composition of the tribunal, on which, besides Great Britain and the United States, only Italy, Switzerland, and Brazil were represented, must have debarred its award from becoming immediately binding upon the great powers unrepresented. But no doubt unanimity would have enhanced its value as an international precedent.

[2] After all awards had been made in answer to the claims for damages there remained a surplus of about 8,000,000 dollars on December 21, 1876!

some other circumstance which has helped to produce the feeling of distrust in arbitration which was excited, and is not perhaps entirely allayed, in this country and elsewhere, by the Award of the Geneva Arbitrators.

That circumstance is the unsatisfactory nature of the principles of interpretation dealing with due diligence and the exterritoriality of warships, upon which, as set forth in the recitals to the Award, the Arbitrators proceeded. *Because of its principles of interpretation.*

It is impossible to deprive Arbitrators of all judicial discretion as to the interpretation of legal rules, but it is hardly to be expected that nations will willingly resort to arbitration, if the court is to be at liberty to lay down and act upon rules at variance with general principles of law which obtain everywhere, or actually opposed to well-settled existing principles of International Law. No country is anxious to submit its legal rights and duties to novel and arbitrary rules of interpretation which, the Geneva Award seems to show, may unexpectedly place it in the wrong.

The standard of "due diligence" laid down by the Arbitrators makes it proportionate not to the results which may reasonably be expected to follow, but *to the actual results of default*, which are beyond all human foresight. It is a preposterous standard, and one unknown to any legal system. *"Due diligence."*

The British view is that the measure of care requisite depends upon the nature of the obligation and upon the surrounding circumstances of each case, no wide and general rule being possible.

With regard to the circumstances of this controversy, it may be freely acknowledged that the British Government did not at the commencement of the American Civil War show itself keenly alive to its responsibilities, and that it was guilty of negligence with reference to the *Florida* and *Alabama*. After the escape of those two vessels, however, it acted with promptitude and success, and failed in no duty of neutrality. In Sir A. Cockburn's words, "After all that has been said and written, it is only in respect of two vessels, both equipped at the very outset of the Civil War, and before the contrivances resorted to had become known by experience, that this Tribunal has been able to find any default in British authorities at home."

The charges of "insincere neutrality" brought by the United States against Great Britain were therefore amply disproved before the Geneva Tribunal. They were only made in consequence of the prevailing irritation in America against England,[1] and ought never to have been brought forward. "He who comes into equity must come with clean hands," and the United States in the matter of Fenian and other incursions into Canada had hardly a clean record of sincere neutrality.

Exterritoriality of warships.
With regard to the principle laid down by the Arbitrators, that the exterritoriality accorded to a ship of war is of a merely provisional character, it can only be said that this doctrine was the *exact opposite* of the generally accepted principle of International Law upon

---

[1] The causes of this irritation were for the most part imaginary. The United States Government was in the first place disappointed and annoyed at the recognition of the "rebels" as a belligerent power by Great Britain and other European States. But the latter were not only entitled but, in defence of their own interests, compelled to extend recognition to the Confederates. Then the fitting out of vessels for the Southerners and the success of British blockade-runners were further causes of ill-feeling amongst the Federals, who seem to have lost sight of the fact that these were only commercial speculations on the part of British merchants, and not acts of national hostility.

At the same time, it must be confessed that there was an undisguised sympathy felt and expressed in England for the Confederates, and it was this fact no doubt that led the United States to ascribe an unfriendly character to the perfectly legitimate actions of Great Britain and her subjects mentioned above.

which Great Britain acted—namely, that the commission of a belligerent power makes a vessel a public vessel, and bars any inquiry by third powers into her antecedents.

The Treaty of Washington provided that the Alabama Claims should be decided by the three rules, "and by *such principles of International Law* not inconsistent therewith as the Arbitrators shall determine to have been applicable to the case."

Great Britain agreed to be tried by the three rules, which, so far as she was concerned, were *ex post facto*. To this no objection can be raised. But she did not agree to be tried by principles laid down by the Arbitrators, which, in addition to being *ex post facto*, were even opposed to already existing principles of International Law.

It cannot be denied, however, that the limitation of a warship's exterritoriality (as laid down by the Arbitrators) would render the discharge of neutral duties an easier matter than it has hitherto been, while it would not prejudice the privileges of a belligerent public vessel which had committed no violation of neutrality. If Great Britain had found herself entitled to inquire into the history of Confederate cruisers in British ports during the war, the Alabama Claims would scarcely have been heard of.

The proposed limitation of the Arbitrators is, as yet, of no authority, but there is no reason why it should not become so in future, seeing that, as pointed out in the last chapter, there is a tendency on the part of all nations to take stricter measures for the preservation of their neutrality as regards the fitting out of ships in their jurisdiction and the use of their ports in time of war.

What form the practice of nations will ultimately assume it is impossible to predict. It may be the absolute prohibition of the sale of certain vessels to belligerents, as already suggested; or it might well be that, if a fourth rule could be added containing a generally acceptable definition of "due diligence," the three rules of the Treaty of Washington might be adopted as the basis of some international agreement as to neutral duty with regard to ships and ports.

CHAPTER V

DUTIES OF SUFFERANCE. CONTRABAND.

THE active duties of a neutral government with reference to its own actions and the actions of individuals within its jurisdiction have now been described. There remain certain negative duties, or duties of sufferance, to be observed by a neutral state. It must suffer or acquiesce in certain interferences with the commerce of its subjects at the hands of belligerent powers, in order that the latter may be enabled to carry on their hostile operations without obstruction, and that the war be not unduly prolonged.

Duties of sufferance.

This general principle has been universally accepted, although the extent and mode of its application has been a matter of debate. In particular it has been contended, as will appear later, that both "commercial blockade" and the "Rule of 1756" are extensions of the belligerent right against neutral commerce going far beyond the true intent of the general principle, which seeks to hold the scales evenly balanced between neutrals and belligerents in the general interests of peace.

Under the head of duties of sufferance, neutral states must allow the cruisers of belligerent powers to prevent the carriage of contraband or breach of blockade by neutral subjects, to capture enemy ships having on board cargoes belonging to neutral subjects, and to exercise the

1. Contraband.
2. Blockade.
3. Capture.
4. Search.

right of search over all private vessels, this being a necessary "act of police," enabling the belligerent to discover whether neutral traders are carrying on a trade noxious to him or not.

Contraband.

Contraband. A belligerent is entitled to treat certain commodities as forbidden (*contra bannum*) objects of neutral commerce. These commodities include arms and munitions of war, and other articles which will assist the prosecution of hostilities by the enemy. There is no universally accepted definition of contraband. Alike in the practice of states and the opinion of jurists, from the infancy of International Law down to the present day, there has been such utter contradiction and inconsistency as to render any authoritative list of articles of contraband impossible.

Inconsistent practice. No single state has pursued for any length of time a consistent policy in its treaties dealing with contraband. There have been a multitude of such treaties since the seventeenth century, and in some cases it has happened that the same state has agreed with different powers to observe widely different lists of contraband under treaties all holding good at the same time.

The reason. The tendency has of course been for every state to wish to secure immunity for its own commerce when neutral, and to extend the list of contraband articles when belligerent. There has further been the tendency for the weaker maritime powers, whether neutral or belligerent, to try to limit the liability of neutral commerce to seizure by a belligerent. Such powers have clearly everything to gain and nothing to lose by such a policy, because, as belligerents, their weakness would prevent them taking much advantage of an extended list of contraband, whilst as neutrals, the more restricted the list the better for their trade in time of war.

A strong maritime power, on the other hand, is interested when belligerent in having a free hand in dealing with commodities likely to be of assistance to the enemy, whilst as neutral its own commerce is vulnerable in proportion only to the maritime power of the belligerents. In other words, a strong naval power gains more as a belligerent and loses less as a neutral proportionately by enlarging the list of commodities liable to be seized as contraband. The contraband policy of most countries has accordingly varied with their naval strength or weakness.

Turning for a moment to the publicists, Grotius divided articles of commerce into three classes—things useful for war only, which are always contraband, things useful for peace only, which are never contraband, and "things *ancipitis usus,*" useful both in peace and war, which are contraband or not according to the circumstances of each case. Similarly, Bynkershoek included as contraband all things capable of use in war, "sive instrumenta bellica sint sive *materia* per se bello apta," according to the circumstances of the case. Grotius.
Bynker-
shoek.

Into the discussions of Heineccius, Vattel, Valin, and other eighteenth-century writers who treated of contraband, it is unnecessary to inquire; because of the two distinct doctrines now existing amongst states, one is identical with that of Grotius, whilst the other, barring things *ancipitis usus* entirely, only recognizes arms and munitions of war as contraband. Two modern doctrines.

The existence of these two opposing doctrines is due to the contending interests of the strong and weak maritime powers already alluded to. Since the commencement of her naval supremacy, Great Britain has with fair consistency adhered to the doctrine of Grotius, although she may have consented in some instances to limit her action with regard to things *ancipitis usus* by various Anglo-
American.

treaties. The United States have adopted the same doctrine with similar partial and occasional limitations.

Continental. The general continental doctrine, confining contraband strictly to arms and munitions of war, was originally based upon the Declarations of the two Armed Neutralities. These were combinations of the Baltic Powers, made to resist what they considered the aggression of England at the end of the last century. Open hostility towards England was their *raison d'être*, and the adherence subsequently given to their Declarations of neutral rights by other powers, such as France, Spain, and Austria, was due to the same cause.

There appears, however, to be a growing opinion on the Continent that this doctrine is too narrow to meet the circumstances of modern naval warfare, in which there are other things, notably coal, of as great an importance as, if not greater than, even guns and ammunition.

The doctrine of occasional contraband. In spite of the hostility still shown in some quarters to the Anglo-American doctrine of "occasional contraband," the opinion of the great majority of modern continental and other writers appears to be that contraband cannot now be limited to mere munitions of war, but includes many articles *ancipitis usus* when essential to the prosecution of hostilities.

Great Britain and the United States have constantly asserted a right to seize as occasional contraband such things as provisions, money, or coals destined for the use of belligerent armies or fleets. Occasional contraband, in fact, consists of Grotius's things *ancipitis usus*, to which the particular circumstances of the case combine to give a hostile character.

The circumstances under which the articles are being supplied to the enemy must be considered in every case, and it must be ascertained whether they are the native product of the country from which they come. It is of great importance to know whether they are raw material or manufactured articles, whether they are intended for ordinary or military consumption, and, above all, what is the character of their port of destination. This latter is the supreme test. Under ordinary circumstances neutral goods bound to a neutral port are safe, and it is only if they are on their way to an enemy port that they are liable to be seized as contraband.

Things *ancipitis usus*, which are the subjects of occasional contraband, must not only be on their way to a belligerent port, but that port must be a port of naval equipment, and not merely a mercantile port, in order to make them liable as contraband.

The captor of occasional contraband does not usually confiscate it as in the case of ordinary contraband, but in the absence of incriminating circumstances buys the articles at a fair price, having regard to their original cost, and their exporter's expenses and reasonable profit, calculated in English practice at 10 per cent. This is called Pre-emption. If the cargo consists of the native products of the exporting country, and they are raw material, and not manufactured articles, it is considered entitled to indulgence, and pre-emption always takes the place of confiscation.   *Pre-emption.*

A right of pre-emption has been wrongfully asserted in times gone by with regard to cargoes of provisions on neutral ships, to which no taint of contraband could possibly attach.

This misapplication has prejudiced it in the eyes of many states, but it is really a peculiarly mild practice if not abused, seeing that it amounts to belligerents paying for goods which as contraband they might seize for nothing. But the hostility with which pre-emption is regarded is mainly due to its intimate connection with the doctrine of occasional contraband, which has been denounced as one which gives belligerents the power of declaring any commodity they please to be contraband, and thus opens a door for the commission of great injustice and oppression with regard to neutral commerce.

The answer to that, from the Anglo-American point of view, is that, so long as Prize Courts discharge their office with integrity, and pre-emption is substituted for confiscation, there appears to be an ample guarantee for due regard being paid to neutral interests.

Two extensions of occasional contraband

Some discredit has, however, been brought upon the doctrine by two unwarrantable extensions in recent times of the hostile destination, which is the essence of occasional contraband.

by the United States.

During the American Civil War the United States Courts applied the English doctrine of "continuous voyages" (cf. chapter vii., *infra*) to contraband, and held that, although the *immediate* destination of a cargo may be a neutral port, yet if there is any presumption of an *ultimate* hostile destination, the voyage must be considered one continuous voyage to the hostile port, and cargo if of a contraband character liable to condemnation.

This extension of contraband destination applied both to contraband proper and occasional contraband.

It can only be explained by the peculiar nature of the then existing circumstances. Cargoes were shipped to neutral ports, chiefly British West Indian ports, and there transferred into ships especially adapted for running the blockade of the Confederate ports.

On principle the United States could only legally seize such cargoes whilst actually on the way to a hostile port, whether as contraband or for breach of blockade. As it was, their irritation led them to seize contraband cargoes bound for neutral ports, and innocent cargoes with similar destination, on mere *suspicion of an intention* to commit breach of blockade.

To cover these illegal proceedings, the United States Courts devised their ingenious misapplication of the doctrine of continuous voyages. "The American decisions," says Hall, "have been universally reprobated outside the United States, and would probably now find no defenders in their own country. On the confession indeed of one of the judges then sitting in the Supreme Court, they seem to have been due partly to passion and partly to ignorance. 'The truth is,' says Mr. Justice Nelson, 'that the feeling of the country was deep and strong against England, and the judges as individual citizens were no exceptions to that feeling. Besides, the Court was not then familiar with the law of blockade.'"

The American doctrine is hardly likely to be again put forward by a belligerent in any future war.

The second extension of the doctrine of the occasional contraband occurred in 1885, when France, hitherto an opponent of the doctrine, proposed to treat as contraband all shipments of rice for any Chinese ports north of Canton. *By France.*

Lord Granville on behalf of the British Government protested against rice being treated generally as contraband irrespective of its ulterior destination, in order to put stress upon the non-combatant population, but agreed to leave the doctrine of the French Government to be tried in the first place by the French Prize Court. Whether the latter would have supported it, it is impossible to say, as during the short remainder of the war no seizure of rice in a neutral ship was actually made.

The action of France was of great importance as showing how easily England's food supply may be attacked by her enemy in time of war, notwithstanding the Declaration of Paris (cf. chapter ix.). The French claim to interfere with neutral commerce (a purely belligerent right) was clearly inconsistent with her contention that the blockade of Formosa was of a pacific character, and that a state of war did not really exist between herself and China.

Penalties for carrying contraband. It is perfectly lawful for a neutral subject to carry on a contraband trade with a belligerent government, but the contraband is subject to the risk of capture *in transitu*, and confiscation by the other belligerent. There is no personal penalty, nor, in general, is the ship which carries the contraband liable to confiscation. Some states have concluded treaties permitting such a vessel to proceed on her voyage upon giving up all the contraband she carries; but the usual practice is for the captor to bring both ship and cargo before his own country's Prize Court. There the ship is *primâ facie* entitled to release, and only incurs the penalty of loss of time, freight, and expenses. She is, however, liable to confiscation if she also belongs to the owner of the contraband, or if her owner has been privy to the carriage of the contraband, or if she uses false papers. Similarly, that portion of her cargo which is not contraband is not generally liable to confiscation unless it also belongs to the owner of the contraband, or its owner is privy to the carriage of the contraband.

The liability of the ship to capture ceases with the sale of her contraband cargo, and the proceeds of that sale cannot be touched on her return voyage. The English Courts have made one exception in holding that, where false papers have been used, the ship can be captured on the homeward voyage with an innocent cargo, whether the latter has been purchased with the proceeds of the contraband or not.

Analogues of Contraband.[1]

The doctrine of contraband has been extended by

---

[1] A few cases have been added to illustrate this branch of the law of contraband, in order, more particularly, to throw light upon the principles involved in the important *Trent* controversy.

analogy to the carriage by a neutral of belligerent despatches, or persons in the naval or military service of a belligerent.

A neutral subject engaging in such a business associates himself more closely with one of the belligerents than by merely selling him articles of contraband. In fact he practically enters his service, and the other belligerent is allowed to stop such acts on the part of a neutral by the same means that he uses to prevent contraband trade, namely seizure. The penalty is appropriately more severe than in the case of ordinary contraband, the ship being liable to confiscation. A neutral ship carrying a belligerent despatch of a character noxious to the other belligerent is liable to confiscation, if either the master or owner is aware of its noxious character. In one case he is presumed to have this knowledge. If a despatch from a diplomatic or consular agent of a belligerent in a neutral country, addressed to persons in the *military* service of the belligerent, is discovered in the custody of a neutral subject, it is presumed to be a noxious despatch, and the neutral cannot plead ignorance of its contents. He can only escape liability by proving ignorance of the fact that it is in his possession, or of the quality of the persons to whom it is addressed. On the other hand, a similar despatch sent from the diplomatic or consular agent to the belligerent *government*, or *vice versâ*, is presumed to be innocent, it being the proper function of such agents to keep up relations between their own government and the neutral state. Thus the bearer of despatches, being ignorant of their contents, is in general judged, as in the case of occasional contraband, by the broad external fact of their destination.

Carriage of belligerent despatches.

The "Atalanta." (6, C. Rob. 440.)   *Cases.*

This neutral vessel was captured in 1807, during war between England and France. In the possession of the supercargo was a despatch from the Governor of the Isle of France—now Mauritius—to the French Government. The vessel and cargo were condemned.

The " Rapid." (Edwards, 228.)

In 1810, during war between England and Holland, this American vessel was captured and brought in. Official despatches for the Dutch colonial minister were sent from Batavia to New York, where they were handed to the master of the *Rapid* by a private person in an ordinary envelope, addressed to a commercial house in Holland. The ship was released on the oath of the master that he was ignorant of the contents of the envelope.

The " Madison." (Edwards, 224.)

France and Denmark being at war with Great Britain, the *Madison*, an American vessel, was captured in 1810 by a British cruiser. She carried a despatch from the Danish Government to the Danish Consul-General at Philadelphia. Sir W. Scott ordered her restoration on the ground that it was not a noxious despatch.

Ordinary mails. Various conventions have been entered into to protect mail steamers, who carry belligerent despatches, in the ordinary course of postal business. Such steamers, like all other private vessels, are liable to search by belligerent cruisers, and no neutral government or its agents can possibly guarantee the absolute innocence of the mail-bags' contents. Therefore, although a belligerent has a strict right of searching the mail-bags, it is improbable, having regard to the enormous interests likely to be affected by interference with the mails, that the right will be exercised in the future except upon very grave suspicion.

In any case, a mail steamer is not liable to condemnation, but is allowed to proceed upon giving up belligerent despatches. By special conventions between Great Britain and France, mail steamers have the privileges of warships in the ports of either country.

With regard to naval and military officers of a belligerent, the rule is that a neutral ship may carry such persons as ordinary passengers in the ordinary course of its business. But if she is hired in such a way as to become a belligerent transport, or evince an intention on the part of her owner to aid belligerent operations, she is liable to be captured and confiscated by the adverse belligerent.

Naval and military officers.

The "Friendship." (6, C. Rob. 422.)

Cases.

An American vessel was hired in 1807, to bring home ninety shipwrecked officers and sailors to France. This was a clear case of a neutral ship being hired as a transport. She was captured by a British ship and confiscated.

The "Orozembo." (6, C. Rob. 430.)

In 1807, during war between Great Britain and Holland, an American ship was chartered ostensibly for trading purposes. Afterwards, by the direction of the charterer, she embarked three military officers of distinction and two civil servants of the Government of Batavia. She was captured by a British cruiser, and condemned by Sir W. Scott, who held that proof of delinquency on the part of master or owner was not necessary, it being sufficient if injury arose to the belligerent from the employment in which the vessel was found.

A neutral ship may therefore be liable even if its master or owner acts under compulsion or deceit, the only remedy of the latter being to apply for indemnity to the belligerent by whose compulsion or deceit naval or military officers have been received on board. Otherwise, said Sir William Scott, such opportunities of conveyance would be constantly used, as it would be almost impossible in the greater number of cases to prove the knowledge and privity of the immediate offender. This judgment has been criticized as an extreme assertion of belligerent right, and it would perhaps seem fairer to the neutral to make him establish his innocence, if he can, by sufficient proof of duress or fraud; and if such proof be forthcoming, to release the ship and only detain the belligerent officers as prisoners of war.

The " Trent," 1861.

In November 1861, during the American Civil War, the *Trent*, a British mail steamer, was stopped on her way from Havana to St. Thomas by the United States frigate *San Jacinto*, and Messrs. Mason and Slidell, two Confederate envoys accredited to London and Paris, were, together with their secretaries, taken out of her and carried as prisoners of war to Boston. The *Trent* was then allowed to proceed upon her voyage. The British Government immediately demanded the surrender of these persons, and an apology, this demand being supported by all the diplomatic agents at Washington.

The United States contended that the envoys were embodied despatches, and therefore liable to be seized as contraband, that the *San Jacinto* had a belligerent right of search, that this right had been properly and lawfully exercised, and that the captain of the *San Jacinto* having found contraband on board the *Trent*, was entitled to seize it.

The British answer may be put briefly as follows:—

The envoys could not be regarded as "living despatches," nor were they naval or military officers, but civilians. They were not, therefore, upon any ground liable to be treated as analogues to contraband. Even had they possessed a naval or military character, they were travelling as ordinary passengers on a neutral ship bound from one neutral port to another neutral port. There was no hostile destination to impose upon them any contraband character whatever. England as neutral state had a perfect right to maintain diplomatic relations with the Confederate States, who were recognized belligerents; and although Confederate envoys to England were liable to be seized on United States soil,[1] nothing could justify their seizure on a neutral vessel bound from and to a neutral port. Lastly, the *Trent* was pursuing her ordinary business, and had done nothing to place herself in the position of a hired transport or to incur penalties for actively assisting the enemy. Finally Mr. Seward took refuge in the irregularity of the *mode* of capture adopted by the *San Jacinto*, and the United States Government surrendered the envoys on the ground that the *Trent* ought to have been brought in for condemnation before a prize court for carrying analogues to contraband.

It is to be doubted if even this contention was correct, the *Trent* as a mail steamer being, according to the usage mentioned above, entitled to proceed upon her voyage on giving up the contraband. That usage is, however, not of absolute authority. Yet, had she been brought in, it can scarcely be doubted that the British arguments must have proved unanswerable, and both ship and envoys have been released. The alternative may be put in the language of "Historicus" (Sir William Harcourt). "If—which it is impossible to conceive—an American prize court should have exhibited an ignorance or a contempt of law equal to that displayed in Mr. Seward's despatch, and condemned the vessel, so gross a violation of the settled principles of the Law of Nations by the tribunal appointed to guard its sanctions would have been in itself a justifiable cause of war."

[1] As in the case of the Maréchal de Belleisle, French ambassador to Berlin, who unwittingly entered Hanoverian territory in 1744, during the war between England (and Hanover) and France, and was arrested as a prisoner of war.

The United States relied upon an isolated quotation from Vattel, made by Sir W. Scott, in the case of the *Caroline* (6, C. Rob. 468)—"You may stop the ambassador of your enemy on his passage." But they carefully ignored the context, which does not support the application of Vattel's dictum to a passage as an ordinary passenger on a neutral ship bound to a neutral port.

The extraordinary feeling against England rife in America at the time, already alluded to in the footnote on p. 222, embarrassed the United States Government in dealing with the *Trent* affair. Congress actually passed a vote of thanks to Captain Wilkes of the *San Jacinto* for his piratical proceedings. It was left for Mr. Seward to devise some means of giving in without actually admitting the justice of the British claims, for to have done so would have raised a storm of indignation amongst the Federals. His remarkable despatch was accordingly written to "mask an embarrassing retreat."

CHAPTER VI

BLOCKADE

A NEUTRAL state must permit belligerents to prevent breach of blockade by neutral subjects.

There are two questions to be settled—what is blockade, and what constitutes its breach?

Blockade is the interruption of access to a place by land or sea. Neutrals are little affected by land sieges. They have no right, and probably no desire, of access to an inland fortress or town which is in a state of siege. But they do not willingly give up their trade with belligerent ports, and their right of access to the latter is only limited by the rules relating to blockade.

Hence for the purposes of International Law blockade is only maritime, and takes effect upon a seaport, the mouth of a river, or a line of coast. It is not confined to fortified places, but any portion of a coast which can be effectively guarded by a belligerent fleet may be placed under blockade. In other words, the institution of a merely commercial blockade is not prohibited, although it can scarcely be termed a belligerent operation. It is condemned by many nations and writers on the ground that it really amounts to waging war against the trade which all neutrals have the right to carry on with each of the belligerents during the war.

It is further urged, that to bring suffering and want

Blockade defined.

Commercial blockade.

upon a non-combatant population, where no immediate military end is to be served, is a grave infringement of the first grand principle of the law. The latter objection answers itself. If such stress is brought upon the non-combatant population as to have due corresponding effect upon the belligerent's fighting force by crippling his resources in food, men, and money, there will be an ultimate if not an "immediate" military purpose served. If, however, a commercial blockade is of such a character as to have no effect immediate or eventual upon the military operations, it does appear open to grave objections. Supposing, for example, the coast blockaded is so utterly remote from the scene of hostilities that the blockade can have no possible effect upon their issue, its institution, merely to annoy the enemy, is a distinct infringement of neutral rights.

The practical answer to these objections, however, is that the line which separates a military and a commercial blockade is an extremely fine one, and the latter frequently develops insensibly into the former. The blockade of the Confederate coasts by the Federal Government in the American Civil War was in its inception merely a gigantic commercial blockade; yet its military importance subsequently became such as to aid materially in bringing the Confederates to their knees.

Hall's comparison of the loss of trade resulting to neutrals from a commercial blockade with that resulting from a land invasion does not seem peculiarly happy. An invasion is, first and foremost, a military operation, and all its consequences are legitimate. A commercial blockade, *ex hypothesi*, is not a military operation, and its consequences are not necessarily legitimate.

The conclusion to be drawn, perhaps, is that, so far as the right of blockade continues to be exercised at all in future wars, belligerents will continue to maintain both commercial and military blockades, and the difficulty of assigning a purely commercial character to any blockade will, except in a case of open and manifest abuse, stifle objections on the part of neutral states.

There are four requisite factors in the constitution of the offence of breach of blockade. <small>Breach of blockade.</small>

(1) There must be a valid blockade effectively maintained.

(2) It must be established under state authority.

(3) The neutral subject must have knowledge of its existence.

(4) There must be some attempted violation on his part.

There are two main streams of doctrine relating to blockade. They may almost be termed two distinct laws of blockade, one containing the doctrines held by England and the United States (who have had far greater practical experience of blockades than other countries), and the other consisting of continental doctrines, theoretical for the most part, and inconsistent with the Anglo-American usage which has at least some claim to authority.

(1) *There must be a valid blockade effectively maintained.* <small>Valid and effective.</small>

Both the Armed Neutralities required that blockade should be effective to have any validity, and the Declaration of Paris similarly requires that " blockades in order to be binding must be effective, that is to say, maintained by a force sufficient to really prevent access to the coast of the enemy."

These requirements were directed against what were formerly known as "paper blockades," that is, blockades not sustained by any actual force or by a notoriously inadequate force. <small>Paper blockades.</small>

A paper blockade, in fact, often merely amounted to a declaration by a government that a particular port or coast was under blockade. The most notorious instance was Napoleon's Berlin Decree in 1806, declaring the whole of the British dominions to be in a state of blockade, when as a matter of fact all the French fleets were themselves shut up "by the superior valour and discipline of the British navy" in French ports! Great Britain replied with a retaliatory Order in Council, which was equally a violation of International Law, the result being that a "Non-Intercourse Act" was passed by the United States in 1809, prohibiting their citizens from all friendly intercourse with France and Great Britain whilst these restrictions on neutral trade remained in force.

A paper blockade is now regarded by all states as illegal, and cannot affect a neutral with any liability.

The effectiveness of blockade. The Armed Neutralities, upon whose declarations the continental doctrine is based, laid down specific rules, making stationary vessels near the blockaded place necessary; but the Declaration of Paris, which is in harmony with the English doctrine, merely requires the blockade to be generally effective, leaving it to belligerent prize courts to judge the circumstances of each case fairly, and to neutral states to protest against any blockade which they deem to be ineffective.

Two examples may be given. In the Crimean War Riga was blockaded by two English ships in the Lyser Ort, 120 miles from the town. The Lyser Ort was a channel three miles wide, and the only navigable entrance to the gulf.

Dr. Lushington held that the distance of the blockading squadron from the blockaded port did not affect the validity of the blockade so long as it was really effective. (The *Franciska*, Spinks, 115.) And again, when the French Government contended that their blockade of Formosa in October 1884 was of a pacific character, Great Britain protested that its incidents were not those of a pacific but of a hostile blockade, and that, as a hostile blockade, it violated the requirement of the Declaration of Paris, in being ineffective.

According to the Anglo-American doctrine, a valid blockade may either be notified by the belligerent government to neutral states, or may exist *de facto* without any such notification. The distinction is of importance in its consequences to the neutral subject with reference to his knowledge of the blockade and the date of its termination. *"Notified" and "de facto" blockades.*

France and most continental states, and the majority of continental writers, do not, however, recognize this distinction.

It should be added that blockade must be against the vessels of all nations, any relaxation by the belligerent in favour of the ships of a particular state rendering the blockade ineffective and therefore invalid.

(2) *The blockade must be established under state authority.* *Authoritative.*

The consequences of a blockade are so important and far-reaching that it can only be declared by an officer in high command whose general powers enable him to do so, or by some officer especially empowered by the government for that purpose.

If a blockade is instituted by an officer without general or special powers, it can only be made retrospectively valid by subsequent ratification by the state.

(3) *The neutral subject must have knowledge of the blockade's existence.* *Notorious.*

On this principle all states are agreed; but they differ as to the circumstances which must be taken to fix a neutral trader with knowledge of the blockade.

The doctrine of France and other continental states, as being the simplest, may be stated first. In French practice a neutral trader, whether he actually knows of the blockade or not, may safely sail to the blockaded port, where he is entitled to be warned once by the blockading *French practice.*

squadron. This warning is endorsed on the ship's papers, and the neutral is then taken to have knowledge of the existence of the blockade. Any second attempt to enter will then render the vessel liable to capture for breaking blockade.

English practice.

In the Anglo-American practice, which has also been adopted by Prussia and Denmark, anything which can be proved to affect the neutral with knowledge of the blockade at the time of his departure for, or before his arrival at, the blockaded port will render his vessel liable.

Notified blockade.

In the case of a notified blockade, if a neutral subject sails after his government has received notice (allowing a reasonable time for the latter to communicate the fact to its subjects), he is conclusively presumed to have knowledge of the blockade, and the mere act of sailing constitutes the offence. If, however, he sails before the notification to his government the burden of proof is on the captor, as in the case of a *de facto* blockade, to show that he has acquired knowledge of the blockade by some means on the way. And if, having sailed before the notification, he arrives at the blockaded port in ignorance, he is entitled to be warned off by the blockading fleet, the fact and date of such warning being endorsed on the ship's papers as in the French practice.

De facto blockade.

A neutral subject is not presumed to have knowledge of a *de facto* blockade unless the fact of its existence is so notorious at the port of departure that he could not possibly have been ignorant of it. Otherwise ignorance will entitle him to an individual warning at the blockaded port, as in the case of a notified blockade.

An exception.

In one exceptional case a neutral subject may sail for a blockaded port with full knowledge of the existence of the blockade.

If the blockaded place and the port of departure are a great distance apart, the neutral may sail on the chance of the blockade terminating before his arrival; but he must be able to show his intention of inquiring whether the blockade is still continued at some intermediate place. He is not entitled to sail straight to the blockaded port and there make inquiry.

(4) *There must be some attempted violation on the neutral's part.* Violation of blockade.

The neutral's offence consists of attempted ingress or egress after the commencement of the blockade.

In the Anglo-American practice a neutral is guilty of attempted ingress if he sails after the blockade has been notified to his government, or its existence is notorious at the port of departure; if, knowing of the blockade, but being entitled by distance to make inquiries on the way, he appears at the blockaded port without having done so; if, having sailed in ignorance of the blockade, he continues his voyage after information; or if, having arrived at the port in ignorance, he does not immediately retire after being warned by the blockading squadron. Ingress.

According to the French doctrine, it is clear from what has been already said that a ship is only guilty of attempted ingress if she tries to enter after receiving individual warning at the blockaded port.

There are certain recognized exceptions to both doctrines, neutral men-of-war being allowed to enter a blockaded port as a matter of courtesy, and neutral merchant ships being accorded a similar privilege under stress of weather, provided that they do not load or unload a cargo.

With regard to egress, it is the universal practice to send notification of the commencement of the blockade to the authorities of the port, at the same time specifying some time-limit within which vessels may come out. During that time vessels may come out in ballast or with a cargo shipped before the commencement of the blockade, but they must not load a cargo after its establishment. If a Egress.

ship does so and tries to come out, the French practice was formerly to give her a special warning, but this appears to have been abandoned in the Franco-Prussian War. Certainly in all other cases the general notification to the port authorities is deemed sufficient. The usual time-limit is fifteen days, and this period was adopted in the Crimean War, the American Civil War, and the Franco-Prussian War. But it may be extended in the case, for example, of a blockaded port at the mouth of a large navigable river, when fifteen days might be too short a period to enable neutral vessels to get down the river and out to sea.

American extension of breach of blockade.

The American extension of hostile destination with reference to contraband and breach of blockade in the Civil War has already been noticed. That misapplication of the doctrine of continuous voyages covered the seizure not only of contraband but of neutral vessels with innocent cargoes on their way to neutral ports, on the mere suspicion of an ulterior intention to commit breach of blockade. The French rule of blockade, allowing every vessel warning at the blockaded port, makes the adoption of this doctrine impossible. In fact, it is only possible according to the Anglo-American practice; but it has been repudiated by England, and, as its origin was only due to the peculiar circumstances of the American Civil War, it is perhaps hardly worth considering in connection with maritime warfare of the future.

The termination of blockade.

Termination of blockade.

A blockade terminates when it ceases to be effective. In a *de facto* blockade the burden of proof that a blockade continues effective is on the captor, but a notified blockade is presumed to continue effective until its termination is notified. This presumption may, however, be rebutted by evidence on the part of the master or owners of the captured vessel.

A blockade ceases to be effective if an enemy force succeeds in driving off the blockading squadron for any period, however short, but a temporary absence caused by heavy weather or the chase of a blockade-runner does not terminate the blockade.

The penalty for breach of blockade.

The ship is always liable to be confiscated and the cargo as well if it belongs to the same owner. Any portion of the cargo, however, which belongs to a different owner, and is not contraband, will be exempt if the owner can prove his ignorance of the existence of the blockade, or that the master of the vessel deviated to a blockaded port, or that he is not personally bound by the acts of the latter. Penalty for breach of blockade.

In the Anglo-American practice a ship having committed ingress or egress is liable to capture during any part of the return voyage, provided the blockade is still in existence. With its termination the ship's liability also ceases. The continental doctrine appears to be that the ship is safe when once it has escaped the blockading squadron.

The development of electricity and steam seems likely to make great alterations in the blockade of the future. The future of blockade.

In the first place, owing to the network of railways now covering the face of every civilized country, the blockade of one or more great maritime ports in a state possessed of a large seaboard will "not arrest trade but only divert it."

In such a case blockade, unless instituted upon a very large scale, may possibly become a *brutum fulmen* in the hands of the belligerent. But a power possessed of a small seaboard and few large trading ports will still, no doubt, suffer in a contest with another state powerful enough by sea to maintain an effective blockade of its coasts.

In the next place, so far as blockade continues to be used as a belligerent measure, the rules relating to its breach will most probably become more stringent. News being spread instantaneously all over the world by electric cables, it will be almost impossible for a vessel to appear at a blockaded port without knowledge of the blockade, and it is obvious that the French rule of allowing approach for inquiry would give a fast and powerful steamer every chance of making a bold dash and running the blockade.

The rules of the future, therefore, may exceed in stringency those at present recognized by Great Britain and the United States.

For example, it is likely that no distance, however great, will be held to entitle a neutral vessel having knowledge of the blockade to inquire as to its continuance on the way, steam having so greatly reduced the length of voyages and rendered their duration certain. Moreover, if the burden of proving the neutral's knowledge is thrown on the captor, as is the present English practice in the case of a *de facto* blockade, no injustice will be done in the rare instances of neutral vessels arriving at a blockaded port in ignorance of the existence of the blockade.

CHAPTER VII

MARITIME CAPTURE AS AFFECTING NEUTRAL SUBJECTS

WHEN an enemy ship carries a neutral cargo, or a neutral ship carries an enemy cargo, a collision of interest arises between the neutral and the adverse belligerent, the latter desiring to seize his enemy's property wherever he can find it, and the former to carry on his trade without molestation.

In order to reconcile these opposing interests, it is necessary to recognize that the belligerent's superior need entitles him to make certain interferences with neutral trade when he finds enemy property associated with neutral property. Nations have differed as to the scope of belligerent interference and extent of neutral liability, but the principle has been universally admitted, that neutral states are under a "duty of sufferance" to permit belligerents to interfere with the trade of neutral subjects where neutral and enemy property are found in close association. *The duty of sufferance.*

At the present time the law relating to the maritime capture of enemy property associated with neutral property may be assumed to have been settled by the Declaration of Paris, which provides that, with the exception of contraband, neutral goods in enemy ships and enemy goods in neutral ships shall be free from capture. *Present law.*

A short historical review of the practice of nations will show that the Declaration has reversed the ancient and well-established rules of International Law, and revolutionized the conditions under which naval warfare must be conducted. It is unnecessary to enlarge upon this subject in the present chapter, the object of which is to describe the law of the past and the present. In order to keep questions of policy distinct from questions of law, England's interest with regard to the law of the future is reserved for discussion in a separate chapter.

The Consolato del Mare.

Turning to the history of national usage, the earliest doctrine on this subject is to be found in the Consolato del Mare, which made the liability to capture of ship or cargo depend strictly upon the nationality of each.[1] This was the doctrine adopted by England, and with the exception of occasional variations by treaty, consistently maintained by this country until the beginning of the Crimean War. Neutral goods in an enemy ship were free, the ship alone being liable to capture, and the captor entitled to freight on duly delivering the goods at their destination. Conversely, enemy goods in a neutral ship were liable to capture, the ship itself being free and entitled to freight at the hands of the captor. Two cases will suffice to illustrate these principles.

English practice.

The "Fortuna." (4, C. Rob. 278. Tudor's L. C. 1041.)

Cases.

During war between Great Britain and the United States in 1801 the American ship *Fortuna*, carrying a neutral (Portuguese) cargo, was captured by a British ship. The ship itself was condemned, but the cargo restored as neutral property and forwarded to the consignees at Lisbon. Sir William Scott, on an application by the captors, held them entitled to freight, having duly performed the contract of the vessel.

---

[1] Enemy or neutral character has ceased to coincide exactly with nationality (cf. Part II. chap. iii.). Therefore the English doctrine may be said to be that of the Consolato del Mare, substituting for the word "nationality" the word "enemy or neutral character."

The "*Bremen Flugge.*" (4, C. Rob. 90. Tudor's L. C. 1045.)

During war between Great Britain and France the *Bremen Flugge*, a neutral vessel, was captured in 1800 by a British vessel. The ship was released, but part of the cargo was condemned as enemy property, and Sir William Scott held that the ship was entitled to her freight as a lien attaching to the cargo, provided there were no unneutral circumstances in the conduct of the vessel to induce a forfeiture of the demand.[1] In this case the neutral claim for expenses in addition to freight was disallowed.

To the rule that neutral ships carrying enemy goods are free from capture and entitled to freight, England laid down one great and important exception. This is usually known as the "Rule of the War of 1756."

The rule of 1756.

In former times it was the policy of all nations to confine their colonial and coasting trade to their own subjects. In 1756 England and France were at war, and the English fleets had practically swept all French shipping off the seas. France then opened her colonial trade to the Dutch to the exclusion of all other neutrals, whereupon England laid down the Rule, declaring that if a belligerent threw open in time of war, either to one favoured neutral or to all neutrals, a trade which was closed to them in time of peace, neutral ships engaging in such trade became practically incorporated in the belligerent's mercantile marine,[2] and were liable to capture by the adverse belligerent. Dutch ships carrying cargoes from the French

[1] Thus in the case of the *Atlas* (3, C. Rob. 299), a neutral ship captured carrying an enemy cargo was released, but deprived of her freight on the ground that she was engaged in the coasting trade of the enemy.

[2] They assist a belligerent to carry on a trade which it is no longer able to carry on itself, to the prejudice of the other belligerent. They must therefore be taken to identify themselves with the interests of the former.

colonies to the mother-country were accordingly captured by the English and condemned as enemy ships.

Before the commencement of the war in 1779, France took the precaution to declare that trade with her West Indian colonies would thenceforth be permanently open, and the Rule was consequently allowed to slumber until the outbreak of the French revolutionary war in 1793, when it revived in more than its former strength.

The "*Immanuel.*" (2, C. Rob. 186. Tudor's L. C. 948.)

In this case the Rule was elaborately expounded by Sir William Scott. The *Immanuel* was a neutral ship which, after quitting a neutral port, sold part of her cargo at Bordeaux and took in other goods for St. Domingo, a French colony, during the war between England and France in 1799. Sir William Scott condemned the goods shipped at Bordeaux under the Rule, but inasmuch as the neutral acted without the notice afforded by former decisions on the subject, decreed restitution of the ship though without freight or expenses.

This was a lenient decision, and, as Phillimore says, the Rule was at first "slowly and mildly restored to its supremacy;" but it was afterwards strictly enforced in English courts, and neutrals thereupon endeavoured to evade it by touching on their voyage between colony and mother country (or *vice versâ*) at a neutral port, where the cargo was landed and dues were paid. The cargo was then re-shipped, and the vessel proceeded to her real destination.

The doctrine of continuous voyages. Neutrals represented this form of trade to consist of two voyages each of which was lawful; but the English courts held that if there existed an intention of carrying goods from colony to mother-country, or *vice versâ*, the proceedings at the neutral port on the way being merely colourable, the two voyages must be construed as one continuous voyage, falling within the principle of the Rule of

1756. If, on the other hand, the neutral could prove an intention to sell the goods at the neutral port, not colourably, but *bonâ fide*, the voyage ended there, and a subsequent voyage from the neutral port to the belligerent country involved the ship in no liability. This was called the "doctrine of continuous voyages." It may be illustrated by the following cases :—

The " William." (5, C. Rob. 385.)

During war between Great Britain and Spain in 1800 the *William*, a neutral ship, took a cargo from La Guayra, a Spanish colony, to a neutral port, landed it, paid duties, and having re-shipped the greater portion of it proceeded to Bilbao in Spain. It was held that this was a continuous voyage from La Guayra to Bilbao, and therefore in violation of the Rule of 1756. Both ship and cargo were condemned, the sentence of condemnation being affirmed by the Court of Appeal in a learned judgment delivered by Sir William Grant, M.R. 11 March, 1806.

The " Maria." (5, C. Rob. 365.)

In this case a neutral ship took a cargo of enemy colonial produce to a neutral port in 1805, re-shipped a portion of it, and sailed to an enemy port in Europe, which was not however a port of the mother-country of the colony whence the produce came. Sir William Scott intimated that he had no disposition to relax the general test of a *bonâ fide* intent to sell at the neutral port, but on the owner of the cargo satisfactorily proving such an intent, held that the voyage was not a continuous one and decreed restitution.

The Rule of 1756 was naturally resented by the neutral states as an extreme exercise of belligerent right, and both the Armed Neutralities declared against it, maintaining that neutral ships might sail freely from port to port of a belligerent in the absence of blockade. *Attitude of the Armed Neutralities.*

At the time the Rule was instituted, however, it was a

Defence of the Rule.

perfectly justifiable belligerent measure, although operating to the detriment of neutrals. In the special circumstances of the case [1] England was being prevented from reaping the fruits of her naval superiority over France by the opening of French colonial trade to neutral ships, and was therefore justified, on the general principle that a belligerent has the right to carry on its operations without obstruction, in treating such neutral ships as being in the enemy's service.

The neutral subject put himself in the wrong by engaging in what was then considered to be an unlawful trade.

But circumstances alter cases, and now that the colonial trade of all or most of the nations in the world is open to the ships of all countries both in peace and war, it may fairly be urged that the Rule has become, if not obsolete, of little practical importance. Such a contention is supported by the fact that England, the author of the Rule, proclaimed by an Order in Council of April 15, 1854, that "the subjects or citizens of any neutral or friendly state shall and may, during the present hostilities with Russia, freely trade with all ports and places wheresoever situate which shall not be in a state of blockade." This, it will

Recent English practice.

---

[1] The American extension of the doctrine of continuous voyages to contraband and breach of blockade, discussed in the last two chapters, has been defended on the ground that it was justified, as its prototype was, by "special circumstances," authorizing high-handed belligerent action. But between the English doctrine of continuous voyages and the American adaptation there was one great difference. In the English practice the neutral vessel captured sailed from an *enemy colonial port.* In the American practice she sailed from a *neutral port.*

In the former case the vessel was engaged *ab initio* in a then unlawful trade; in the latter the vessel was necessarily and entirely innocent whilst bound from and to a neutral port.

In the former case there was a taint of wrong-doing about the vessel, in the latter there was none.

be observed, abandons the Rule of 1756, and affirms the doctrine put forward by the Armed Neutralities.[1]

There only remains the theoretical possibility, that the Rule might still be applied if a belligerent invited neutrals to carry on its coasting trade, which a state usually keeps in the hands of its own subjects; but from a practical point of view any maritime state would probably be driven to surrender before it was in so sore a strait as to be unable to protect and carry on its own coasting trade. Hence the occasion for any revival of the Rule of 1756 seems unlikely to arise.

The Rule in the future.

The English practice, therefore, from early times down to the Crimean War was regulated by the doctrine of the Consolato del Mare, subject at one time to the one exception of the Rule of 1756, and subject to variations by treaties from time to time giving temporary recognition to exceptional principles and practices advocated by other states.[2]

[1] England's waiver of her belligerent rights in the Crimean War, her abandonment of the Rule of 1756, her adoption of the principle of " free ships free goods," her waiver of the right to issue letters of marque to privateers, were due partly to the fact that the scene of the war was very remote, and Russia was not a strong naval power, and partly to the fact of her alliance with France. She paid the penalty for her concessions by being hustled into the Declaration of Paris.

[2] Two lapses from the path of consistency are usually quoted to the discredit of England.

1. In 1793 she agreed by treaty with Russia, Spain, the Empire, and Prussia to prevent neutrals affording any protection to French commerce. This amounted to a prohibition of all neutral commerce with France. The mere fact of the treaty indicates an exception to the general rule, and the French Revolution was a crisis in the world's history which demanded exceptional measures. In any case, whatever blame there may be attaches to the other parties to the agreement as well as to England.

2. By the Orders in Council retaliatory upon the Berlin and Milan Decrees, she again prohibited neutral commerce with France. That they were retaliatory does not entirely justify them, it is true, but

French practice.

The French practice has been far less consistent. In the Middle Ages France, in common with all Western European nations, accepted the doctrine of the Consolato del Mare, and still adhered to it late in the fifteenth century.

Fifteenth century.

In 1474 Ferdinand King of Sicily wrote to Louis XI. of France, to complain that his "subditus" Christopher. Columbus had captured two Sicilian vessels trading with Flanders and Britain and carried them to Normandy. By his letter, dated December 8, 1474, he demanded that Colombus should restore the vessels with their cargoes. "Igitur hortamur ac obtestamur majestatem vestram ut triremes in potestatem ejus perventas ita restituendas putet, ut . . . omnia ita incommoda recompenset ut absque detrimento redeant, ablata omnia reddi restituique curet, *tam nostrorum quam alienorum.*" In January 1475 Louis XI. wrote back defending the action of Columbus in seizing the vessels, but at the same time restoring them and the *Sicilian* property found on board them. "Tantum tamen fuit et est apud nos dilectionis et amicitiæ vestræ zelus ut his omnibus allegationibus et excusationibus post positis *omnia vestra subditorumque vestrorum* extemplo fecerimus restitui."

The enemy property on the vessels was, however, confiscated. "Quantum autem ad merces hostium et bona quæ vestris in triremibus adinventa captaque esse dicuntur, habet hoc *usus inter propugnatores in hoc occidentali mari indelebiliter observatus, res hostium et bona, etiamsi infra amicorum aut confoedatorum triremes seu naves posita sint aut recondita, nisi tamen obstiterit securitas*

England may fairly plead the extenuating circumstance of enormous provocation.

It may also fairly be asked, what state has so clean a record that it can throw a stone against England ? Has any other state departed so seldom from its principles regarding maritime warfare?

specialiter super hoc concessa, impune et licite jure bellorum capi posse, naulum (freight) *propterea debitum exsolvendo."*

That doctrine was admittedly in favour of belligerents, because it enabled them to prevent the enemy trade from being carried on under a neutral flag.

But in the sixteenth century France enunciated a doctrine even more favourable to belligerents. By an Édit of Francis I. in 1543, it was declared that a neutral ship carrying enemy goods was liable to confiscation as well as the cargo. This was followed by an Édit of 1584, declaring neutral goods in an enemy ship lawful prize.[1] In 1650 the latter Édit was repealed by a Royal Declaration, granting the freedom of neutral goods in enemy ships; and after this date France also pretended to relax the severity of the Édit of 1543 by entering into several treaties, granting the principle "free ship free goods," the acceptance of which the Dutch were making strenuous efforts at that time to secure. These relaxations on the part of France did not, however, represent her real policy, for in the midst of these treaties, and in spite of the Declaration of 1650, the severe regulations of the Édits of 1543 and 1584 were repeated in Louis XIV.'s famous Ordonnance de la Marine of 1681, enacting that neutral property was compromised by association with enemy property and liable to confiscation. Enemy goods confiscated a neutral ship, and an enemy ship confiscated neutral goods. "Robe de l'ennemi confisque celle de l'ami."

With loss of power France was content to abandon some of her high belligerent pretensions, and by an

_{Sixteenth century.}

_{Seventeenth century.}

_{Eighteenth century.}

[1] To be quite accurate, the Édit declared the goods of French "subjects or allies" on enemy ships to be lawful prize. But by interpretation it was extended to neutral goods, *i. e.* the Édit was taken to mean that all goods on an enemy ship, *even* those of a subject or an ally, were to be liable to confiscation.

s

Ordonnance of 1744 declared a neutral ship carrying enemy goods to be free, though the goods continued liable to seizure. This was a partial return to the doctrine of the Consolato del Mare, but by a Règlement of 1778 enemy goods on a neutral ship were freed from liability to capture. In 1778, therefore, France adopted the Dutch principle "free ship free goods," at the same time retaining the other half of her own doctrine, *i. e.* "enemy ship enemy goods," which it may be observed she never formally abandoned until the beginning of the Crimean War in 1854.

In 1793, at the outbreak of the revolutionary wars, France returned to the rule of the Consolato del Mare as regards enemy goods in neutral ships, declaring such goods to be good prize, but the neutral ship free and entitled to freight. But the tale of her inconsistencies was not yet complete. Under Napoleon she threw all principles to the winds. By his Berlin Decree, 1806, Napoleon decreed the confiscation of all neutral vessels and property in any way connected with British commerce; and by the Milan Decree, 1807, declared *all* vessels submitting to search by British cruisers, which they had neither the right nor the power to resist, to be lawful prize. These were simply acts of wrongful might, and after her humiliation in 1815, France reverted once more to the principle of "free ship free goods."

From that date until 1854 she maintained this principle, and embodied it in a number of treaties, inconsistently retaining at the same time her old doctrine of "enemy ship enemy goods."

It may be briefly noted in passing, that Spain has closely followed the lead of France. She adopted the regulations of the French Ordonnance de la Marine of 1681, and re-enacted them by various ordinances in the eighteenth century. Like France, she gave her adhesion to "free ship free goods" in 1780, at the same time upholding "enemy ship enemy goods"; and, not being a party to the Declaration of Paris, probably adheres to the latter principle in theory at the present day, though it is unlikely that she would be able to actively assert it in a modern war.

In the middle of the seventeenth century the Dutch commenced to promote a new doctrine, making the cargo follow the flag. "Free ship free goods; enemy ship enemy goods." They did not assert their doctrine as a right, but endeavoured to obtain its concession by treaties as a privilege. Their statesmen and jurists alike recognized the rule of the Consolato del Mare to be the accepted principle of the law of nations. But as a maritime and mercantile nation, the Dutch perceived that the right of carrying the trade of all states at war would be a very valuable concession for neutrals when war was the rule and peace the exception in Europe. This concession, says Hall, they "steadily kept before their eyes as an object to be striven for, to such purpose that they induced Spain, Portugal, France, England, and Sweden to grant or confirm the privilege in twelve treaties between the years 1650 and 1700." Spain was the first country to grant it by a treaty in 1650, and similar treaties with Portugal and France quickly followed. Cromwell refused the Dutch terms in 1654, and concluded a treaty with them confirming the ancient English practice; but in three later treaties in Charles II.'s reign England conceded the privilege of the neutral flag to Holland. At first the principle of "free ship free goods" was always accompanied by its converse, "enemy ship enemy goods." In fact, the consideration offered by the Dutch for the neutral privilege was the belligerent right of seizing neutral goods in enemy ships. As, however, all neutral subjects were likely to prefer to trust their goods to the absolute security of

Dutch practice.

Its early history.

neutral bottoms, the proffered sacrifice of neutral property in enemy ships was not a very substantial consideration.

> "In matters of commerce the fault of the Dutch
> Is giving too little and asking too much."

The two principles did not really depend upon each other, and were soon separated. "Free ship free goods" became the great neutral watchword. "Enemy ship enemy goods" merely continued as representing the exceptional practice of France.[1]

The Silesian Loan.

In the case of the Silesian Loan, Frederick the Great claimed that the English had wrongfully seized Prussian vessels carrying enemy cargoes on the ground that "free ship free goods" was the acknowledged principle of the law of nations. This proposition was easily disposed of by the English Government in the State Paper dealing with the Prussian claims. (Cf. Part I. chap. v. p. 59.)

The first Armed Neutrality.

In 1780 the first Armed Neutrality adopted the principle "free ship free goods" whilst rejecting that of "enemy ship enemy goods." The declaration of the Armed Neutrality was directed against England as the alleged aggressive upholder of belligerent rights, and, as English practice, based upon the true rule of International Law, had always amply recognized the freedom of neutral goods in enemy ships, neutrals had no demand to make upon that account. The Armed Neutrality remained silent therefore as to neutral goods in enemy ships.

The Declaration of Russia was not originally aimed especially against England, but it was acceded to by the Baltic powers, by France and Spain in direct controversion

---

[1] The French and Dutch doctrines may be reduced to these formulæ:—

French. Enemy ship makes enemy goods;
Enemy goods make enemy ship.
Dutch. Free ship makes free goods;
Enemy ship makes enemy goods.

of their own doctrine, and by other countries, out of hostility to England.

How little these nations were influenced by principle is evidenced by the fact that all of them, without exception, on the first opportunity of becoming belligerents, gave up the principles which they had laid down as neutrals and returned to their former practice.

The second Armed Neutrality, in 1800, was due, even more than the first, to hostility towards England, Sweden and Denmark having fallen foul of the English doctrines of search and convoy. It re-asserted the declaration of its predecessor, that enemy goods on neutral ships should be free except contraband. War followed, chiefly owing to the claim laid by the Czar Paul, who was mad, to the island of Malta recently ceded to England. Thanks to Nelson at Copenhagen, and the assassination of the Czar, the second Armed Neutrality was short-lived, and once more its members found no difficulty in laying aside their "principles," the treaty between England and Russia in 1801, to which Denmark and Sweden afterwards acceded, providing that enemy goods in neutral ships should be liable to capture and confiscation. *The second Armed Neutrality.*

A sketch of the history of the principle "free ship free goods" would be incomplete without some account of the attitude adopted towards it by one other great maritime power, the United States. On the outbreak of the French revolutionary wars the United States declared that the English doctrine of capture was that of the law of nations, and that the Dutch principle, "free ship free goods," only subsisted between particular states in virtue of particular treaties. The United States further declared that they had concluded such treaties with France (1780), Holland (1782), Sweden (1783), and Prussia (1785), and were willing and anxious to enter into similar engagements with other nations. Upon this declaration of law *Attitude of the United States.*

and policy the United States have acted consistently ever since. American statesmen, diplomatists, judges, and writers have recognized, over and over again, with unbroken unanimity the rule of the Consolato del Mare, *i. e.* the English doctrine, to be the undoubted rule of International Law. At the same time, the United States Government has in the course of this century entered into a number of treaties embodying the principle " free ship free goods."

It is true that, as a belligerent, the United States has occasionally put forward remarkable pretensions. The affair of the *Trent*, the Alabama Claims, and the application of the doctrine of continuous voyages, will be recalled as examples of attempts to extend belligerent rights as against neutrals. But on the whole it is fair to say that the general policy of the United States has been to uphold neutral privilege.

State of the law in 1854. In 1854, at the commencement of the Crimean War, the position was briefly as follows:—

England still held, as she had ever done, to the rule of the Consolato del Mare.[1] France adhered to the principles "free ship free goods" (favouring neutrals) and "enemy ship enemy goods" (favouring belligerents). This, it will be observed, was the old Dutch doctrine as originally introduced in 1650.

On entering into alliance it seems to have been considered necessary to arrange some compromise between the English and French practice.[2] [France agreed to abandon the relic of her old belligerent pretensions, the

---

[1] England has so thoroughly identified herself with this rule, and upheld it so consistently until the Crimean War, that it is commonly and conveniently called the "English rule of capture."

[2] The necessity is not altogether apparent, seeing that no attempt was made to reconcile other inconsistencies between English and French practice, notably as regards the law of blockade.

principle "enemy ship enemy goods," whilst Great Britain *accepted provisionally*, for that present war, the Franco-Dutch principle "free ship free goods," but in so doing expressly declared that she "waived a part of the belligerent rights appertaining to her by the Law of Nations."

The war was brought to an end by the Treaty of Paris, and a Declaration appendant to that Treaty was signed on April 16, 1856, by the Plenipotentiaries of Great Britain, Austria, France, Prussia, Russia, Sardinia, and Turkey.

<small>The Declaration of Paris, 1856.</small>

That Declaration adopted two principles.

From the French doctrine it took the part most favourable to neutrals—"that enemy goods in a neutral ship are free except contraband." And from the English rule it likewise took the part most favourable to neutrals —"that neutral goods in an enemy ship are free except contraband."

The two other provisions of the Declaration were to the effect that privateering is and remains abolished, and that blockade in order to be binding must be effective.

The Declaration is, in short, the Magna Charta of neutral privilege, and England by becoming a party to it renounced the ancient right of capturing enemy goods in neutral ships which she had maintained and exercised for centuries.

It has been already seen, that maritime states such as Holland and the United States, whilst recognizing the English rule to be the undoubted rule of law, had pursued the policy of securing by treaty the immunity of the neutral flag; and the interests of probably every other state except England lay in the same direction. Therefore it is not surprising to find that the Declaration of Paris has secured the adherence of every civilized state except the United States, Spain, Mexico, and Venezuela.

The United States were unable to agree to the abolition

of privateering unless all the other states would consent to concede the total immunity of all private property from capture at sea in time of war. They regarded privateering as the most effective weapon of defence for the weaker maritime powers, and one which relieved them from the pressure of maintaining large standing navies in time of peace. Therefore they have not as yet acceded to the Declaration.

It cannot, however, be denied that, although not an entirely unanimous international act, the Declaration of Paris is of sufficient authority to determine for the present the conduct of maritime warfare as affecting neutral property at sea.

CHAPTER VIII

THE RIGHT OF VISIT AND SEARCH

A BELLIGERENT has the right, within the limits described below, to visit and search every merchant ship at sea in time of war, whatever flag it may be flying, in order to ascertain what is the true character of both ship and cargo, and of the trade in which they are engaged. This right has existed undisputed from the earliest times, and is admitted by all English, American, and Continental writers of any distinction, not excluding such prejudiced and strenuous upholders of neutral privilege as Hübner and Hautefeuille. <small>Object of the right.</small>

It is for the very purpose of satisfying search that every merchant vessel is bound by the municipal law of her own country to carry papers, which render her character and that of her cargo certain. Hence it is that Bynkershoek says, "Velim animadvertas licitum esse amicam navem sistere, ut non ex fallaci forte aplustri sed *ex ipsis instrumentis in navi repertis* constet navem amicam esse." These papers differ slightly according to the laws of various countries, and this very difference makes them the clearest possible evidence of the nationality of the ship. <small>Ships' papers.</small>

In English practice a ship's papers include the register, specifying the owner of the ship and its name and tonnage, the passport or sea-letter issued by a neutral state in time of war, the muster-roll containing the names and descriptions of the ship's company, the charter-party if the ship is chartered, the invoices of the cargo, a duplicate copy of the bill of lading, and the ship's log kept by the captain. The papers which other states require their ships to carry are, speaking generally, of a very similar character.

In time of peace.

The right of visit and search is essentially a belligerent right, and may not be exercised in time of peace except upon reasonable ground of suspicion that the ship is a pirate, against whom all warlike measures are always lawful, or in virtue of a treaty, as, for example, the Treaty of Washington, 1862, by which Great Britain and the United States agreed to concede a mutual right of visit and search in certain latitudes where there was reasonable ground to believe that the flags of the two countries were being used by vessels to cover the African slave trade. This agreement did not of course give British cruisers a right to search vessels flying any foreign flag except that of the United States, and *vice versâ*.

There is no real distinction between visit and search, although it has been hinted (rather than stated) by some authorities that there is a right of visit, or what the Americans call a "right of approach," as distinct from search, in time of peace. If this means that vessels may approach each other and ask questions by means of signals, etc., it hardly requires stating as a rule of law, but the contention that any right of visit can be exercised in time of peace, except upon suspicion of piracy or in virtue of a treaty, as above stated, is altogether unsound.

In time of war.

The right may be exercised in time of war by all belligerent public vessels, and formerly also by privateers, but not by ordinary private vessels. They may search all merchant vessels in their own or in enemy territorial waters, or upon the high sea; everywhere, that is, except in neutral territorial waters.

The warship approaches the merchant vessel, hoists her flag, and fires a gun, called the "semonce" or "affirming gun," warning the latter to heave to. She then sends an officer on board, who examines the ship's papers, and, if there are any circumstances of suspicion, the ship and cargo as well. If there is no ground for suspecting fraud the ship is of course permitted to continue on her voyage. But if she resists search, or if, having submitted to search, her papers are found to be fraudulent or unsatisfactory, she may be captured and taken in for adjudication. So also if she has no papers at all, or if she destroys or conceals them, "spoliation" or concealment creating a strong presumption of fraud. The lawful exercise of the right extends to ships and property, but not to persons on board ships. *Mode of exercise.*

Objects of search.

In 1812 there were a great number of English sailors serving on American merchant vessels, and Great Britain claimed the right to search such vessels, and press British seamen found in them into service in the Royal Navy. The United States resisted this claim, and war resulted. It must be admitted that this was an unwarrantable extension of the right of search on the part of Great Britain, and though impressment for the navy is not obsolete, no attempt is likely to be made in future to press British seamen serving in neutral merchant vessels by means of search.

The action of Great Britain in 1812 may be partly explained by the fact that the United States based their objection on the theory that a private vessel on the high sea is territory, and search therefore a violation of neutral territory, a fiction which Great Britain has always uncompromisingly rejected. The theory was first put forward by Prussia to support its claim in the Silesian Loan; but the law as to contraband and breach of blockade in time of war, and the fact that a private vessel is subject to local jurisdiction in a foreign port in time of peace, are sufficient to demonstrate that it is a mere fiction.

It is not a harsh right.

The right as lawfully exercised in time of war must not be considered an aggressive right against neutrals. As Wheaton very justly points out, the right exists to determine the character of a vessel which is *unknown*. The neutral flag under which she very probably sails is no guarantee of her neutral character, which can alone be tested by search. Therefore whatever may be the character of a ship or her cargo, she is liable to search.

Resisting search.

If she is an enemy ship she will resist, and resistance on her part is fully justified, for, as Sir William Scott put it, "lupum auribus teneo, and if he can withdraw himself he has a right to do so." Hence, if an enemy ship is captured resisting search, confiscation will not extend to her cargo if the latter is neutral. Whereas, if the master of a neutral ship resists search, he is not acting within his rights, and if captured both ship and cargo become liable to confiscation.

The above principles as to resistance of search by individual enemy or neutral merchant vessels are universally accepted. Where, however, neutral property is confided to the care of an *armed* belligerent ship, whether as part of its cargo, or in the case of belligerent convoy, a difference of doctrine has arisen between Great Britain and the United States. And in the case of convoy proper —where a number of neutral merchant vessels sail under the convoy of a man-of-war of their own country, the belligerent right of search for which England has always contended has been disputed by various Continental powers.

Right of search disputed. A. By United States. (1) Neutral property on armed belligerent ship. (2) Neutral vessel in belligerent convoy. B. By continental powers. (3) Neutral vessel in neutral convoy. Neutral property on armed enemy vessel.

(1) And first of all with regard to single ships.

It has been already seen that neutral goods loaded on an unarmed enemy merchant vessel which resists search are regarded as free from confiscation in the practice of all nations, including England and the United States. But the case of neutral goods loaded on an *armed* enemy vessel is different.

In American practice such goods are also held to be free from confiscation; whereas they are condemned by English courts on the ground that their owner by loading them on such a ship betrays an intention to resist search, and therefore his property acquires an enemy character.

<small>United States.</small>

<small>England.</small>

Public vessels may be dismissed from consideration. No right of search can be exercised over vessels of war, and therefore neutral property found on enemy public vessels is condemned not for actual or constructive resistance to search, but because the property on board a public vessel shares its fate as a matter of course. The captor is entitled to assume that it is enemy property, and is not bound to inquire into its character.

<small>Public vessels.</small>

But in the case of neutral property placed on armed enemy private vessels, there is certainly constructive resistance to search, and very often actual resistance as well.

<small>Armed private vessels.</small>

The two following cases explain and illustrate the divergent practice of the English and American courts.

The "Fanny." (1 Dods. Adm. Rep. 443.)

<small>Cases.</small>

In 1814, during the war between Great Britain and the United States, the *Fanny*, a British privateer,[1] with a cargo consisting partly of Portuguese property, was captured by an American cruiser. She was subsequently recaptured, and the captors claimed salvage in the English court in respect of the Portuguese property, on the ground

---

[1] The *Fanny* was, in fact, a merchant vessel furnished with a letter of marque ; but Sir W. Scott stated in his judgment, that the distinction which once existed between such a vessel and a privateer, the latter being entitled to head-money and the former not, had been entirely done away.

that it would have been liable to condemnation by the United States court as neutral property found on an armed enemy vessel.

<small>Sir William Scott.</small> Sir William Scott held that a neutral subject may put goods on board a merchant vessel belonging to one belligerent without giving the other belligerent a right to condemn the property. "But if the neutral puts his goods on board a *ship of force*, which he has every reason to presume will be defended against the enemy by that force, the case then becomes very different. He betrays an intention to resist visitation and search, which he could not do by putting them on board a mere merchant vessel, and so far as he does this he adheres to the belligerent; he withdraws himself from his protection of neutrality, and resorts to another mode of defence; and I take it to be quite clear that if a party acts in the association with a hostile force, and relies on that force for protection, he is *pro hac vice* to be considered an enemy."

The usual salvage to the recaptors was accordingly decreed.

The "*Nereide.*" (9, Cranch, 388.)

In 1813, during the same war, the *Nereide*, a British merchant vessel mounting ten guns, was chartered by a neutral subject, and sailed with a cargo partly neutral under convoy of a British man-of-war for Buenos Ayres. She became separated from her convoy, and was captured after a conflict by an American privateer. The neutral portion of the cargo was condemned by the District Court of New York, the condemnation being affirmed by the Circuit Court. On appeal this sentence was reversed in the Supreme Court by a majority of two judges to one, <small>Chief Justice Marshall.</small> and Chief Justice Marshall laid down, in effect, that a neutral may lawfully employ an armed belligerent vessel to transport his goods, and that such goods do not lose their neutral character by the armament, nor by the resistance made by such a vessel, provided the neutral do not aid in such armament or resistance, and even although he charter the whole vessel, and be on board at the time of the resistance.

In answer to the argument that a neutral subject, by loading his property on an armed belligerent vessel, withdraws it from search and connects himself with the enemy in such a way as to affect his property with a hostile character, the Chief Justice said, "If the property be neutral, what mischief is done by its escaping a search? In so doing there is no sin even as against the belligerent if it can be effected by lawful means. The neutral cannot justify the use of force or fraud, but if by means, lawful in themselves, he can escape this vexatious procedure, he may certainly employ them. . . . The object of the neutral is the transportation of his goods. His connection with the vessel which transports them is the same *whether that vessel be armed or unarmed.*"

That is the essence of the American doctrine on this point. By the law of nations, they said, neutral goods on an enemy ship are free, and whether the ship is armed or unarmed is immaterial.

Mr. Justice Story in his dissenting judgment upheld in the clearest and most unmistakable language the British doctrines with reference to search and convoy. He argued that if a neutral ship by accepting the convoy of a neutral armed vessel is guilty of constructive resistance to the belligerent (see below as to neutral convoy), *a fortiori* the same guilt attaches to him if he accept the convoy of an armed ship belonging to one of the belligerents.[1]

Mr. Justice Story.

---

[1] It may be remarked that the *Nereide*, though she started under belligerent convoy, was not a case of a neutral vessel in belligerent convoy, but of an armed enemy merchant vessel carrying neutral goods. The immunity claimed by the Americans for a neutral ship in belligerent convoy was based upon precisely the same principle

"In the latter case," he said, "it is necessarily known to the convoyed ships that the belligerent is bound to resist, and will resist until overcome by superior force. It is impossible, therefore, to join such convoy without an intention to receive the protection of a belligerent force in such manner and under such circumstances as the belligerent may choose to apply to it." He referred to the dispute between the United States and Denmark as to belligerent convoy, approving of the principles laid down by the Danish Government, which were identical with the doctrine upheld by Great Britain. And he went on to say, "On the whole, on this point my judgment is, that the act of sailing under belligerent or neutral convoy is of itself a violation of neutrality, and the ship and cargo if caught *in delicto* are justly confiscable; and further, that if resistance be necessary, *as in my opinion it is not*, to perfect the offence, still that the resistance of the convoy is to all purposes the resistance of the associated fleet."

In this divergence of English and American practice it may perhaps be submitted, that the English doctrine, supported as it is by such a weight of authority as the names of Sir William Scott, Mr. Justice Story, and Chancellor Kent combine to carry, is the correct legal principle.

Neutral ships in belligerent convoy.

(2) The next point to consider is the question of belligerent convoy. The American principle, that the

---

as the immunity they claimed for a neutral cargo on board a belligerent armed ship. It was, in fact, only a wider application of the same principle, viz. that neutral property protected by a belligerent ship (armed or unarmed) is not liable to condemnation by the other belligerent.

The greater includes the less, and Mr. Justice Story's argument as to belligerent convoy consequently covers the case of a neutral cargo loaded on a belligerent armed vessel.

protection of a belligerent armed ship does not affect its neutral cargo with an enemy character, was extended, by an easy expansion, into a claim that the protection of a belligerent armed ship does not impose an enemy character upon a fleet of neutral merchantmen under its convoy. (See footnote above, p. 271.) In this contention it has been already seen that the United States had not the support of one of the most distinguished judges that has ever adorned the Bench of their own or of any other country. ^{United States.}

The doctrine of the English courts as to belligerent convoy was, similarly, an expansion or rather a corollary of the doctrine they held concerning neutral goods in an armed enemy vessel. Just as a neutral cargo on board an armed enemy vessel was liable to confiscation for resisting search, so also were neutral ships sailing under an armed enemy convoy. ^{England.}

The circumstances of the dispute between the United States and Denmark as to belligerent convoy, to which reference has been already made, were briefly as follows:— ^{Dispute between United States and Denmark.}

During war between Great Britain and Denmark in 1810 many American merchantmen engaged in the Russian-American trade placed themselves under the convoy of British men-of-war in the Baltic. Denmark thereupon issued an ordinance declaring all neutral vessels availing themselves of belligerent convoy to be good prize. Several American vessels were captured and condemned by the Danish courts.

In negotiations that ensued the United States contended, that the presumption that a merchant vessel in enemy convoy is itself an enemy vessel, is one which may be rebutted by evidence; and that, if proved to be a neutral ship, it is no more liable to confiscation for being under enemy convoy than are neutral goods on an enemy ship, whether armed or unarmed, which resists search.

The Danish Government, on the other hand, upheld the

T

English doctrine as expressed in the Danish Ordinance, and maintained that an intention to resist search was sufficiently manifested by a neutral ship which joined a belligerent convoy, that such a settled intention amounted to actual resistance, and that a neutral ship acting in such a manner ranged itself upon the side of the enemy and abandoned its neutral character.

Twenty years later the dispute was settled by a treaty, under which Denmark, whilst expressly declaring that its concession was not to be regarded as a precedent, paid an indemnity to the United States for the Amercian property which had been seized.

Wheaton alone of American jurists, who in fact negotiated the treaty just mentioned, upholds the doctrine of the United States Government; Kent and other American authorities regarding the English doctrine as unquestionable.

If to this fact be added the extract from the judgment of Mr. Justice Story in the *Nereide*, quoted above, there appear to be good grounds for submitting that the American doctrine as to belligerent convoy is unsound. It is also apparent that if the main doctrine as to the immunity of a neutral cargo on a belligerent armed ship is, as has been already submitted, erroneous, its corollary as to belligerent convoy must necessarily be likewise condemned.

Neutral ships in neutral convoy.

(3) The third question to be determined is, under what circumstances the right of search may be excluded by neutral convoy?

English doctrine.

The ancient doctrine, to which Great Britain has always adhered, is that the presence of a neutral man-of-war with a fleet of the merchant vessels of its country does not exempt the latter from the belligerent right of search; and that the so-called "*right* of convoy" has no existence except in virtue of a treaty between two states mutually conceding that right.

The contrary doctrine, of a later origin, is to the effect that the declaration of the officer in command of the ship of war, that the vessels under his convoy and their cargoes have no taint of enemy character, exempts all the vessels from search. Continental doctrine.

This right of convoy was first claimed as a neutral right existing independently of treaty by Queen Christina of Sweden in 1653, during war between England and the United Provinces. It was revived by the Dutch in 1759, in order to attempt to cover their trade between France and her colonies, which was prohibited by the Rule of 1756. And in the American War of Independence they again asserted the existence of this right.

In both those wars, however, England maintained her previous practice, and Dutch merchantmen, whether under convoy or not, were subjected to search.

Towards the end of the eighteenth century Russia, Sweden, and the other Baltic powers accepted the principle of the immunity of convoyed vessels from search, and embodied it in various treaties amongst themselves. The mere existence of these treaties of course shows that the parties to them knew themselves to be adopting an exceptional usage, and they are the best possible evidence of the *primâ facie* liability of convoyed neutral vessels to search.

The new doctrine very soon brought its upholders into conflict with England.

The "Maria." (1, C. Rob. 340.)

In January 1798, a British squadron fell in with a Swedish frigate in the Channel with a number of Swedish merchantmen under her convoy. War was at that time going on between England and France, and both the frigate and the merchantmen had instructions from their government to resist search. On the Swedish Commander refusing to allow search, the British squadron followed and England and Sweden.

took possession of most of the Swedish vessels in the night. They were eventually brought in for adjudication, the *Maria* being one of them. Sir William Scott in his judgment laid down, in effect, that the right of search is an incontestable belligerent right, and one which can only be excluded in the case of convoy by express agreement between particular states. Both the ship and cargo were accordingly condemned.

England and Denmark.
This case was followed by disputes with Denmark on the same subject. In 1799 the Commander of a Danish convoy fired on the boats of an English search party in the Straits of Gibraltar. In this case the Danish convoy was not captured, but on complaint to the Danish Government the latter denied the right of a belligerent to search merchantmen under neutral convoy, and maintained that reparation was due not from but to Denmark. In 1800 the *Freya*, a Danish frigate convoying six merchantmen, refused to submit to British search in the Channel, and the whole of the vessels were captured.

The negotiations that followed this occurrence led to a temporary convention in August 1800, by which Denmark agreed to suspend her convoys until some definite arrangement could be made between the two countries.

The second Armed Neutrality.
The hostility of the Baltic powers to the rule of search, together with other circumstances, led to the formation of the second Armed Neutrality. This combination, whilst reiterating all the principles maintained by its predecessor of 1780, added to them, with reference to convoy, the principle, that the declaration of an officer commanding a ship in charge of a convoy of merchant ships, that the latter have no contraband on board, is final and excludes search.

Denmark, by joining the second Armed Neutrality in December 1800, broke her convention of the preceding August, and England declared war. That war came to a speedy termination with Nelson's great victory of Copenhagen, April 2, 1801.

By the treaty of June 1801, between England and Russia, and by treaties with Sweden and Denmark embodying the same terms in 1802, the English rule of search was adopted, but, in consideration of the three Baltic powers abandoning their principle of " free ship free goods " (cf. *supra*, p. 261), in a somewhat modified and softened form. It was agreed that the right of search should only be exercised by public vessels, and should not extend to privateers; and that ships under neutral convoy should only be subjected to search upon reasonable ground for suspicion. This compromise was terminated by other treaties in 1812 and 1814, and the Baltic powers returned to their former principle.

Since 1815 many treaties have been concluded by various states, except Great Britain, stipulating for the freedom of convoyed merchant vessels from search. At the present day France, Germany, Austria, Spain, Italy, and the Baltic powers have adopted this principle, and provide by their naval regulations that the declaration of a convoying officer exempts the vessels under convoy from search. *Present policy of nations.* *Continent.*

England alone still maintains the ancient doctrine upon which her practice has been always based. *England.*

With regard to the United States, American judges, as evidenced by Mr. Justice Story's judgment in the *Nereide*, and American writers such as Kent and Wheaton, are fully in accord with the ancient English practice, both as to search and neutral convoy. But, as has been noticed in the last chapter in the case of enemy goods in neutral ships, it has been the policy of the United States Government to abandon what it recognizes to be the correct principle of International Law, and to adopt by its treaties a principle more favourable to neutral interests. *United States.*

The immunity of convoy has accordingly been the

subject of United States treaties with Sweden and Italy, and various South American states.

<small>Objections to the alleged right of convoy.</small> Search being a belligerent's only means of testing the character of merchant vessels and their cargoes, it seems clear that the right of convoy, if it exists, may be so exercised so as to defeat all belligerent rights at sea.

Even if it be exercised honestly, and *a fortiori* if it be exercised dishonestly by neutral nations, all neutral vessels by sailing under convoy will escape search, belligerents will regard with distrust "an innocence which cannot be tested," and occasions of international dispute will be multiplied.

<small>Convoy in future.</small> If a right of convoy were to be asserted apart from treaty in a future naval war, there can be no doubt that Great Britain as a belligerent would be brought into serious collision with many neutral states. It may therefore be regarded as a happy circumstance, that steam has in all probability rendered the system of convoy obsolete. Superior speed having become such an important factor in commercial success, it seems probable that fast merchant steamers, especially if their character and that of their cargoes is innocent, will prefer to make their voyage alone, and will take their chance of being stopped for search instead of joining a convoyed fleet whose speed is only the speed of its slowest member. If a ship and its cargo are innocent it has nothing to apprehend from search, although the exercise of this right may occasion some slight annoyance and some small delay. A belligerent's superior need certainly entitles him to expect that neutral states, in fulfilment of their duty of sufferance, will not make use of convoy to defeat his acknowledged right of search.

On the whole, it seems that a right of convoy would now only be of actual advantage to neutral merchant steamers if their states exercised that right *dishonestly* (*e.g.* to cover contraband trade, or to protect vessels on their way to break blockade), and it is necessary to assume that this would not be the case.

The conclusion is, that the right of convoy, whilst distinctly injurious to belligerents, is not likely to be of any great commercial advantage to neutrals in the modern conditions of maritime commerce. It cannot be said to ever have been an authoritative rule of International Law, and the circumstances indicated appear likely to prevent its ever attaining such authority.

Assuming a neutral ship to have been captured for resisting search, or on the ground of the fraudulent or unsatisfactory character of her papers, the following consequences ensue.

Procedure on capture for resisting search.

The captor must bring her in with all reasonable care and speed for adjudication. If he fails to exercise due care to preserve the ship and her cargo from loss or damage, or makes unnecessary delay in bringing her in, he will lose his costs and expenses, and is also liable to penalties for negligence.

Property in neutral ships and goods is not transferred by mere capture, and until she is duly condemned by a Prize Court she accordingly remains neutral property. It is for this reason that, if she is destroyed at sea instead of being brought in for adjudication, the neutral owner gets full restitution in value, and English courts give him costs and damages as well.

The crew must not be treated as prisoners of war as they would be if belligerents, and if maltreated in any way can recover damages. If detained as witnesses they are kept at the cost of the captor's state; otherwise they are handed over to the consul of their state to be sent home.

CHAPTER IX

ENGLAND AND THE DECLARATION OF PARIS

IN times past a naval war has been fought out by the means of battles between armed vessels and attacks upon the enemy's commerce. The Declaration of Paris, therefore, which regulates the capture of private property at sea, provides for the conduct of what will be shown to be the most important branch of naval warfare.

It is proposed to consider in this chapter how England's interests will be affected in a future naval war by the provisions of the Declaration, and what should be her future policy with regard to them.

Under those provisions a belligerent cruiser may only seize enemy ships, and, if possessed of an enemy character, their cargoes, but may not touch a neutral ship or its cargo unless it is guilty of unneutral conduct, such as carrying contraband, breaking blockade, or resisting search.

This law which enables a belligerent to carry on his ordinary trade unmolested by the enemy, by transferring it to the security of a neutral flag, was made simply for the benefit of neutral states. That it tells enormously in favour of the lesser maritime powers when neutral, and of belligerent states possessed of no considerable carrying trade, is self-evident; and a little consideration will make it equally clear that England, as a neutral, will reap no marked advantage from it, and will find, as a belligerent, that it has paralyzed her maritime power.

First of all, how will England be affected in the position of a neutral? *England as a neutral.*

English ships in common with the ships of all other neutral states will, subject to the exercise of the right of search, enjoy an immunity from belligerent interference, provided that they do not carry contraband for the use of either belligerent. Therefore, at first sight, the advantages likely to be gained by England seem to be the same as those accruing to every other neutral power.

But England's position is in reality different from that of all other states. In time of peace, she not only carries her own commerce, but also no small portion of that of other nations as well. Her carrying trade is already so enormous, that in war she would have proportionately far less to gain than other neutral states by the transfer of the belligerent's trade to neutral flags. It may indeed be doubted whether England would reap any substantial benefit at all.

It is a matter of common knowledge, that the vast proportions to which English commerce has grown are a source of constant jealousy and hostility amongst most, if not all, foreign nations. It is therefore quite possible that, all neutral ships being equally safe in time of war, if a transfer of belligerent commerce took place, the ships of other neutral countries would be preferred to those of England. Even if this were not so, and England obtained her share of the trade diverted by war into neutral bottoms, the comparatively small commercial advantage she would be likely to gain thereby would be infinitesimal when weighed against the absolutely certain national loss which, it will be seen below, the Declaration of Paris would inflict upon her as a belligerent.

England as a belligerent.

The next point to consider, then, is the position of England as a belligerent under the Declaration.

The ancient practice of England has been described in chapter vii. She obtained her maritime supremacy not merely by the brilliant naval victories of her fleets, but by driving her enemy's commerce off the seas. English cruisers and squadrons scoured the seas, and the rule of the Consolato del Mare, upon which England consistently acted, afforded the property of her enemy no protection from association with neutral property. Enemy ships carrying neutral cargoes and enemy cargoes in neutral ships were alike liable to capture, and by exercising this right, and by blockading her enemy's ports, England was able in time of war to ruin and destroy her enemy's commerce, and by that means more than by any other to bring him to terms.

Under the Declaration of Paris, on the other hand, a vigorous attack by England upon her enemy's commerce would very soon drive the latter to seek the security of neutral flags, and England would thenceforth be deprived of what has proved in former times to be her most effective weapon.

The Declaration therefore diminishes England's power of attack. To this it will very possibly be objected, " Why England's more than other states' ? The law is the same for the belligerents on both sides. The rights of all states under the Declaration are the same. England is not deprived of any weapon which is left available to her enemy. English commerce can be protected no less than that of her enemy by temporary transfer to neutral flags."

These objections, however, rest upon the fallacious assumption that the circumstances of England and other countries are identical. This is not the case. The object of this essay is to show that, though her rights under the Declaration are theoretically the same as those of other states, she is prevented by her circumstances, whether as a strong or a weak power, from enjoying the same power of exercising them.

As already stated, England's position is unique. An island of small area compared to her enormous population, she can produce neither sufficient raw material to supply her manufactories nor sufficient food to feed her people. Her very life and existence, therefore, depend upon the raw materials and food supply which she imports; in other words, her very life and existence depend, as no other country's do, upon her ocean commerce and carrying trade.

England's peculiar position.

England imports the necessaries of life; other states chiefly import only its luxuries. Most of the latter can grow enough wheat to feed their populations, and even if the supply ran short, and it became necessary to import food, a complete blockade of all their ports, if such a thing were feasible, could not prevent its importation, because the great extension of railways would enable such states to obtain supplies imported from neutral territory across their land frontiers. England, on the other hand, can only import supplies by sea.

To all other states therefore the temporary transfer of their ocean commerce to a neutral flag, although entailing a very great loss, would not be a matter of life and death; but to England it would mean starvation, ruin, and defeat.[1]

---

[1] One objection may be dealt with in passing. It may be said, "Granted that the loss of her carrying trade would be an enormous blow to England, it would not necessarily result in her being starved out, because she could at least import supplies, as other belligerents would, *in neutral ships*."

The answer is, that not even so would England's food supply be safe. By an extension of the doctrine of "occasional contraband" similar to that propounded by France with reference to China's rice-supply in 1885 (cf. p. 231), England's food supply could be cut off by her enemy if shipped in neutral no less than in English bottoms; and the Declaration of Paris, when likely to operate for the benefit of England, could be rendered ineffective.

It is absolutely imperative for England at all hazards to maintain and keep in her own hands her carrying trade in time of war, and it is the fact that, owing to her peculiar circumstances, she cannot avail herself of the protection which it holds out to belligerent commerce that forms the foundation of England's case against the Declaration of Paris. It is fatal to her interests as a belligerent because it has enormously increased her vulnerability. It has diminished her power of attack, while leaving her enemy's power of attacking her undiminished.

The Declaration has increased England's vulnerability.

It has diminished her power of attack because her enemy's commerce can find safety in neutral ships, and it has left her enemy's power of attack undiminished, because her own commerce, upon which her wealth, her prosperity, her prestige, and her very existence depend, must necessarily remain under her own flag, and consequently exposed to the enemy's attack.

The case of England against the Declaration is unaffected by her maritime strength or weakness. If her position as a strong maritime power would be untenable in naval warfare under the Declaration, *a fortiori* in proportion as she was weakened by loss of sea power, or by reason of overwhelming foreign combinations, the more desperate would her struggle become.

England's power of attack.

If England should unhappily be engaged in a naval war in the future, it is fair to assume that she will enter upon it in the full possession of the naval supremacy which she has held so long, and which at the present time of writing there seems no reason to anticipate that she will in any way relax her efforts to maintain.

Therefore, as the paramount naval power, holding the command of the sea, she would be able to attack the commerce of any possible single opponent with such success as to drive it within a very short space of time to seek the protection of neutral flags.

Supposing, on the other hand, that England ceased to be the paramount naval power, or that her maritime supremacy were counterbalanced by the combination of two or more powerful maritime states against her, in either case she would cease to have the command of the sea, enabling her to drive her enemy's commerce to take refuge under neutral flags, and enemy commerce as well as English would remain exposed to attack.

Under these circumstances it may be readily conceded that England would have the same power of exercising the right of attack as her enemy. But this "power" would *ex hypothesi* accrue to her in virtue of her impotence!

Let us turn from England's *power of attack* to the other side of the question—her *exposure to attack*.

It is from this point of view that the utter fatality of the Declaration to England's interests as a belligerent can be most clearly seen and appreciated. It seems unnecessary to further elaborate the point that it is impossible for England to transfer her commerce to neutral flags. It is a statement of fact which no serious politician would attempt to deny. If England were driven to such a course it would be a clear proof that she was in extremities, and upon the verge of surrender. As long as England has power of resistance her commerce must and will remain beneath the Union Jack. This being the case, the great question then arises—as to which experts differ—whether England's power of protection is commensurate to the vast proportions of her mercantile marine.

In the first place, let us assume England to occupy her present position of paramount naval power.

Assuming this to be the case, and taking into consideration the extraordinary amount of damage inflicted upon commerce within a very few months by the *Alabama* and *Florida* in the American Civil War, it is a matter for serious doubt whether England, however powerful and

England's exposure to attack.

numerous her fleets and cruisers, would be strong enough to adequately protect her vast and widely scattered commerce in a naval war.[1] She might, and, assuming her to be the paramount naval power, she would be able no doubt to overcome enemy fleets in pitched battles and drive enemy merchant shipping off the sea. But could she possibly prevent a few swift enemy cruisers getting to sea and preying upon English commerce ? Such vessels would be independent of coaling stations, as the coal-bunkers of their prizes would afford them a supply enabling them to keep the sea indefinitely; and though it is reasonable to assume that every such cruiser would ultimately be captured or destroyed, the history of the *Alabama* clearly shows that such vessels during even a brief career would be able to do such an enormous amount of damage as to weaken our prestige, undermine confidence abroad, and thereby strike a deadly blow against our carrying trade. For what would be the result? Parliament might possibly prohibit English goods to be carried on neutral ships, but all neutral goods would undoubtedly be transferred to the absolute safety of neutral bottoms, in order to save war rates of insurance, and to avoid loss by delay arising from capture, to which British ships would be liable. In short, a great part of England's carrying trade would fall away from her, English ships and sailors would

---

[1] It is urged by supporters of the Declaration, that the abolition of privateering enormously reduces the power of weaker maritime states to attack English commerce at sea. Experience has, however, already shown that this provision can be evaded by the creation of a "Volunteer Navy"; and the enemy of England would undoubtedly commission a number of fast volunteer cruisers, which would perform the function of the old privateers without constituting a breach of the Declaration. The change will in reality be little more than one of name. (Cf. Part II. chap. iv. p. 113.) The provision "La course est et demeure abolie" consequently will afford little protection to English commerce in a future naval war.

be out of employ, and a blow would be dealt to capital and industry which would weaken the country more surely and disastrously than a succession of naval defeats.

It is impossible to resist the conclusion that this fate would await England in a naval war, however great her maritime strength might be, and it is almost unnecessary to point out the corollary, that the less power of protection she possessed the more speedily and completely would she lose her carrying trade, and be reduced to impotence and surrender.

It may perhaps be said, with reference to England's power of attack, that owing to the modern internal communication by railway amongst Continental powers already alluded to, the exercise of the right of capturing enemy property at sea has become a far less effective and valuable measure to England than it was in former times, and that she is therefore not greatly prejudiced by being deprived of a weapon whose edge has become blunted. Admitting that there is an element of truth in this, there is still neither justice nor reason in the proposition that England alone should be deprived of the exercise of a right when the circumstances are such that her enemy, so far from being similarly deprived, would find its exercise to be his most valuable weapon!

But, whatever arguments may be raised to show that England's power of attack has not been seriously affected by the Declaration, it is a fact beyond all controversy, that it leaves England more than any other nation exposed to attack, and there is grave reason to fear that its result under all circumstances to England must be the loss of her carrying trade and consequent humiliation and defeat.

The mere fact that the United States are not bound by the Declaration is in itself a circumstance of serious menace to the interests of England as a belligerent, and one which will render one of two events inevitable in the *The relations of England and the United States.*

future—the acceptance by the United States of the Declaration or its repudiation by England.

If England were at war and the United States neutral, England would be justified in excluding the United States from the privileges of the Declaration and capturing her enemy's goods on American ships. This would probably result in sufficient "Yankee bluster" to induce England to concede those privileges to the United States, a concession for which she would receive no consideration whatsoever.

If the United States were at war and England neutral, neither England nor any other neutral state would reap any advantage from the Declaration by which the United States were not bound.

If England were at war with the United States, American commerce would be safe under neutral flags, if England continued to observe the Declaration, whilst English goods on neutral ships would remain liable to capture so long as the United States were not bound by that agreement.

Consequently, except in a war in which both countries were neutral, England would infallibly be the loser so far as her relations with the United States are concerned unless she repudiated the Declaration, a course which, it is submitted, she would sooner or later be obliged to adopt.

Conclusion.
I. It is England's interest to repudiate the Declaration.

The first point then is, that *the safety and welfare of England demand that she should repudiate the Declaration of Paris.* The next question to be settled is, whether England has the right to repudiate it. Could she justify repudiation?

In considering this question, it may be well to briefly recall what has been the attitude of England, as expressed by Parliament, towards the Declaration both at the time when it was first entered into and subsequently.

The Declaration of Paris was signed by Lords Clarendon and Cowley on behalf of England on April 16, 1856.

On May 5, 1856, in the House of Lords, on the Address to the Crown with reference to the Treaty of Peace, Lord Derby said, "The minister sent and trusted by the country to conduct negotiations for restoring peace on certain bases known to the country, took advantage of his position to make an important alteration in the maritime law of England, without the knowledge of Parliament, and without our having the least idea that such our birthright was being given away." It was answered by Earl Grey and Lord Campbell, that it was the prerogative of the Crown to enter into treaties without the advice and assent of Parliament.

Attitude of Parliament towards the Declaration.

In 1856.

On May 6, in the House of Commons, Mr. (afterwards Sir Robert) Phillimore, who had already raised his voice in protest when England provisionally accepted the principle of "free ship free goods" at the beginning of the war in 1854, made a powerful speech in support of the ancient English rule of capture. He said, "It was quite true that the alteration of our ancient law was within the abstract power of the prerogative of the Crown, . . . but it was not the custom of the Crown to make any great change in any great question of public policy without first soliciting and receiving the advice of Parliament. He thought there was the more necessity for such a constitutional course in the present instance, because the public and the Parliament were perfectly unapprised that the question was about to be so summarily and perhaps so irrevocably disposed of."

Lord Palmerston in reply said, the only question was whether the policy of the change was not one which deserved the approbation of a commercial country, and described the Declaration as a "wise and politic measure."

On May 22, 1856, Lord Colchester moved a series of resolutions in the House of Lords, condemning the

U

Declaration, and deeply regretting that the old right of capture "should in the recent conference at Paris have been suddenly abandoned without the previous sanction or knowledge of Parliament by Plenipotentiaries assembled for the purpose of discussing the terms on which peace with Russia might be concluded, and the affairs of the East satisfactorily adjusted."

Lord Derby, in strenuously supporting these resolutions, went so far as to say, " My lords, I look upon this act of the Government as cutting off the right arm, as it were, of the country," and " you have sacrificed the maritime greatness of England."

Lord Clarendon, in defending himself and Lord Cowley, practically confessed that they had exceeded their original attributions, although they were apparently authorized to do so by the Government. He said, " If we had confined ourselves within the strict limits of our attributions, we should have lost an opportunity, when the representatives of the principal powers of Europe were met together, of discussing many important subjects which, although they did not relate to our quarrel with Russia, it was most desirable should be arranged. . . . Lord Cowley and myself did not hesitate—*of course with the consent of her Majesty's Government*—to affix our signatures to a Declaration which changed a policy that we believed it would be impossible, as well as against the interests of England, to maintain."

The resolutions were lost by a majority of fifty-four.

In 1862.
As a consequence of the outbreak of the American Civil War, Mr. Horsfall moved, on March 11, 1862, in the House of Commons, "That the present state of International Maritime Law as affecting the rights of belligerents and neutrals is ill-defined and unsatisfactory, and calls for the early attention of her Majesty's Government." A full and interesting debate on the Declaration of Paris

followed. It was adjourned until March 17, when the motion was by leave withdrawn.

In 1866 and 1867 the subject was again brought before the House of Commons, but no resolution against the Declaration was adopted, no particular question of International Law being before the Powers of Europe at the time.   *In 1866.*

But on April 13, 1875, Mr. Baillie Cochrane moved, "That in consequence of a Conference having been held at Brussels in 1874 on International Law, and the proposed renewal of the Conference this year, a favourable opportunity is afforded to the country of withdrawing from the Declaration of Paris of 1856, and thus maintaining our maritime rights, so essential to the power, prosperity, and independence of the Empire." After a debate, in which Sir William Harcourt (amongst others) opposed the motion, it was not pressed to a division.   *In 1875.*

On March 22, 1878, Sir John Lubbock moved what was practically the same motion as that of 1862 over again, and a debate followed, in which the total abolition of the right of capture and search was advocated as an alternative, or rather perhaps a supplement, to the Declaration of Paris. As in 1862, the motion was by leave withdrawn.   *In 1878.*

Thus it will be seen that Parliament has never directly pronounced against the Declaration by a formal resolution, though there has always been a strong body of opinion adverse to it both in the country and in the House ; and the debates mentioned above, if they have done nothing else, have at all events made it clear that the position of England with regard to the Declaration was not regarded at the time of their occurrence, and cannot yet be regarded, as a question which has been finally settled. It is a question which, so far from being settled, ought to be considered from time to time in connection with the changes and developments which maritime commerce and naval warfare are constantly undergoing.

What, then, are the arguments against the repudiation of the Declaration by England?

Arguments against repudiation.

It will be said that the Declaration was validly and constitutionally entered into by the English Government, and is therefore still binding upon this country; that it has been upheld on many occasions in Parliament, which has always refused to condemn it by an adverse vote; that a treaty is an engagement of a peculiar sanctity; that England has enjoyed the benefits of this particular treaty as a neutral for forty years, and has joined in inviting other states to become parties to it, and cannot therefore now repudiate her obligation with honour; that if she were to attempt to do so she would meet with a storm of opposition, and have to face a renewal of the Armed Neutralities; finally, that her interest as well as her honour is concerned in upholding the Declaration.

England's interest.

The last point has been already dealt with, and it has been submitted that the little England has comparatively to gain as a neutral is not to be weighed against the loss of carrying trade and consequent ruin that would overwhelm her as a belligerent.

The Declaration is valid and binding.

It must of course be admitted that the Declaration is at the present time binding upon England. If it were not, the question of repudiation could hardly arise. It is true that England entered into it somewhat blindly and hurriedly, and that the British Plenipotentiaries had not the mandate of Parliament and the nation to discuss questions of maritime law at all, nor were they originally authorized to do so by the Government; but Lord Clarendon's assertion in the House of Lords that the Declaration was signed with the consent of Her Majesty's Government was unchallenged, and the act of the Government of 1856 therefore still holds good. But that act is not absolutely irrevocable, and if ever the day comes when the people of England—the true political sovereign—make certain and clear demand for its revocation, the Government which serves the people will have to obey its master's voice.

It is also true that England has held by the Declaration —it is believed with little consequent profit—as a neutral in the wars which have occurred during the last forty years; but it is absurd to endeavour to attribute to such passive acquiescence the consequences of a legal estoppel. A far more notable fact is that *England has never yet been a belligerent under the Declaration.* She has never yet been brought fairly face to face with her position, and has not been forced into taking action in the matter. The Declaration has, in fact, never been tested by a great naval war, in which the combatants have been naval powers of the first importance. Consequently England has hitherto refrained from stirring up an international controversy which might disturb the peace of Europe; but no lapse of time, however great, can confer immunity from revocation upon a treaty. *[Lapse of time.]*

It would be unnecessary to point this out, but for the existence of an erroneous idea, that a treaty is a solemn engagement which can never be broken without bad faith.

The peculiar sanctity of a treaty is a matter of sentimental superstition rather than of fact. A treaty is nothing but a public contract, and differs essentially from a private contract only in that it has a moral instead of a legal sanction, and that there exists no International Court to enforce it or set it aside. If a private individual may upon good grounds be released from the burden of his contract without the consent of the other party to it, the logical conclusion is that a public contract may also, *upon good grounds,* be set aside without the consent of the other party or parties to it. *[The sanctity of a treaty.]*

Two obvious questions then arise. Who is the judge as to the existence of good grounds? Can any good grounds be suggested for the repudiation of the Declaration of Paris?

In the absence of any omnipotent International Court, every state must judge for itself whether sufficiently weighty reasons exist to justify it in repudiating any of its public obligations; and it forms that judgment in the full knowledge that it will have to justify its action to the other parties to the contract and to the world at large. No nation courts the ill-will or open hostility of its neighbours by lightly breaking treaties. But it is part of the weakness of International Law, that a state's conduct can only be tested by the sense of equity or fair play possessed by its fellow states; and there is a very great danger that a country which happened to be regarded with general enmity or jealousy would not obtain the strict justice upon which a private individual in a court of law might rely.

Arguments for repudiation. The next question is, what are England's good grounds for repudiating the Declaration of Paris?

It has been asserted, both by writers and speakers, that the Declaration is not in itself a treaty, but merely an appendage to the Treaty of Paris, and consequently of no more binding force than the Declaration in favour of arbitration, which was also appended to that Treaty; that, if it ever was binding, it has ceased to be so, since Russia was allowed in 1870 to break the Treaty to which it was appended by repudiating Articles 11 and 13, restraining Russian action in the Black Sea; lastly, that the Declaration itself was practically broken by Russia in 1875, when she took steps to equip privateers in view of probable war with England. These arguments may, however, be set on one side.

It is the wiser course, as it certainly is the more honest, to base England's case against the Declaration upon arguments untainted by any suspicion of quibble or sophistry. Let it be freely admitted that the Declaration is a valid and binding treaty, and that England is at present still bound by it. Then let England, disdaining any technical subterfuge, boldly assert her right to repudiate it upon the broad single ground of self-preservation. *The true ground for repudiation.*

The Declaration of Paris means utter ruin and irretrievable disaster for England as a naval belligerent, and the right of self-preservation which every state possesses, and which outweighs all its obligations (cf. p. 43), justifies England in cutting herself free from the coils of a treaty which ties her hands and places her at the mercy of her enemy. To sum up the whole argument, England's safety not only demands *but justifies* her repudiation of the Declaration. *Conclusion. II. It is England's right to repudiate the Declaration.*

At the same time, it cannot be denied that such a course on her part would meet with the strongest opposition from the other nations of the world, who are ultimately the judges of her conduct. They are, moreover, not only judges but parties in the case, nearly every state having now acceded to the Declaration; and this is a fact which enormously increases the difficulties of England in freeing herself from its obligation. The Declaration has been commonly regarded on the Continent as a notable triumph over England, and there is the great danger already pointed out, that this country, however righteous its claims, would obtain scant measure of justice from the Court of Nations. It is more than probable that there would, as the supporters of the Declaration assert, be a repetition of the Armed Neutralities, and England might again have to face the world in defence of her rights as she did at the beginning of this century. Yet it can hardly be doubted that she will one day be forced, in self-preservation, to repudiate the Declaration, and the longer she delays doing so the greater expectation she creates among other nations *Foreign opposition.*

that she intends to abide by it, and the greater opposition on the part of neutral states will she encounter when she finally finds herself compelled to take that course.

England's true policy.

The conclusion is obvious. England should act without delay in a time of general peace, and not wait until she is involved in war, when a repudiation of the Declaration would be regarded by neutral states as an act of perfidy, and probably convert them into additional enemies. It is not sought to minimize the difficulties of withdrawing from the Declaration. A government has usually sufficient difficulties and complications to contend with abroad without gratuitously adding to their number. It is content to "let sleeping dogs lie," and to leave this question to be dealt with by the government of some future day when its settlement will brook no longer delay. But one thing at least is certain, and that is, that the longer repudiation is postponed the more will the difficulties which attend it increase.

Two alternatives to the Declaration.

Assuming England to have repudiated the Declaration by fair notice in time of peace—which, it is submitted, is her true policy—it would be possible for her to resume her ancient right of capturing enemy goods on neutral ships, or to proclaim her adhesion to the doctrine of the total immunity of all private property from capture at sea.

The immunity of private property from capture.

Of these two policies the latter has found considerable favour in England since 1856 (*e. g.* Sir John Lubbock's motion in the House of Commons in 1878), because it promises security to England's carrying trade, which has been placed in jeopardy by the Declaration of Paris.

Two fictions.

This doctrine has been somewhat discredited by the arguments which have been used to support it, and especially by the two fictitious theories, previously noticed in these pages, that war is a relation of states and not of individuals (whose property should therefore be untouched), and that a ship is a portion of territory (on which private property is consequently safe).

It has already been pointed out, that the ordinary incidents of land warfare demonstrate the first theory to be a fiction (cf. p. 74). Every individual subject of one belligerent becomes an enemy both in person and property to all the subjects of the other belligerent. Consequently his property is liable to seizure. The adherents of the second theory argue that a neutral ship is a piece of neutral territory, and that as enemy property is safe from capture on neutral territory, it must likewise be secure on a neutral ship. But the immunity of enemy property in neutral territory merely rests upon the fact that it is out of the belligerent's reach, and if the theory is applied to enemy, instead of neutral, ships it ceases to support the immunity of commerce at sea. If a ship is territory, an enemy ship is enemy territory, and neutral goods which can lawfully be captured on enemy territory (because they *are* within belligerent reach) should also be liable to seizure on an enemy ship.

The doctrine has also been supported on the more plausible ground of humanity; but it is difficult to see any reason in such a proposition, because maritime capture is certainly the most bloodless means of bringing an enemy to terms; and if it were entirely abolished, naval warfare would be reduced to duels between armed vessels or fleets, bloodshed would be the only weapon, and so far from humanity being served in any way, war would only become more protracted and more bloody. "How war is to be humanized by shooting at men's bodies instead of taking their property I confess surprises me."—*J. S. Mill*. The plea of humanity.

The United States refused to join in the Declaration of Paris owing to the abolition of privateering, but were willing to agree to such abolition if accompanied by the complete freedom of commerce from capture. They have Practice and opinion.

advanced the doctrine as neutrals and in time of peace, adopting it in a treaty with Italy in 1871, but have shown no disposition as belligerents to relax any of their belligerent rights. In 1866 Austria and Prussia proclaimed the immunity of enemy ships and cargoes on the outbreak of war subject to reciprocity, a precedent followed by Prussia in 1870. The Institute of International Law also adopted two resolutions (in 1875 and 1882) in favour of the immunity of commerce.

Thus it appears that there is some slight body, both of practice and opinion, in favour of the doctrine which might be supposed to tend to procure its acceptance in place of the Declaration of Paris. But it may be doubted whether certain of the weaker maritime states, whose weakness is, in general, likely to keep them neutral, will readily forego the privileges which the Declaration holds out to neutral states, and abandon the opportunity which it gives them of profiting by war to "poach" the carrying trade of the belligerents. Such states would equally resent the adoption of immunity of commerce, and the resumption by England of her ancient right of capture, because either course would deprive them of the chance of acquiring a share of the English carrying trade if England was at war. It therefore seems clear that the argument that England should adopt the doctrine of immunity of commerce, because she could more easily procure its acceptance than that of the ancient rule of capture, is not well-founded.

The doctrine would not be acceptable;

And is impracticable.

Moreover, on all practical grounds the doctrine appears to be objectionable and impossible. It is utterly unreasonable and preposterous that enemy property should be liable to capture on land, in case of invasion, and exempt at sea; and it is impossible to believe that such a doctrine, even if adopted by the world in general, could stand the strain put upon it by the outbreak of actual war. The mischief and danger which would result from the close commercial intercourse of the subjects of the respective belligerents are obvious. In Sir William Scott's words, "a military war and a commercial peace is a thing not yet seen in the world," and the truth of the matter is, that the doctrine is an Utopian dream incapable of realization until the days when "nation shall not lift up sword against nation, neither shall they learn war any more." It is a visionary scheme beyond the pale of practical politics.

On the other hand, the arguments in favour of a return to the ancient rule of capture seem unanswerable and overwhelming. That rule is no shadowy chimera, but a practical rule which has stood the test of some centuries' observance; and it is one which holds the scales far more evenly balanced between the opposing interests of neutrals and belligerents than does the Declaration of Paris or any of the principles described in chapter vii. of this Part, which it has been attempted to substitute for it. *The ancient rule of capture. Practically.*

On moral grounds, maritime capture may be defended as one of the most humane and effective of warlike measures. It conduces to the speedy termination of the war, because it is the only form of hostility which strengthens the captor in proportion as it weakens his adversary. It does not consist in mere waste and destruction. It is no harsher a measure than contributions and requisitions; it is not so harsh as bombardments and other acts of land warfare. It is a formidable weapon which deranges trade, arrests importation of food, deprives the enemy of his naval reserve, and yet causes less individual misery than any other weapon, because "it takes no lives, sheds no blood, imperils no households, and deals only with persons and property voluntarily embarked in the chances of war for the purpose of gain, and with the protection of insurance." *Morally.*

It will be said that the rule of capture favours the strong naval power, and therefore directly ministers to English *An objection.*

aggression. The answer to such a "Little-England" objection is, that a rule which strengthens the hand of England at sea, tends to act as a counterpoise to the "rampant militarism of continental states," and becomes therefore one of the strongest influences which make for peace. J. S. Mill in supporting the old principle of capture used these weighty words—" Above all it is for the interest of the world that the naval powers should not be weakened, for whatever is taken from them is given to the great military powers, and it is from these alone that the freedom and independence of nations has anything to fear." It is therefore to the interest, not only of England, but of the whole civilized world, that the ancient rule should be re-established. It has been seen that the freedom of the neutral flag threatens England with ruin by the loss of her carrying trade, and it has been acknowledged as open to doubt whether England's commerce has not outgrown her power of protecting it in time of war. If this is so, it may be asked, how will England be able to preserve her carrying trade under the ancient rule any more than she could under the Declaration?

<small>Another objection.</small>

This objection is easily disposed of. Of course it is probable that England under the old rule would lose a great many ships by capture. But the value of capture on both sides is not equal. England might lose more ships than her enemy, and yet annihilate the latter's commerce. But in any case, whatever her loss by capture, she would at least *retain her carrying trade.* Under the old rule, an English subject would not forsake his country's ships, because neutral ships would hold out no superior advantages to him. His goods would be equally liable to capture, and he would have to pay the same rate of insurance if they were loaded on a neutral ship as would be the case if they were loaded on a vessel of his own country. In fact, the latter vessel would probably be the safest, because, even if the means of protection were not complete, the presence of English cruisers guarding the trade-routes would render English merchant vessels less exposed to hostile attack than absolutely unprotected neutral vessels carrying enemy goods. English vessels would have the best chance of escaping capture, and also of being re-captured if made prize. And, if this is so, the foreign carrying trade would also not fall away from English ships, because "commerce always seeks the safest ships," and English ships would be in the future under the old rule, as they have been in the past, the safest ships.

But it is not merely the commercial nor even the national interest of England that is concerned in this question. The repudiation of the Declaration of Paris and the restoration of the ancient rule of capture is a policy not only essential to the interests of England, but one which, judged by the standard of utility, will be productive of the greatest good to the majority of states. England's independence and very existence is menaced by the Declaration of Paris, and it cannot be for the general good of all nations that one of them should be extinguished in order to confer a mere commercial advantage upon the rest. Under the Declaration, England's loss as a belligerent is national as well as commercial. The neutral suffers no loss at all, but reaps a commercial gain. *The restoration of the ancient rule* *on the ground of utility.*

Under the ancient rule of capture, neither belligerent nor neutral is prejudiced for the other's benefit. The belligerent fights with his hands free, and his enemy's property cannot escape him by neutral interposition. The neutral has liberty to carry on his trade as in time of peace, and any loss he may suffer by delay, in case of his ship being captured, he can more than recoup by the increased freights he is able to charge. If he suffers any loss at all, it is not a loss of anything he already possesses, but he simply loses the opportunity of making profit out of the necessity of his belligerent neighbour.

<small>For the good of England and the world at large.</small>

To sum up. If England adopts the policy of repudiating the Declaration, and leads the way to a revival of the ancient rule of the Consolato del Mare, she will do so, not only in her own interest, but in the interests of peace and of the general good of the greater number of states in the civilized world.

INDEX

[The Names of Cases are printed in *Italics*.]

Alabama, The, 210, 218
Alabama Claims, The, 186, 192, 208-224
Alcinous v. *Nigreu*, 86
Allies, 88
American Civil War, 51, 175, 186, 200, 206, 230, 240, 246
Amnesty, 164
Amphyktionic League, 12
Analogues of contraband, 101, 232
André, Major, case of, 122
Angary, 139
Anglo-American War, 1812, 149, 267
Antoine v. *Morshead*, 87
Arbitration, 51
Archer, The, 210, 219
Armed Neutralities, The, 32, 228, 241, 253, 260, 261, 276
Armistice, 153
Army Instructions, 30, 132
Assassination, 120
Assignment of ships during war, 102
Asylum, 48, 173
Atalanta, The, 233
Atlas, The, 251
Austin, 4, 5, 41
Austro-Prussian War, 51, 298
Ayala, 21, 22

Bacon, 67, 73
Balance of power, 6, 44, 69, 74
Balloonists, 123
Banda and Kirwee Booty, case of, 142

Barbarous states, 40
Bentham, 3, 38, 53
Bentzon v. *Boyle*, 100, 137
Berlin Congress, 1877, 56
—— Decree, 1806, 242, 255, 258
—— Treaty, 1877, 40
Blockade, commercial and military, 239
—— hostile, 63, 103, 239
—— notified and *de facto*, 243
—— pacific, 62
—— paper, 241
—— penalty for breach of, 247
Bluntschli, 179
Boards of arbitration, 33
Boedes Lust, The, 60, 101
Bombardment, 116
Bons de réquisition, 140
Booty, 141
Bremen Flugge, The, 251
Breviarium, 18
Brussels Conference, 1874, 56, 109, 110, 115, 117, 118, 120, 122, 123, 125, 129, 130, 133, 136, 138, 140, 155, 156, 174
Burke, 56
Burot v. *Barbut*, 6
Bynkershoek, 11, 22, 25, 35, 46, 67, 74, 78, 88, 145, 146, 172, 181, 227, 265

Calvo, 36
Canals, 45
Capitulations, 157
Caroline, The, 237
Cartels, 157
Cartel ships, 87, 157

INDEX

Cessation of hostilities, 152, 159, 161
Charlemagne, 16
Chino-Japanese War, 75, 80, 153
Chivalry, 17, 19, 73
Clarence, The, 210, 219
Cockburn, Sir A., 216, 222
Columbus, 256
Combatants and non-combatants, 107
Commissions, issue of, in neutral states, 193
Confederate States, The, 38, 41, 71, 149, 191
Conquest, 135, 160, 186
Consolato del Mare, 17, 28, 146, 250, 256, 282
Continuous voyages, 230, 246, 252, 262
Contraband, 101, 226
Contracts in time of war, 86
Contributions and requisitions, 140
Convoy, 103, 274
Coutumes d'Amsterdam, 18
Creasy, 35
Crimean War, 79, 88, 90, 151, 191, 242, 246, 250, 254, 255, 258, 262
Cromwell, 58, 259
Crusades, 17, 20, 73

Declaration of war, 77
Devastation, 115
Diplomatic Notes, 30
Divine Law, 5, 22, 25, 27
Domicil, 94
Don Pacifico, case of, 61
Droits of Admiralty, 91
"Due diligence," 192, 204, 221
Duties of abstention, 179
—— prevention, 188
—— sufferance, 225

Effects of war on treaties, 83
—— persons and property, 86
Egypt, 40, 104
Elector of Hesse Cassel, case of, 166
Eliza Ann, The, 80
El Monassir, The, 208
El Tousson, The, 208

Embargo, 50
Emperor and Pope, rivalry of 16, 17
Enemy character, 93
—— persons, 89, 94
—— property, 91, 96, 134, 164
—— territory, 103
Enlistment, 191
Exchange of prisoners, 127
Exterritoriality, 47, 96, 222

Fanny, The, 269
Flad Oyen, The, 145
Flags of truce, 155
Florida, The, 208, 219
Formosa, blockade of, 63, 231, 242
Fortuna, The, 250
Franciska, The, 242
Franco-Prussian War, 51, 79, 90, 110, 113, 116, 130, 132, 133, 136, 139, 143, 149, 151, 166, 181, 183, 191, 195, 206, 246, 298
Francs-tireurs, 110
Freya, The, 276
Friendship, The, 235

Gauntlet, The, 201
General Armstrong, The, 172
Genêt, M., case of, 193
Geneva, Arbitration, 216-224
—— convention of 1864, 7, 31, 56, 74, 84, 120, 129, 132
—— convention of 1868, 133
Gentilis, 3, 18, 21, 22, 67, 78
Georgia, The, 213
Gideon Henfield, case of, 192
Gladstone, 189, 216
Great Britain and the Two Sicilies, 61
Grey Jacket, The, 87
Griswold v. Waddington, 87
Grotius, 3, 14, 18, 19, 20, 21, 22, 25, 27, 34, 36, 46, 53, 67, 71, 73, 74, 78, 115, 146, 227

Hale, Sir M., 81
Hall, 7, 8, 43, 53, 75, 91, 107, 135, 150, 167, 184, 190, 207, 231, 240, 259
Hallam, 22

INDEX 305

Halleck, 8, 49, 179
Harcourt, Sir W., 36, 237, 291
Hautefeuille, 36, 265
Heffter, 36
Heineccius, 227
Hoop, The, 87, 99
Hostages, 131, 150
Hostile expeditions, 194-204
Hübner, 265
Hughes v. Cornelius, 6

Immanuel, The, 252
Immunity of private property from maritime capture, 296
Indian Chief, The, 97
Inherent right of states, 42
Institute of International Law, 7, 56, 63, 298
International, The, 201
International Conference, 56
—— Court of Arbitration, 51, 69
—— Law, classification, 1, 37; definition, 2; nature and title, 8, 10; public and private, 9; history of, 11; sources of, 25
—— persons, 37
—— tribunals, 33
Intervention, 43, 50
Irregular troops, 109

Jameson, Dr., 72, 202
Jenkins, Sir L., 30
Johnson-Clarendon Convention, 214
Jonge-Klassina, The, 99
Jurisdiction, 47
Jus belli, 15
Jus fetiale, 13, 78
Jus gentium, 3, 14, 21
Jus inter gentes, 3
Jus naturale, 14

Kant, 53
Kent, 2, 8, 26, 35, 75, 179, 184, 272, 274, 277
King's chambers, 46

La Santissima Trinidad, 197, 206
Lakes and rivers, 44
Langrel, 115
Lateran Councils, 19, 114
Law of nations, 1, 3, 8

Law of nature, 2, 14, 20, 21, 22, 25, 26
Lawrence, Rev. T. J., vi, 21
Laws of Antwerp, 18
Lee, Sir George, 31, 59
Leges Wisbuenses, 18
Letters of Historicus, 36, 237
Levée en masse, 109, 137
Levies in neutral states, 181
Lex Rhodia, 18
Lex Romana Burgundorum, 18
Licence to trade, 158
Loans to belligerents by neutrals, 182, 189
Lockwood v. Coysgarne, 7
Lois de Westcapelle, 18
London, Conference of 1831, 56
Ludwig, The, 149

Madison, The, 234
Maine, Sir H., 4, 55, 119, 120
Manifestoes, 29, 79
Mare Clausum, 46
—— Liberum, 46
Maréchal de Belleisle, case of, 129, 237
Maria, The (2), 253, 275
Maritime capture, 144, 249
Maritime territory, 45
Marshall, Chief Justice, 34, 270
Mediation, 50
Mentor, The, 168
Milan Decree, 1807, 255, 258
Military combatants, 108
—— occupation, 135
Mill, J. S., 53, 297, 300

Napoleon, 90, 138, 167, 242
National status, 38
Naturalization, 48
Naval combatants, 111
Nayade, The, 88, 97
Negotiation, 49
Neptunus, The, 88
Nereide, The, 270
Neutral cargo on armed enemy vessel, 268
—— duties, classified, 177
—— ports, use of, in war, 205
—— property associated with enemy property, 249   [139
.—— property in enemy country,

INDEX

Neutral rights, 171
—— vessel in belligerent convoy, 272
—— vessel in neutral convoy, 273
Neutrality Act (U.S.A.), 7, 28, 192, 195, 200
Neutrality, history of, 23, 24
Neutralized states, 40
Norwaerts, The, 149

Occasional contraband, 228, 230, 231, 283
Ocean, The, 98
Ordonnance sur la Marine, 1681, 59, 257
Orozembo, The, 235
Ottoman Empire, 38, 40

Paris Congress, 1856, 56
—— Convention, 1873, 53
—— Declaration, 1856, 32, 34, 59, 84, 102, 103, 112, 149, 231, 241, 249, 255, 263, 280-302
—— Treaty of 1763, 23
—— Treaty of 1856, 38, 40, 51, 85, 263
Parole, 131
Passage over territory, 183, 185
Passports, 156
Phillimore, Sir R., 20, 25, 35, 36, 51, 60, 62, 67, 81, 113, 138, 145, 148, 167, 180, 184, 252, 289
Phœnix, The, 100
Pirates, 47, 112, 147
Pope, The, 15, 16, 19
Portalis, M., 74
Portland, The, 99
Positive law, 5
Postliminium, 142, 165
Potts v. Bell, 88
Pre-emption, 229
Prisoners of war, 127
Privateers, 112
Prize, 144
Prize Courts, 6, 23, 33, 148, 186
Property exempt from seizure, 138, 150
Publicists, 34
Public vessels, 111
Puffendorf, 22, 25, 35, 74

Qualified neutrality, 179
Quarter, 124
Questions of prize, 186

R. v. Carlin, 202
R. v. Jameson, 202
R. v. Sandoval, 201
Ransom, 127
Ransom-bills, 150
Rapid, The (2), 87, 234
Rebel provinces, 40
Recapture of prizes, 146
Reprisals, 57, 81
Retortion, 57
Rights of property, 44
Roman Law, 3, 18, 73
Rooles of Oleron, 18
Rousseau's theory of war, 74, 83, 151
Rule of 1756, The, 101, 225, 251
Rules of Peace, The, 1, 19, 37, 41, 176
Russo-Turkish War, 79, 151

Safe-conduct, 156
Safe-guard, 158
Sailing under false colours, 121
St. Petersburg, Declaration of, 1868, 74, 115
Sale of arms by neutrals, 181
Salvador, The, 202
Scott, Sir W., 27, 34, 75, 80, 268, 299
Seizure, 64
Selden, 46
Semi-sovereign states, 39
Seven Years' War, 79
Shenandoah, The, 212, 219
Ships of war constituting hostile expedition, 197
Siam, 63
Sick and wounded, 132
Sieges, 154
Silesian Loan, 59, 91, 260, 267
Sitka, The, 175
Spanish Armada, 78, 174
Spanish Succession, War of, 79
Spies, 121
State Papers, 33
Status quo ante bellum, 160, 165

Statutes:
  4 Henry V., c. 7, 59
  7 Anne, c. 12, 7
  Foreign Enlistment Act, 7, 28, 192, 195, 197, 200, 201
  Magna Charta, 89
  Naval Prize Act, 142, 146, 148
  Statute of Staples, 90
  Territorial Waters Jurisdiction Act, 7, 46
  Treason Act, 88
Story, Mr. Justice, 34, 271, 277
Stratagems, 119
Suarez, 18, 21, 22
Suez Canal, 45, 105
Sumter, The, 207, 213
Supply of troops, etc., by neutrals, 180
Suspension of arms, 152
Swineherd, The, 162
Sybille, The, 119

Tacony, The, 210, 219
Tallahassee, The, 213
Terceira affair, The, 194
Territorial property, 44
Territorial sovereignty, 14, 20, 23, 188
Teutonia, The, 80
Text-writers, 34
Thalweg, 45
Thirlwall, 12
Thirty Years' War, 19, 73, 79, 140
Three rules of the Treaty of Washington, 32, 198, 214
Trading with the enemy, 87
Trading Corporations, 40
Treaties, 31, 83-86
Treaty of peace, 160
Trent, The, 236, 262
Trenga Dei, 12, 53
Triquet v. *Bath*, 6
Truce, 153
Tuscaloosa, The, 212, 219
Tuscarora and *Nashville, The*, 207, 213

Twee Gebroeder, The (2), 185
Twenty-four hours' rule, 207
Union, Confederate, 39
—— Federal, 39
—— Incorporate, 39
Uti possidetis, 135, 160
Utrecht, Peace of, 1713, 23

Valin, 227
Vattel, 35, 49, 68. 115, 120, 122, 145, 181, 184, 227, 237
Venus, The (2), 87, 98
Vienna, Treaty of, 1815, 23, 85
Volunteer cruisers, 113, 286

Walker, 215
War, definitions of, 67; just causes, 67; different kinds, 70; limits to violence in, 73; declaration of, 77; effects of outbreak, 82; conduct of, 106; termination of, 159
Waraker, vi
Warfare against savages, 72, 126
Washington, Treaty of 1846, 52
—— Treaty of 1862, 266
—— Treaty of 1871, 32, 52, 198, 199, 204, 214
Weapons, lawful and unlawful, 113
Wellington, 118
Westlake, 17
Westminster, Treaty of, 1756, 60
Westphalia, Peace of, 1648, 19, 20, 23, 44
Wheaton, 25, 68, 179, 198, 214, 268, 274, 277
William The, 253
Wolff, 115, 145
Wolff v. *Oxholm*, 86, 91

Xenia, 13

Zouch, 3

www.ingramcontent.com/pod-product-compliance
Lightning Source LLC
Chambersburg PA
CBHW030805230426
43667CB00008B/1077